Praise for *Survivor's Game* from Kirkus Reviews:

Eminently readable and largely remarkable

Karmi's debut, a matter-of-fact memoir focusing on his ordeals in Nazi concentration camps, strikes a relatively upbeat chord largely discordant with works by other Holocaust survivors.

Born into a Jewish family in the then-Hungarian city of Satu Mare, a young Karmi grows up in a country that is increasingly hostile to its Jewish population. With Hitler's rise to power in Germany, the hostility becomes a matter of official policy; despite his valiant service to Austria-Hungary in World War I, David's father's foreign heritage results in the family's expulsion to Poland. There, the Karmis attempt to bunk with unhelpful relations, then undertake great risks to return to Satu Mare, only to find their home and possessions seized. Soon the family is deported once again, this time to Auschwitz, where young David is separated from his parents and sister amid horrific rumors of their likely fate. David survives not only Auschwitz, but a transfer to a second camp in the ruins of the Warsaw Ghetto and then a death march to Dachau in Germany as the Allied armies close in.

The author ascribes his improbable endurance to the fact that he never gave up hope—he writes in an afterword, "I always look forward to tomorrow and try to forget yesterday"—and indeed, the book lacks the tonal despair employed by fellow survivors such as Primo Levi and Elie Wiesel, instead echoing the optimism of Anne Frank's pre-camp diaries. But perhaps just as important to David's survival as his sunny outlook are his quick wits, good fortune and knack for making the right kinds of friends—ranging from fellow inmates who share his pluck to a sympathetic Wehrmacht lieutenant who even invites David out of the camp to his family's home for meals.

Though Karmi's narrative loses steam once he details his postwar emigration to Palestine, his prose moves along at a respectable clip and rarely lingers on trivial details, until a handful of later chapters profiling Karmi's successful but relatively dull American real-estate career.

Eminently readable and largely remarkable.

"You don't usually associate terms like 'nail-biting,' 'suspenseful,' and 'page-turning' with Holocaust books, but Mr. Karmi's memoir is just that: an extraordinary, compelling depiction of what it took for one kid to survive the terror and monstrous machinery of the death camps. Give this remarkable book to every kid (and adult) you know!"

—Aaron Rosenberg, best-selling author of titles in the Stargate Atlantis, World of Warcraft, Star Trek, Transformers, Daemon Gates, and Ben 10 series; winner, Scribe Award and Origins Award

"Although it's a true story, *Survivor's Game* reads like a best-selling novel. The author immediately engages the reader as he describes a pleasant life with his parents, brothers, and sisters in a small town in Romania. But this idyllic existence begins to unravel as he experiences anti-Semitism—and then it falls apart with the violence and death that came under the Nazis' rule. Karmi expertly sets the stage with his depiction of an innocent, carefree life that is suddenly, violently shattered when his family is deported. Separated from them, Karmi lives through a nightmare of horror, going from Auschwitz to Dachau and then the Warsaw ghetto.

"Karmi's narrative is compelling and his dialogue real and natural. This is a moving story full of suspense, adventure, intrigue, tragedy, and survival against all odds, and the fact that the author has written it for the young-adult market is impressive. It's crucial the world never forgets that Hitler and his political machine tried to wipe out an entire race, and Karmi has made sure the next generation, and generations to come, will always remember. This is an awesome, important work that should be in every school library in the world."

—Charlene Keel, author of *Dark Territory* and *Ghost Crown* (The Tracks series)

"*Survivor's Game* reads not so much like a memoir but a novel, replete with tension, drama, and twists and turns. The vivid moment-by-moment recollections are as immediate to the reader as they were when they occurred so many years ago. *Survivor's Game* holds a powerful message of hope—not just for Holocaust victims but for the world. Recommended."

—Diane Donovan, Midwest Book Review

"There are reading experiences that can be so different, so gripping, yet so visceral they can change your perception of the world around you. *Survivor's Game* by David Karmi is one of these experiences. Karmi's ability to deliver it to young adult readers is an amazing, remarkable achievement."

—Richard Steinberg, author of *Nobody's Safe, The Gemini Man,* and *The Four Phase Man*

"I do not know how many books have been written by survivors of the Nazi concentration camps and the Holocaust which took the lives of six million Jews and another five million Christians, gypsies, homosexuals, and assorted 'enemies' of the Nazi state. David Karmi has written a memoir, *Survivor's Game*, about his life as a teenager in the death camps. We need to read such books to fully grasp the horror of the deliberate genocide of Europe's Jews and the fate others shared as well. The author survived almost by pure instinct and after being liberated by the Allies made his way to what was then the Palestinian mandate, administered by the British until a Jewish state was proclaimed in 1948. Later he moved to the US and had a thriving career in construction in New York City."

—Alan Caruba, *Bookviews*

"*Survivor's Game* is a thriller with real substance. It provides a fine history lesson on the Holocaust and encourages independent thinking about how to be responsible for yourself. I'm going to buy copies for my grandchildren."

—James Bankes, retired school administrator; historian; contributor to *Highlights for Children* and *Cobblestone*

"*Survivor's Game* teaches the timeless lesson that a teenager's cunning mind and will to survive can conquer even the worst brutality. David Karmi's action-packed thriller inspires readers to hang on through their own difficult circumstances—no matter how bleak life gets—until they too achieve victory."

—Barbara Bendall, TV producer, news reporter

"David Karmi lived through historic times, including the Nazi takeover of Poland, the rise of Auschwitz and Israel's War of Independence. Despite all the suffering he endured, he remained proud to be a Jew. His story is an inspiration."

—Anna Olswanger, author of *Shlemiel Crooks* and a Koret International Jewish Book Award finalist

"From the first scene, David Karmi evocatively conveys the theme and spirit of *Survivor's Game*. This is a story we all need to know, remember, and teach our children; the cost of forgetting is too high. *Survivor's Game* is a reminder not just of the human and spiritual costs of irrationality and hatred but of the transcendence of wit, wisdom, and courage."

—Maya Kaathryn Bohnhoff, *New York Times* best-selling author

Dear Karen
Thank you for your interest
in my Book. Best regards
[signature]

Survivor's Game

David Karmi

D.K. Montague

Survivor's Game

Published by D.K. Montague

For more information: dkarmi28@aol.com

Book design by:
Arbor Books, Inc.
www.arborbooks.com

Printed in the United States of America

Survivor's Game
David Karmi

1. Title 2. Author 3. Memoir

Library of Congress Control Number: 2010915586

ISBN 13: 978-0-615-41295-5

In memory of

My parents Gabriel and Lea,
my brother Moshe
and my sister Rachel.

And all the other millions who perished
in the Holocaust, all murdered by the Nazis.

You had to believe that you would get through it in the end, and that there would be another life waiting for you in a place where the world had not gone insane. That was what mattered the most. If you lost your belief or will to endure and suffer, you might as well have walked out toward the nearest fence and let the guards shoot you down.
—David Karmi

Foreword

There are lives too complex and painful to believe in. There are hardships that you just can't wrap your mind around. No matter how you try, no matter how much you study and think and believe that you understand, there are experiences that are too personal to be truly shared. Still, we try. When we get the chance, we make the effort to listen, and to walk through the memories of others and learn.

The book you are holding in your hand is such an opportunity. In fact it's one of the most unique opportunities of its type you will ever encounter. David Karmi has lived through adversity. He has experienced things most of us can't even imagine. Those experiences alone are enough to mark him as unique, but that's not where it ends. When I say David has lived through adversity, I don't just mean that he simply survived. I mean that he lived.

There are two kinds of men in the world: those who think about doing things and those who do them. David Karmi is a doer. He'll be the first to tell you that he's not alive because he's a genius, or because he's faster, or stronger than other men. He's alive because when life held out a hand, he took it. When there was a way to get ahead, he didn't hesitate.

Through deportation, three death camps and two forced marches that left fields strewn with the lives and dreams of others, David lived by a few simple rules: He kept a little money, no matter what. He kept a positive attitude. He remembered his family. And when others around him gave up hope he turned away and followed his own road. He never believed that he could not do a thing—but instead just set about doing it.

Beyond the Holocaust and the suffering of his childhood and young adult years, he worked to help free Israel, to make a home for his people. Finding that home—a place he could call his own—was a driving force in his life. His childhood home had been taken from him and destroyed. Everyplace he went he was an outsider, but he kept looking forward. As with all the important things in his life, he made it happen. Now there are thousands of families in New York City who also have homes thanks to David—homes that he has built.

Against one of the most powerfully stacked decks in history, David Karmi played his hand, and he won. He has his life, his health and his sense of humor, and he has his family. He is blessed in many ways, and those blessings were earned and are well-deserved.

This plot of this book is intense and cinematic, but it is simply the story of one man's life—a very real story, and a very real man. And it is a story you will never forget. I am humbled by the power and drama of it and proud to call David Karmi my friend, and to have even a small part in telling his story.

Turn the page and prepare yourself. It's quite a ride.

—David Niall Wilson
author of *Deep Blue* and *The Orffyreus Wheel*;
CEO of Crossroad Press

Acknowledgments

My deepest gratitude to my son, Glenn Karmi, who surprised me on my birthday by making arrangements for me to write and publish my life story. It is because of him that this book is being published.

My thanks to my sister Irene who helped me fill in some of the details of our family's history.

Special thanks to David Niall Wilson and Anna Olswanger for the help they provided while writing this book.

I sincerely hope that the people who will read this book, including my daughter, Cora, my son-in-law Michael, and my grandchildren, Jessica, Lauren and Kimberly, will realize how lucky they are that their generations did not have to live through these unimaginable, horrible times and that they will appreciate more than ever the wonderful world that they live in now. I hope they will take this message to the next generation.

Introduction

When people think of Transylvania they usually think of horror films and Bram Stoker's *Dracula,* but the Transylvania of my childhood was a very different place. I was born in the small town of Halmi in Transylvania, then part of Romania, and the early days of my life were very happy times.

We lived in a large home—not fancy, but comfortable—with a wraparound terrace and a large yard. We had a lumberyard and an attached workshop in back as well as a barn. We didn't have a lot of money in the bank, but we never went without the things we needed.

The streets of Halmi were unpaved, and there were no electrical appliances, no bathrooms and no kitchens with running water. These were not conveniences and luxuries that the people of the town missed—we didn't know any other way of life.

My family was a large one, eight children in all. My sisters were Irene, Ilana and Rachel, and my brothers were Armin, Mendu, William and Moses. I was the youngest. My nickname was "The Leftover" because I came nine years after the birth of my closest sibling, Irene, at a time when my mother did not expect to bear more children.

My sister Irene served as my mother's helper. During much of my early life, she acted as a second mother to me, and so the two of us were very close. This, of course, made Irene my favorite sibling—she was the one who was there for me most often and who I knew the best. Hers is the story that, over the years and through the horrors to come, most closely mirrored mine. To Poland, back to what became Hungary, to the concentration camps, to Israel and even to America and a new life, our lives have been similar and at the same time very different. Irene chronicled her own memories in her book *Life at the End of the Tunnel, a Survivor's Story.*

My father, Gabriel, was born in Poland and immigrated to Transylvania, then part of Austria-Hungary, when he was seventeen years of age. He served in the Austro-Hungarian army during World War I. After the war, when Transylvania became part of Romania, my father settled down in Halmi, where he married my mother, Lea. He owned a successful furniture business and kept the wood for his business in the lumberyard behind our house. He employed several workers to help in the design and creation of fine bedroom and living room sets. Not many families in those days could afford the luxury of furniture like he created, but there was enough demand to keep him busy. He also owned a shop in town where he sold the furniture, and he divided his time between the two places.

My father was a very hard-working man. He spent long hours in his shop, working six days a week, resting only on the Sabbath when no work was allowed. He often came home for lunch and, after eating, would lie down for a short nap. Only our mother was allowed to wake him and when she did, he returned to the shop and to his work. For him, a trade was a person's most important possession. He believed that idle time was wasted time, and he was careful that all his children were occupied during any hours that might otherwise have been wasted.

My father's first concern was education. He wanted all his

children to apply themselves to their studies, both standard education and religious, and to learn professions. We attended public school in the morning and Hebrew classes in the afternoon.

"In life," he said, "you can lose all of your possessions, but if you have a trade you will never go hungry."

My father was a good man, respected in the community for his work and his kindness. Although our family was not wealthy, he often made loans to those in need. If it were possible, the people who borrowed from him paid him back, but there were many times when he was never repaid. It did not change his attitude toward others—if he could help someone, he did. He didn't believe in letting others suffer.

My oldest brother, Armin, became a teacher. Rachel, my oldest sister, learned to make hats. My sister Ilana was a seamstress and my brother William studied to be an artist. At the time when things started to go badly, my youngest brother Moses and I were still in school. Irene was home, assisting my mother, acting as permanent babysitter for me.

My mother, Lea, was a fine woman. She was born in Transylvania when it was part of Austria-Hungary, and the members of her family were Hungarian citizens. She was slender and attractive even after giving birth to eight children. My father managed the business at his furniture company, but he gave the money he made to my mother, and she managed all the family's affairs. She cooked, cleaned, raised the children and did the laundry. She did it all with a smile and a caring heart. My father and mother were well-liked in the community, and our house was always open. My mother was a gracious hostess, and she loved people. There was always company in our home, and when she cooked no one ever left hungry.

Friends and neighbors used to ask her how it was that she always had enough food no matter the number of guests.

She would smile and explain that the magic was in her pots. She said that they were made of rubber, and whatever the number of guests, the pots stretched to accommodate them.

In addition to the house and the workshop, we had a two-story barn that housed our cow. This became the playground for my friends and me—there was nothing in Halmi like the parks of today. We played hide-and-seek in the straw and made up our own games. On very warm days I would lie on my back beneath the cow and one of my friends would milk the cow directly into my mouth. That milk was warm and sweet, and though not pasteurized it never made any of us sick.

In Halmi, there was nothing like the toy stores of today. For amusement, we children were on our own, and this included manufacturing our own toys to play with. Around Chanukah, we made our own dreidels. My brothers and I took a broomstick and cut off a length of about eight inches. We cut that into four parts. On one side of each we carved the symbols that belong on the four sides of the dreidel. These symbols represent the phrase "a great miracle happened there." It was important to get the right symbol on the right side.

We took the four pieces of broomstick and bound them together with wire so they formed a bundle. Then we drilled a hole in the center. Next we slipped off to steal seltzer bottles—which were very expensive—so that we could get the lead caps that sealed them. We lit a fire and melted the lead, which we then poured down into the hole drilled in the broomsticks. Once the lead had sufficient time to cool, we untied the wire and we had a dreidel with the proper symbol appearing on each of the four sides.

My sisters made dolls out of scraps of cloth and rags they managed to salvage. When the dolls had been sewn, our brother William painted on the faces to bring them to life.

Every day shepherds came to our house and took the cow, along with the cows of all our neighbors, off to the fields to graze. Each cow wore a handmade bell with a unique tone, and we could tell the sound of our cow returning from the fields. All the bells sounding together made a sort of music that I found pleasant to the ear.

Clothing was very expensive. Hand-me-downs circulated through every generation of the family. Most of the clothing was made of wool. One thing about wool: when it ages, the material has a tendency to wear out and grow shiny all over the outer surface. When this happened, and it got bad enough that it seemed ragged, the solution was to take the suit to the tailor. The tailor would then reverse the material so that it was inside out. The interior of the cloth did not have the shiny appearance, and the clothing would look almost new when the tailor was finished, but you could always tell when someone had this done because the vest pocket would be on the right side instead of the left.

In my childhood, I learned five different languages. With my father, I spoke Yiddish. Sometimes my sisters spoke to him in Hungarian, but he answered in Yiddish. With my mother and her family, I spoke Hungarian. My religious studies included lessons in Hebrew, and the official language of the country was Romanian. My father also brought in a tutor to teach my siblings and me German. At the time, this was considered the most important European language, and he wanted us to be able to communicate in German.

My siblings were all born about two years apart. With the large gap in age between my sister Irene and me—nine years—and even more between the others and me, I was not very close to my older siblings. They had more serious concerns than I did as a young boy and, on top of this, my mother tended to spoil me.

Being the last of the children, I received preferential treatment from her while my older brothers and sisters sometimes screamed at me and chased me from the room quite often and even slapped me—though I often deserved it.

My brother William, for example, had a private drawer where he kept his most prized secret possessions. This drawer was always locked, and William had the only key. Whenever I got the chance, I stole the key and went through the drawer. If William caught me, I knew, I would get a beating, but I was never really worried because I knew that I could count on my mother to protect me if things got out of hand.

Not all of my childhood was spent pursuing mischief, however. It was about this time that I started to take an interest in working and earning money. On Friday afternoons, I would go to town and visit the candy store. While there, I bought a box of 100 chocolate wafers, and when Saturday came, I took the box to the synagogue. There were long periods of time on Saturday when the adults were busy and the children were left to their own devices. During this time, I sold my box of wafers for the equivalent of a penny apiece on credit—no money was allowed to change hands on the Sabbath. I collected my money on Sunday in Hebrew school.

My family and I lived in a very religious, Orthodox community. This meant that dating between young men and women was forbidden and never took place in the open. Of course, the fact that it was forbidden in public did little to discourage it from taking place—it only made things more interesting.

I was a bright child and learned very early on to keep my eyes and ears open, particularly when in a position to overhear gossip. Over time I became somewhat of an expert on who was dating whom in the town. When this came to the attention of others, they began coming to me for their gossip. For the price of a few *lei*, which was about a nickel, I told them who was dating whom and all that I knew.

From that time forward, there was never a period when I didn't have at least a little money or something of value. This grew important over the days and trials to come. It gave me a sense of security. Sometimes all it takes to keep a person from losing hope is the knowledge that he has something of worth to fall back on.

When I was five, our cow became pregnant. Friends and neighbors showed up to watch and to lend a helping hand if necessary. Once the calf had been born, it struggled and eventually got up on its feet. I walked over and stood beside it. I turned and told one of my friends that the calf must have been five years old when it was born because it was already as tall as I was.

This early period of my life, with its happy memories and simple pleasures, came to an end abruptly around my sixth year. There were limited opportunities in Halmi for business and for my siblings to branch out and begin their lives. My parents decided that the family should move to a larger city. The city they chose was the largest of those nearby, a place called Satu Mare. It was the birthplace of Hasidic Judaism, and there was a very large Hasidic community there. Some of the most famous rabbis in history taught there.

The rooms we rented in Satu Mare were on the second floor of a very large home. The main floor was commercial, filled with stores and vendors. The basement was rented to a poorer family. My new home was a large space with high ceilings and big windows that let in a great deal of light. There was a good-sized kitchen, a living room, two bedrooms and a foyer that served as a den.

There was, of course, no running water in any of the city's houses at the time. There was a well out in back of the house from which we drew water, but this water was only for washing. Drinking water had to be carried from a fountain a few blocks away.

The intimacy and security of the small town I had grown up in was not in evidence in Satu Mare. Our outhouse was separated from the house by a large yard. Sometimes, late at night, when it was very dark, I was afraid to make that walk on my own.

The house was owned by a peasant who had gone off earlier in his life to America. He had worked in the United States for a time, raised capital and moved back to Satu Mare, where he built that large house and rented it out. He moved outside of town to a large farm where our family would sometimes go for milk and vegetables. We had no place to keep a cow in the city, but we had a large chicken coop out in back. It was my job to collect the eggs daily and bring them back to my mother.

Since we lived on the second story we had direct access to the attic, which was very large. It ran the length and width of the lower floors and had eight-foot ceilings, so it was quite spacious. The home was heated by fireplaces, and the main chimney ran on up through the attic. There were metal access doors in the chimney. We made use of them by turning the attic into a smoke room, which we used to smoke quartered goose breasts and other meat.

Beneath the basement was a cellar. Down there, the air was very cool all year long, and this was where we stored food that needed to be kept cooler. We bought our milk and butter daily as needed, so it wasn't as difficult as it might seem to live without the convenience of a refrigerator or ice box.

I remember those happy years of my life in sharp contrast to the years that were to come. Our family had moved to Satu Mare the same year that Hitler assumed his chancellorship. Hungary signed a pact with Germany almost immediately. As early as 1924 there were restrictions on university seats for Jewish students, and anti-Semitism was firmly taking root. Initially, these things had little effect on my family and me, but as we lived longer in the city, chinks and cracks appeared in our world that no amount of familial love could patch. It wasn't long before our entire world was shattered by hatred, violence and needless death—and we were powerless to stop them.

Journeys of David Karmi Pre-Liberation

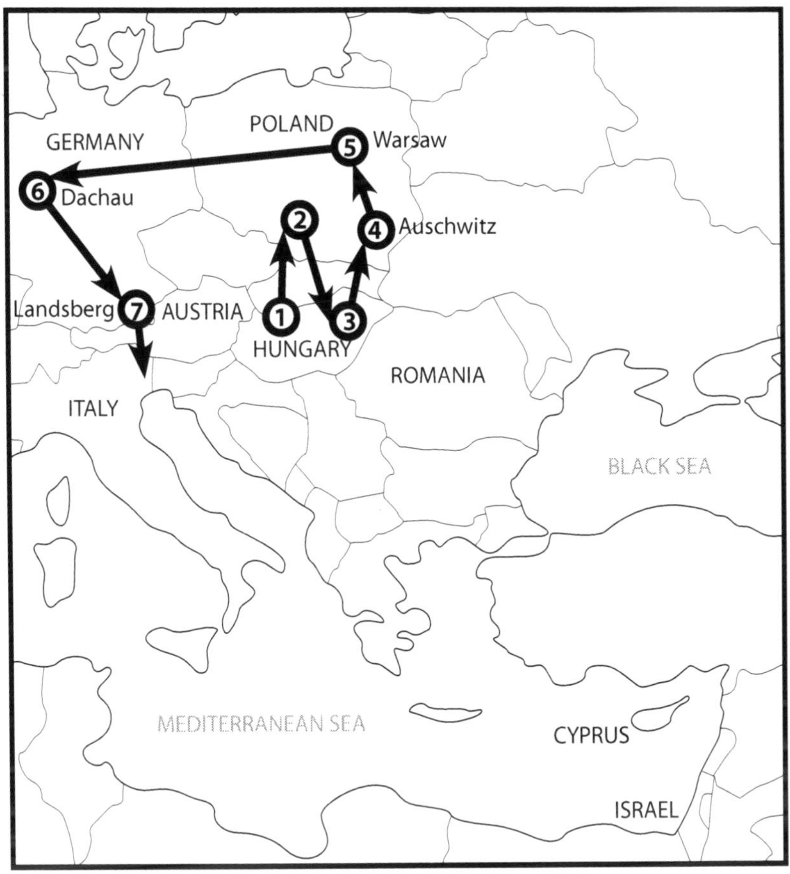

1 Deported from Hungary to Poland.
2 Returned to Hungary.
3 Transported from ghetto in Hungary to Auschwitz death camp in Poland.
4 Transported from Auschwitz to a concentration camp in the Warsaw ghetto.
5 Death march from Warsaw ghetto to Dachau concentration camp in Germany.
6 Transported from Dachau to concentration camp in Landsberg, Germany.
7 Death march from Landsberg to the Tyrol Mountains near the Italian border. Liberated by Americans here.

Journeys Post-Liberation

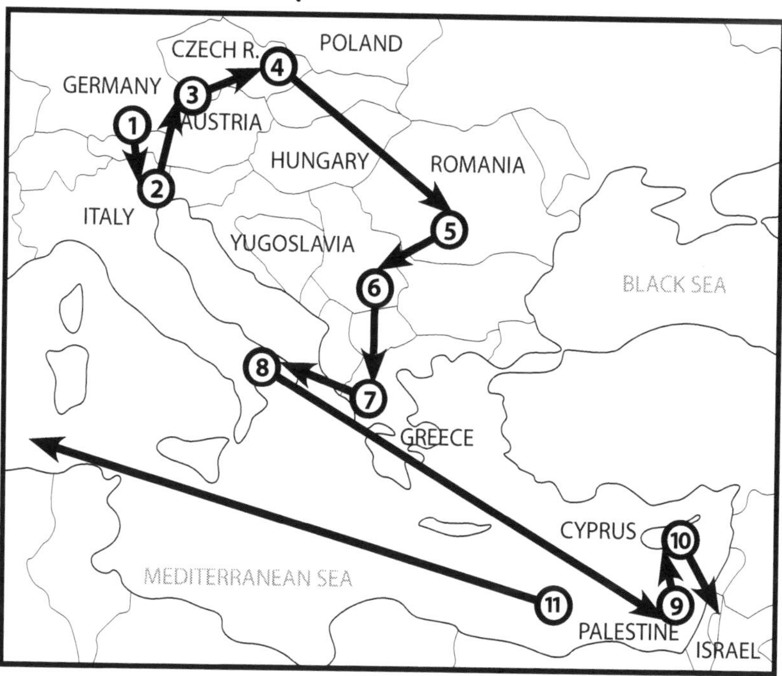

1 Departed Feldafing, Germany, to a UN refugee camp in Modena, Italy. Smuggled across the border by Jewish volunteers from Palestine—part of the British Army.

2 Departed Italy following cigarette smugglers through the snow-covered mountains to Austria (occupied by Russians).

3 Departed Austria with the help of the Hagana, who were helping Jews to cross the border into Czechoslovakia, illegally en route to Palestine.

4 Departed Prague (occupied by Russians) to Satu Mare, Romania (Russian zone).

5 Departed Romania with counterfeit passport to Yugoslavia by train.

6 Departed Yugoslavia with false Greek papers to Greece.

7 Departed Greece as Italian refugees went back to Italy.

8 Departed Italy with 700 refugees on a fishing boat, after thirty-five day journey, arrived at the port of Haifa, Palestine.

9 Departed Port of Haifa on a British transport ship to Nicosia, Cyprus—a British Camp.

10 Departed Cyprus by boat to Palestine.

11 Eight years later, departed from Israel on a four-week journey by freight ship to New York.

Chapter One

The afternoon was warm, and it was nearly time for school to let out for the day. I was looking forward to bathing at the river with my friends. When the bell rang I was the first to the door, where I grabbed my bathing suit and my book bag and took off at a run.

My best friend, Solomon, and a small pack of boys hurried along at my heels. Because I was the oldest of our group, the other boys often followed me and counted on me to lead them safely. The Somosh River ran through the center of the city and, if the weather permitted, we always stopped there before going home.

When we reached the river, I stopped. The others gathered in behind me and stared. The river was high. Always fast-moving, the water had picked up its pace and crawled up over its banks. It was muddier than usual, and white-capped ripples showed the power and speed of the current.

A group of older boys and adults were gathered near the water a little bit downstream. Some of them splashed and laughed in the shallows. I looked away from them and back at the river. I was a small boy but, even so, I was the largest of our group. I knew that the boys who had come to the river with me were waiting to see what I would do.

The sight of that rolling water left a tight knot in my stomach, but I didn't want to go home without swimming, and after seeing the older kids downstream braving the river, I didn't want to look like a coward in front of my friends. I set my book bag down on the bank and took off my shoes. The others followed my lead, and in moments we had slipped into our bathing suits, littering the shore with our bags and belongings.

I stepped into the swirling water and waded out from shore. The others followed, staying in a close group. We never went very far out. Even on a lazy day the current was strong, but for some reason, that day, the high water felt like a challenge. I kept moving, passing the point where the water wet my trunks. It felt good and cool, but the current was very strong.

I turned and looked over my shoulder. The others were following me closely. In that instant, my feet slipped. I tried to regain my balance, but the current was far too strong and my legs were swept out from under me in a rush.

The boys made half-hearted attempts to grab me, but it was no use.

"Go back!" I called. "Go back, it's too strong!"

They retreated, crying out for help.

I wasn't a strong swimmer. I could float on my back, kick my legs and wave my arms to remain afloat, but I couldn't fight the current. It gripped me and swept me out and away from my friends so quickly, I was in shock. The water was very powerful, and it was a horrible, helpless sensation to be caught in its grip.

"Help!" I screamed. I whirled in the grip of the river. I looked to the shore and, through water-blurred eyes, saw the men and boys downstream staring out at me. I tried to wave to them, calling out again and again for help, but water filled my mouth and I choked. That moment seemed to last forever. I saw their faces and I heard them calling out to me, but my mind could not process the words.

"Look!" I heard a tall, tousle-haired boy shout, pointing. "The Jew boy is drowning!"

Others called out as well, and I heard their laughter rolling out across the water. It pounded at me and I fought harder, flailing at the river helplessly as it drew me away from the shore.

"Help!" I cried again. My friends had reached the group by then. I heard them pleading with those gathered.

The current turned me so the shoreline was no longer in sight. The water, cool and inviting when I'd first stepped in, felt like ice, and the waves washing in and out of my ears caused sounds and voices to echo strangely. In that instant I believed that I was on the brink of death, that I would be swept away, drowned and forgotten.

I saw the faces of those on shore and etched their hard, staring eyes into my memory.

Nearby, the water suddenly erupted with the sound of splashing. A large hand gripped my arms and yanked me back toward the shore. Strong arms curled beneath me and lifted me. I was moving back toward the shore.

The man who rescued me placed me gently on the bank of the river. My friends gathered around me, all talking at once, but I barely heard them. Shivering uncontrollably, I glanced up into the face of the man who had saved me.

"Thank you," I said.

"Will you be all right?" he asked. His voice was deep, and his face was awash in conflicting emotions. He glanced over his shoulder at his companions of a few moments ago, shook his head in disgust and turned back.

"I think so," I said. I coughed as I spoke.

The man nodded. "Next time, be more careful. I don't believe there are many left to help you." He turned away and, in a moment, disappeared into the nearby streets of Satu Mare. I rose, hurried back to my clothes, and dressed.

I still heard the laughter in my mind, and the words: "The Jew boy is drowning."

I led the young boys away from the river as quickly as possible. My best friend Solomon, once again at my side, broke the silence.

"David, are you all right?"

I looked at Solomon and tried to force a smile, but I gave it up. I shook my head. "They were going to let me die."

He nodded and stared at the ground. Somehow the river at our backs no longer held the same appeal, and the streets and buildings loomed over us, stark and ominous.

Chapter Two

It was another hot day. Solomon and I and a few others trudged across the city from school. We made this same journey daily, two miles both to and from school. It was a chance to spend some time talking and dreaming without our parents, families or teachers around, and all of us enjoyed it. We kicked stones in the street as we discussed our plans for that evening.

We passed a row of shops, some closing as evening approached, others open and waiting for the working men and women to pass by on their way home to make last-minute purchases and finish their daily shopping. Alleys, casting lengthening shadows, sliced from street to street through the buildings and apartments.

"I think we're having smoked goose for dinner," I told Solomon. "We've had it hanging in the attic for days now."

"I'll ask if I can come to your house for dinner," he said.

No one was ever turned away from the table when my mother cooked, and she was very good at it. All of the boys had found their way to her table on one occasion or another, and she never seemed to mind.

"You'd better ask early," I said. "The goose won't last long!"

Before Solomon could reply, four shadowed figures stepped from an alley just ahead of us. I stopped. I recognized the boys from school. The largest was named Yonosh. All four were from gentile families, and more than once I had been the victim of their taunts and threats.

This felt different. It was still more than a mile to my home, and suddenly that was a very long distance.

"Look what we have here," Yonosh said, stepping forward. "Looks like the Jew boys have gotten lost."

"Let us pass," I said. My voice wavered slightly, but I stood my ground. My friends gathered in close, but Yonosh and his companions were older and larger.

"Why would we do that?" he asked. "You don't belong here. None of you do. Papa says you people are taking our jobs and our money. He says you shouldn't be allowed in our school."

"We have no fight with you," I said. "We're just on our way home."

"Well," Yonosh said, turning to his companions. "I guess they'll have to go through us to get there."

The others nodded. They stepped up beside him and the four fanned out, blocking the street.

I took a step toward them and then hesitated. I glanced at my friends and then shouted, "Run!"

We took off with a quick burst of speed, hoping that surprise would be on our side.

But Yonosh, quick for his size, grabbed me by the arm and dragged me to the side. I felt my feet slip, and I cried out as I spun in the air and fell hard. Before I could roll to my feet or pull away, I felt the larger boy's knee slam into my stomach and pin me to the ground.

I was overmatched in size and age. I struggled and cried out again as Yonosh, blind hatred in his eyes, punched me hard in the ribs. As the older boy drew back for another blow, I wrenched away with all my might and managed to slip from beneath his knee, which still pressed me to the ground.

Yonosh growled and reached for me again, but I was too

quick. I crab-walked back a few feet and spun, finding my footing and taking off at a run. There was no time to look for my friends, to see how they were doing. I lowered my head and ran.

"You can run, Jew boy," Yonosh called after me, "but you have to come this way again and again. When you do, I'll be here—waiting for you."

Tears of frustration and pain streamed down my cheeks, but I didn't look back. I ran until I had passed several blocks and turned the final corner. Once my home was in sight, I glanced back. I saw Solomon about a block behind, and I slowed to let my friend catch up.

We didn't speak for several moments. We were both fighting for our breath.

"What are we going to do?" Solomon asked. "There aren't very many other ways we could go to get home, and this is the shortest. If they wait for us every day…"

When I saw that Solomon's eye was dark and puffy, my anger returned. "Don't worry," I said. "I think I know what to do."

"What?"

"Just wait," I said. "For now, it's time to see about that smoked goose."

Solomon took off for his home in search of permission, and I continued more slowly, deep in thought.

That night, after dinner, I wandered through the house and Papa's workshop to gather the things I needed. I didn't tell my parents about the confrontation—I knew it was mine to handle. Any interference by the family would only make things worse and might include them in the danger.

When I was satisfied, I took everything I had gathered to my room and set to work. I'd found a piece of rounded wood in

Papa's workshop and some long, thin strips of leather Mama had left out. In my room, I had hidden away a number of bits of lead, and I gathered these as well.

I attached the leather strips to the wooden handle firmly. Then I took the small bits of leather and slowly braided them into the strands of leather. When I was done, I laid this makeshift weapon beneath my bed and lay down. It was a long time before I slept.

When I left school the next day I had the makeshift whip secreted beneath my jacket. I had shown it to Solomon and the others, but as they neared the area where we had been ambushed I could see that they weren't convinced it would help.

At first it seemed we would be left alone, but just as we were passing the alley where Yonosh and his friends had hidden themselves on the previous day, a voice called out from the far side of the street. It chilled my blood.

I turned. Yonosh had stepped to the edge of the street, flanked by the same gang of boys with glaring expressions. They smiled and spread out across the street. Yonosh stepped forward.

"You don't learn quickly, do you, Jew boy?" Yonosh said.

"We have to pass this way to get home," I replied, holding the larger boy's gaze. As I spoke, I inched my hand beneath my jacket and wrapped my fingers tightly around the wooden handle of the whip.

"If you come this way, you will have to pay the toll," Yonosh said, stepping a little closer.

My heart hammered. I wanted to look around to see if my friends were still with me, but I didn't want to release Yonosh's gaze. The larger boy took another step forward. He grinned and something snapped in my mind. I pulled out the whip and ran straight at him.

The leather straps whistled through the air. When they struck Yonosh across one side, the lead weights bit deep. I didn't hesitate. I drew the whip back and slashed out again and again. Yonosh raised his hands and cried out. His friends stepped back, confused, and I heard Solomon and the others calling out to me, though I couldn't make out the words. I took a final slash with the whip and then stepped back.

Yonosh stood, stunned, clutching his sides. Small ribbons of blood seeped into the material of his shirt. I held the boy's shocked gaze for a moment longer and then, with a cry to the others to follow, took off down the street toward home at a dead run. Yonosh didn't follow.

Our journey from one side of the city to the other was no less dangerous after that day, but the fear—which only my friends and I had felt—now spread to our attackers. Fear and a small amount of respect. It would do nothing to stop the bigotry and hatred spreading through the city and the country, but for a while it made it easier to survive.

Chapter Three

We entered a dark alley and stayed low, speaking only in hushed whispers. I glanced over my shoulder to make certain no one had seen us. The building to our right presented a solid wall to the alley. At the very base of that wall, windows with heavy iron bars vented the basement area beneath the shop.

"Hurry!" Solomon called. "Someone will see us."

I followed my friend to the first of the low-slung windows. We knelt on the packed-dirt floor of the alley and placed our faces tight to the bars of the window to scan the interior. Inside were tables piled high with apples, stored in the cool basement to prevent their going bad.

Solomon glanced up the alley again. No one was in sight.

"We're clear," he said.

I held a long pole at my side. On the tip of the pole we had affixed a sharp spike. With a quick, careful jab, I poked the pole through the hole and into the nearest pile of apples. I felt it sink in.

"Got one!"

I worked quickly. It might only have been a matter of minutes until someone walked by the end of the alley and saw us, and to be caught stealing was unthinkable. Beyond the beatings we would no doubt receive, it could draw unwanted attention to our families. We got two apples apiece, stood up, hid the fruit under our jackets and slipped back out of the alley.

"Will you be going to the *mikveh* this afternoon?" Solomon asked. We both ate the apples greedily as we headed down the street toward home.

"Of course," I replied. "Papa would never allow us to miss the ritual bathing, and even if he slipped there is always my brother Moses to help him remember."

Both of us laughed. Moses was the closest of my brothers to my own age and the most carefully religious member of our family. This was no mean feat in a household containing Papa.

"You'd better hurry, then," Solomon said. He began running toward his own home.

I waved to my friend and took off in a slightly different direction. I covered the distance quickly, keeping my eyes out for trouble. In my own end of the city, I was rarely confronted, but there was no way to tell when Yonosh or one of his friends might decide to look for trouble.

When I reached home, I heard raised voices inside, and I hurried up my steps yet again.

"It's not proper!" Moses cried. "It's forbidden to create graven images, and you do us a dishonor by bringing it into our home."

"Calm down, Moses," Papa said. "William is a student of art, and this is his creation. We will not be making offerings to it or worshipping it—it is his likeness, and a very good one."

"It should not be here," Moses said.

I entered the room. In the center of the dining room table, a ceramic bust stood, staring back at me. It was an uncanny likeness of my brother William, who stood beside Papa, ready to defend his work if Moses made a sudden move. It was a tense moment, and I wished I'd had the forethought to wait for it to end before entering the room.

Mama stood in the corner. I glanced at her, and she looked up.

"Both of you go," Papa said. "I will take care of William's work of art, and we will hear no more of it."

Grudgingly, Moses turned away, casting a last, poisonous glance at the bust that seemed to mock him from the table. There was no time to continue the discussion. Of all the members of the family, Moses was least likely to do anything to cause a disruption on Friday afternoon. The ritual bathing was an important part of the week, and we had to walk to the *mikveh.*

"This is not over," Moses said, brushing past William close enough that their shoulders bumped.

I waited until the others had left the room, then stepped over to examine the bust of William's head. It was very well done and showed talent. William had always been the one who could draw or sculpt better than the rest of us. It was a gift, and it was hard to understand why Moses couldn't see it.

I turned and left the room. Not long after, Papa, my brothers and I left for the *mikveh.* We visited the ritual bath every Friday before the Sabbath. Not all the Jewish men in the city participated weekly, but this Orthodox practice was a part of what held my family so close together.

Nothing else was said that day, or for several days following, about the bust. William hovered near it when he was home. It was displayed proudly, and when company visited it was a conversation piece. Life progressed normally, and I breathed more easily. It seemed as if, despite the tension, the modern world had begun to infiltrate our home as well as the city.

Then it happened.

I was out in back when the loud crash sounded. I rushed for the door to find out what had happened. When I entered, I found Moses, wild-eyed, standing over William's bust. His expression shifted from triumph to guilt to anger. The bust lay on the floor. It was mostly intact, except that the nose had broken loose.

"What have you done!" I exclaimed.

"You know the laws as well as I do," Moses said. "It is wrong. This statue does not belong in our home—or in any home. I have fixed it."

"Fixed it?" I asked, incredulous. I glanced down at the smashed nose.

"Yes," Moses said. "The law says that a marred or imperfect image can be displayed. I have found a way that William's work can remain in our home."

"But Papa had already approved... You should not have..."

At that moment William and Papa entered the room. It grew very silent, and I backed away so that I wouldn't be caught between the two brothers. William stepped over to where Moses had returned the broken statue to its place—minus the nose. The broken piece still sat on the floor where it had fallen.

"What have you done?" Papa asked softly. "Oh no, Moses, what have you done?"

William paid no attention to either of them. He ran his hand over the ruined face of the statue as if unwilling to believe what he saw. Moses backed to the far wall but, by the time William finally turned, had worked up to a righteous rage.

"You should thank me, brother," he said.

When William hesitated, confused, Moses pressed his attack. "The statue can stay now. It is still a remarkable likeness of you, and now that it is marred—now that it is not an exact likeness of a human being, God's creature—the law allows it."

Up to that moment William had focused on his ruined art—the work of many weeks—lying broken on the table. But suddenly his anger boiled over. "Do you speak for God then, brother?" William demanded. He started walking across the room toward Moses. “Is it now your place to tell our father what is and is not proper in his home?”

“I did not create the law,” Moses said. “But it is my duty—the duty of all of us—to obey it. You should never have brought that…abomination into our home.”

That was all it took. William lunged at Moses and would have knocked him to the floor, but Papa stepped between them.

“You will not fight in this house!” he said. “Moses, we will talk of this at another time. William, I am sorry, but there is nothing any of us can do to reverse a thing that is done.”

The two brothers faced one another across the room. The tension was thick.

Then, as suddenly as it had begun, it was over. Moses spun on his heel and stormed out of the room and the house. William stood and watched until his younger brother was out of sight and then turned back to his statue. Papa took a step toward William and then stopped. He turned and gestured for me to follow, and we left the room.

The rift was deep, and the problem between William and Moses was only the tip of a very large iceberg. As the city split at its spiritual seams, Gentile and Jew squaring off against one another, other cracks formed, and what had been a very strict community, spiritually, became less cohesive and more diverse. The more the modern world seeped into our Orthodox lives, the more things shifted and came apart at the seams.

Chapter Four

I learned early to be careful with my money. Much of this came from Papa, who passed on to me what he knew. One day I went with him for a walk into town. I didn't realize that, before we left, he had hidden some coins beside the sidewalk.

"You should never just walk," Papa said. "When you walk, you should always be watching where you are going. There's a lot you can miss if you aren't observant. As we walk, I want you to pay attention."

I did as I was told and, not far from the house, I saw the coins beside the street. I bent quickly and scooped them up, then slid them into my pocket.

"Now you see what I mean," Papa said.

I felt the money jingling in my pocket. I knew the importance of money, of learning how to get it and of keeping it once you had it in your grasp. I did everything I could to build my own meager savings. I did chores and errands for my brothers and sisters, worked at whatever I could whenever it was available, and was careful with what I earned.

Although William was the artist in the family, I decided that I would like to try my hand at music. I had heard and very much loved music played on a violin. A shop in town sold instruments, and I had my eye on one of the violins for some time. When I had enough money saved to buy the instrument and still had enough held back to feel secure, I went to the shop, picked out the instrument I'd been watching and paid for it.

I had no idea how to play the violin or even why I bought it, other than the fact that I liked hearing the sound when someone else played one. When I carried the violin home and showed it to my parents, they were surprised. No one in our family had gone to music school. But it was the first possession that I bought with money I had earned, and I prized it dearly.

When I had been born in Halmi, Transylvania was part of Romania, but in the early 1940s Hitler gave all of what was Transylvania to Hungary. This marked the beginning of the end for the Jewish communities throughout Hungary. The government immediately began passing a series of anti-Semitic laws regarding employment, education and citizenship.

The Hungarian Jews were not immediately deported, but my family had a problem. Jews born in Poland were to be deported almost immediately, and since my father had been born in Poland, my family was in danger. Suddenly, the fact that Papa had served in the Austro-Hungarian army and lived in the country most of his life meant nothing. Neither the police nor the government cared that Mama, all my siblings and I had been born there.

"They are deporting all families with Polish heritage," Papa said. "We aren't safe here—they might come for us at any time."

"There must be something we can do," Mama insisted. "We have citizenship papers. We must have them verified. Rachel can go—in Budapest they have records. If she brings back the proper paperwork, surely, with your military service, they won't deport us."

"Nothing is sure any longer," Papa said. "Still, we can try.

We‘ll send Rachel immediately to see what she can do. There are already families that have been taken. If I were not the only one of Polish descent, we would have been deported already, and I‘m sure I‘m on their list."

Standing in the hall and listening from just outside the room, I told myself that it was a bad dream. I loved my home, the city and our house. I had friends, my school and the new violin, which I hoped to learn to play soon. I came to a decision. Making no secret of the fact that I‘d overheard my parents, I entered the room.

"I will not go," I said.

They stared at me.

"If they try to deport us, I will not go," I repeated. "I will run away and I will hide. I will find a place to live and work. I do not want to leave."

"We are a family, David," Papa said, almost absently. "We will find our way through this."

"No one has come yet to take us away," Mama added. "We talk about it and worry about it, but we are good people, and we are Hungarian citizens. They will straighten it out."

"If they do not," I said, "I will run away."

They stared and said nothing. I turned and left the room, and as I went I heard them begin to speak again. I didn't think that they believed me, but I had made up my mind. I had never been to Poland, and the fact that Papa did not want to go back was enough for me. I had no friends there, no place to live, and I had no intention of acquiring those things. I was not Polish; I was Hungarian.

The next day, when the postman came and delivered the mail, I was in my room. There was no reason to be excited about the mail on most days, and I paid no attention until I heard my mother cry out.

In the kitchen, I found Papa clutching an official envelope

from the police. Since Hungary had begun its proliferation of anti-Semitic laws, such letters had taken on an ominous aspect. At first, no one spoke. My sister Irene stood beside Mama, who had dropped onto one of the kitchen chairs. Irene's face was very pale, and Mama was sobbing openly.

"What is it?" I asked. I stepped closer to Papa, trying to get a glimpse of the letter.

At first, it seemed that no one had heard me.

Papa turned, ashen-faced, and held out the letter. I took it and scanned it quickly. I had trouble holding on to the letter and shook my head to clear the haze.

"Deported," I said softly. "You are to report to the police—to be deported."

Then my face brightened. "But it says only if you do not have citizenship papers! I heard you and Mama talking. You are a citizen… You can tell them!"

Papa shook his head.

"We don't have the papers yet," he said. His voice was thick with emotion. "Rachel was to have sent them from Budapest, but they haven't arrived and I'm out of time."

"I'll go," Irene said. "If you go down there, they will surely arrest you. I'll go, and I'll tell them that you are ill, that you can't come down, but that when you have recovered we will come and bring your papers."

"They won't listen," Papa said. "They are not in the business of helping Jews to remain in Hungary. They are trying to drive us out."

"But you fought for them in the Great War," Irene insisted. "You married Mama, a Hungarian, and all of your children were born here. If you are not a citizen of Hungary, who is?"

"Go and see what they tell you," Papa said. "It will give me time to think."

Irene took the letter from my trembling hands and ran from

the room. I helped Papa to a chair. He said that it would work out, that they would find a way to fix things. He said this over and over, but there was no comfort in the words.

Irene was gone for almost an hour. During that time we huddled together. We talked, but with no purpose. The shock of what was happening hit us all, and it was impossible to concentrate on details. Papa repeated several times that it was a blessing that the older children had all moved away. The letter had called for the deportation of every family member by name. All of the children, with the exception of Irene, Rachel and I, had left the city, and Rachel was out of town.

When Irene returned, tears streamed down her face.

"They wouldn't listen," she said. "They sent me home to bring you back. They said if you are ill, you must take a cab. They wouldn't tell me anything."

"I must go," Papa said. "Staying here will only anger them, and if we make them come to me, we may end up worse off than we already are. So far, they have only asked me to come. If we wait for them to come here…"

Mama launched out of her chair and wrapped her arms around Papa. The two stood there for what seemed a very long time. I hated seeing my mother crying but could think of nothing to say or do.

Finally the two separated, and Papa turned toward the door.

"Come," he said to Irene. "Take me down there and we will see what they are going to do. You have told them I am ill—it won't do for me to just walk in on my own power as if nothing were wrong. I don't want them angry at you."

"Oh, Papa," Irene said.

He took her by the arm, and together they headed out into the street and on toward town. Some neighbors had gathered. They had seen—or somehow known about—the letter, and they knew what it meant. They watched from a distance, but they didn't come to comfort or even to say goodbye.

An hour later Irene returned from the police station accompanied by four policemen. She moved very stiffly, and I saw that she was crying. When she stepped into the kitchen, the officers moved in behind her, blocking the exit.

"They say that we have to pack, Mama," Irene said. "We have only two hours. They say we are allowed only two valises and twenty *pengo* each for money."

Mama rose very slowly. She turned away from Irene and from the police, and walked slowly into her bedroom to pack. Her shoulders were slumped, and her face was streaked with tears, but she carried herself with grace. The police officers remained near the door. They didn't look comfortable with their current duty, and they didn't press the opportunity to be cruel.

My mind reeled. The thought of leaving our home and all of our possessions behind was hard to conceive. I didn't know if we would ever return. What would happen to our furniture and our clothing?

I had only one valuable possession of my own, and that was the violin. I rushed to my room and grabbed the instrument case. No one paid any attention to me as I left my room and ran up the stairs that led to the attic. If we made it back to the house, I wanted the violin to be safe.

When I reached the attic, I worked quickly. I pulled out some boards in one corner, tucked the violin behind them, and hurriedly pounded them back into place. As I worked, I kept glancing at the stairs, expecting one or all of the police to follow me. No one came.

I finished what I was doing and then slipped back down the stairs. No one was watching the door at the rear of the house, and when I saw that I was alone, I opened it, stepped out into the yard and closed it quietly. I stood very still for a moment to see if anyone had noticed, or if they would follow. I saw and heard nothing. More frightened than I'd ever been in my life, I turned and ran from the house.

Down the street was the home of a neighbor and distant relative. I knew the woman as Aunt Margarit. She had a large backyard with tall trees and bushes, and, keeping low to remain out of sight, I entered her yard and found a place in the deep shadows. The police would look for me, but I didn't believe they would spend much time or effort on it, and I thought—maybe—that I could wait them out. If they left, I would find a place to sleep and something to eat, and then get out of the city to a place where I could make a new start. I had no real plan, but anything that kept me in Hungary was preferable to deportation.

I was standing in the shadows, peeking out at the road every few moments, when I heard a shuffling step behind me and turned to find myself face to face with Aunt Margarit. I saw a mixture of fear and concern in her eyes.

"What are you doing in there, David?" she asked.

I thought it was obvious what I was doing and wondered why she didn't walk away before she drew attention to me.

"They are taking my family," I said. "We are being deported to Poland because that is where Papa was born. I am not going."

Aunt Margarit half turned, as if she might walk away, but instead she stepped closer.

"You should not be doing this, David," she said. "I have been in the street, and I heard your mother. She was crying—wondering where you had gone and what would become of you. She wants you back there, with your family."

I frowned. My decision had been made, and I'd already told my parents what I planned to do, but I hadn't planned on this. I had seen Mama crying when the letter arrived and when Papa was taken away. If she were crying now and it was because of me, I didn't think I could bear it.

"She knew that I planned to run away," I said.

"She is frightened," Aunt Margarit said, "and she needs you."

For a long moment, I hesitated. Everything I knew told me that I would be a fool to go back. I'd seen the hard, emotionless faces of the police. I'd heard stories of Poland, and I knew other families had been taken away. Here I would have to struggle, but there might be a way to find shelter and work. Here I could blend in, be Hungarian and find a way through whatever was to come.

In the end, the thought of my mother's tears was more than I could bear. I stepped from the cover of the trees and walked slowly back down the street to my home. When I arrived, the officers saw me at once. They hurried me in with my family, just in time for us to gather the last of our things and be swept out the door and into the awaiting transport.

"Why are you doing this?" Irene asked one of the officers. He was a young man, and she had recognized him.

The officer frowned. "I am doing my job," he replied. "Our orders are to bring you to the station. It isn't my decision."

He looked troubled, as if the words tasted sour in his mouth, but that was all the answer we got.

We were ordered into the back of a police sedan and driven away from our home. Once we were alone in the car, Mama turned and met my gaze. Her face was streaked with tears and her eyes filled with dread, but there was something more. She leaned over, whispering so that only I could hear.

"Why did you come back?" she asked fiercely. "You might have escaped."

I stared at her. Aunt Margarit's words came back to me, but I couldn't say them aloud to Mama. I knew in that instant that what I'd heard all my life was true: no mistake went unpunished.

I glanced out the window of the car into the street and watched as my life swept away behind me.

The drive was a quick one and, before we knew it, Mama, Irene and I were escorted into the room where Papa was being held. The room was long and narrow. Benches ran up and down the sides, and the floor was piled with heaps of straw. The windows were barred.

Papa rose to greet us, and he tried to smile but the expression did not light up his face as it normally would have. There were others in the room, men and women, families uprooted in the same way and bound for Poland.

We were kept in the room without food and without water. All that we had were the small parcels and bits of things that neighbors had brought as we packed. Food was already growing scarce in Satu Mare under the new laws, but people did what they could. They couldn't prevent the deportation, and they all lived under fear of what might happen if they were associated with those who were deported. But there were good, honest people in our town.

As darkness fell, we found a small corner of the room, piled up the straw on the floor to make beds, and slept fitfully, our meager possessions close about us. As night stole the daylight, our lives as we had known and lived them ended.

Chapter Five

The next morning, we were led out of the room where we'd been kept, still without food or water. We were loaded into cars that transported us directly to the railroad yards. Though many wished to return to their homes for items they'd forgotten, or to get messages out to family and loved ones, it was not allowed. If they insisted, they were cuffed and herded along.

At the railroad yard my family and I were loaded onto trains that were so full it was difficult to find a place to sit or even stand. There were hundreds of deportees in each car. Again, no food or water was offered. The doors were closed, and it was so claustrophobic that it became hard to breathe.

Everyone was talking at once, but few were listening. I heard a woman cry out. No one knew for certain where we were going or what was happening.

"We will die of thirst," a woman said, pounding on the doors.

All around me was misery. It was bewildering. One day I had been sitting in my room in my family's house, contemplating learning the violin, and the next day I was here, everything gone. My family huddled together and the train began its journey.

It took three days to travel from the station in Satu Mare into Poland. There was little food, only what we'd brought with us, and we were afraid to deplete the supply. There was nothing to drink, which was worse. It was August, and the sun was high in the sky. The trains were hot and far too full. It was difficult to breathe, and there was always the palpable, plaintive sound of crying women and children, the cursing and wailing of men, and the steady clack of wheels on the rails, driving us away from all that we knew. The air became a thick, fetid cloud of odor, and the constant clatter and rattle of the train, knocking us from side to side and providing a background to the moaning and tearful sobs, was nearly impossible to bear.

When the train finally came to a stop, no time was wasted. Though many were sick, starving or dehydrated, we were herded like animals from the train onto the beds of open trucks. Our questions were ignored by the officers assigned the task of moving us. The trucks rolled out and away from the train and into the broad, empty fields of Poland.

Compared to the endless train ride, our time on the trucks was limited. We bumped and bounced over uneven roads, passing no homes or towns, only desolate farmland. No consideration was given to pregnant women, children, the sick or the elderly. When the trucks rolled to a stop, I looked around in dismay.

We were in the middle of a road. Fields lined either side of the road, dusty and dry. There were no farms or homes in sight. There was nothing—it was like stepping onto the face of another planet.

We were quickly unloaded and, when we gathered in a confused group, one of the commanders of the guards who had driven us stepped up onto the bed of a truck to address the crowd.

His voice was loud and harsh. It rang out over us like the tolling of a bell.

"This is the land that your messiah has led you to," he said. "This is your reward. Do not drink the water—it is poisoned.

Stay away from the locals—they will rob and kill you if they can. If you dare to try to return to the border, or to cross back into Hungary, you will be shot."

Then, without a backward glance, and ignoring the cries of those they'd left behind, the guards piled back into the trucks, started the engines and roared back down the road the way they'd come.

I turned and stared at all of those who had been deported. There were mothers, fathers, small children, pregnant women, old and infirm men and women; they came from all walks of life. Many among them prayed loudly, but others cried.

"There is no God!"

"How can there be a God when a thing like this can happen?"

"What will we do?"

I turned to my family. My father, remarkably calm in the face of the situation, gathered us into a small group and moved us off the road, into one of the fields. It was already late afternoon and, without a plan, the deportees spread out into the fields but did not immediately leave the area. Those who had food huddled together and made whatever small meals they could. Others rested or tried to find some meager shelter against the coming night.

The entire group was in shock. Some still cried or rocked back and forth in endless prayers. The air was heavy with despair. For me, it was like walking from childhood into a nightmare adult world. I sat in the dirt, with nothing to see for miles but a road, dust and the setting sun.

I thought about my life and wondered what it was that I had done to deserve this fate. I remembered the orchard where I had stolen fruit and the times my friend Solomon and I had stolen candy from Solomon's father's store. I thought of stabbing apples through the windows in Satu Mare. None of it made sense. Solomon had not been deported, yet he had shared in each of the mischiefs that now stood out in my mind. How could it be that the same God who would send me from my home and destroy my world would turn his eyes from Solomon?

Darkness dropped swiftly and we sat close together, exhausted and hungry, unable to sleep. There was not much talk. My father spoke of what relatives he remembered from his childhood. He had vague plans to find his way to them and seek aid, but it was hard to believe any of it was real. I leaned back and stared into the blackness of the sky, and after a while I dozed. It wasn't sleep, exactly, and when cries broke out around us and the sound of stones thumping into the soil broke the silence, it took a moment to register.

"What is it?" I asked Papa. "What's happening?"

"Ukrainians," Papa hissed. "Keep low and be quiet. We must go, and quickly."

All around us the families that had ridden with us on the train and the trucks scattered. There were screams and grunts of pain. Women and children wailed and I heard heavy breathing and the struggles of men fighting for their families and their lives.

The Ukrainians fanned out and surrounded us. They held sticks and kept throwing stones. All around us people were struck with stones or dragged out through the ring of attackers and beaten. It was a nightmare as the invaders bore down on us, lashing out and calling to us in harsh, foreign tones.

My father got us on our feet and, with our belongings clutched tightly, the four of us started straight off across the field. A man leaped at us with a stick held high over his head, but Papa managed to sidestep the blow and sent our attacker sprawling.

"Run!" he cried out.

We did as he said, and he kept us low as we moved as quickly as possible. There was no way to stay completely out of sight, no cover, but the attackers concentrated their efforts near the road and, before long, the sounds of the struggle fell away behind us.

My father drew us all down into a trench in the field. We huddled down as deep as we could. The darkness helped to shield us from sight. The other deportees scattered, screaming and crying out, and their attackers followed.

"Who are they, Gabriel?" Mama asked. "Why would they do that? What do they want?"

"They want food and money, anything we might have," Papa said. "This is a poor place—the lower classes are little better than beggars. They knew we were coming—and they were waiting. This...is the life we have come to. We will have to be very careful who we speak with, where we are seen and how we spend what little we have."

"What will we do?" Irene asked.

Papa drew her close and leaned back into the trench. We all huddled close together and kept our heads low.

"We will do as I have said," Papa replied. "We will find our way to my family. We have a little money, and we have our lives and our health. I have my trade. We will live, and we will work. God will provide."

I heard the words, but thinking back over the past twenty-four hours—the pain, the loss, the cruelty—I wondered if God would indeed provide.

When the sun rose, I poked my head carefully up over the edge of the trench and scanned the field. No one was in sight. There was no traffic on the road. All of those who had been on the train, and all of those who had attacked us in the night, had disappeared. It was as if they had never existed.

We crawled up out of the trench and brushed ourselves off.

We stood and stared back along the way toward the railway station and the border beyond. All we saw were empty, barren fields and the road stretching off into the distance.

My father turned us away, down the road and deeper into Poland. We were out of sight of any homes or towns and, no matter what else was going to happen, there was no way we could survive without finding food and some form of shelter. We walked slowly, conserving our energy. There was nothing to drink, and we had very little food left.

A little after noon, we heard an engine in the distance. We stepped off the side of the road.

"What do we do?" Mama asked. "Will they attack us again? Should we hide?"

Papa stared back down the road behind us. Dust rose where a wagon rolled steadily toward us. He shook his head.

"I will speak with them," he said. "Maybe I will be able to arrange for us to ride to town."

We stood and waited as an old farm wagon approached. The bed of the trailer was half full of covered crates and boxes, but there was some room. The driver was a short, swarthy man. When Papa stepped out into the road, he slowed and stopped.

I listened carefully as Papa greeted the man. Though born in Poland, my Papa's linguistic skills were rusty. The driver stared at him with distrust and glanced up and down the road, as if making sure that he wasn't being observed speaking with a Jew.

After a few moments' bartering , Papa returned and opened one of our bags. He rummaged inside for a moment and then drew out a shirt. It was one of only three he had with him, but it was clean and in good condition. He carried it back to the truck and handed it to the driver, whose smile was more genuine, if not exactly friendly, at the sight of the shirt. They spoke a moment longer and then Papa turned back to us.

"Get into the back," he said. "We're going to ride until we are just outside of town. We'll have to get down before anyone sees him helping us, but it's a long way from here, and this will give us a short time to rest."

We clambered onto the flat, uncomfortable bed of the wagon. I slid over and leaned against a pile of crates. The horses started off down the road with a lurch. The sun hung high above us, and the day had grown hot and dry. The farmer had a small jug of water, and he shared it reluctantly. We each took a sip, trying not to gulp it down. It took a couple of hours to come within sight of town. As we rode, Papa spoke quietly and we listened.

"Things have already changed here," he said. "The Nazis are in control, and we are going to have to be very careful. These are poor villages. People have very little—not much more than we do. There is not much food, and to make things even worse, they do not like Jews. Even before the Germans, there were problems. What they told us when they left us in the road last night was true. The Germans aren't the only danger here… The peasants will beat us, rob us, even kill us if it can bring them food or money. We will have to keep moving, and we will have to blend in as well as we can."

"How can we do that, Papa?" Irene asked. Her eyes were wide, and I saw that her lip trembled. "How can we blend in when we can't even speak their language?"

"I don't know," Papa said, "but I know that we will find a way. We have no other option but to go forward and to trust. We will find my sister, and from there we will find our way."

"It's been a long time since you saw her, Gabriel," Mama said. "Are you sure she'll be happy to see us?"

"I don't believe anyone will be happy to see us," Papa said. "But we will go and we will see."

The driver slowed and rolled to a stop near a small patch of trees. He glanced over his shoulder with an apologetic smile. Papa waved. He climbed down, took the suitcases and then helped Mama. Irene and I jumped down on our own and, moments later, we were alone again, standing on the road leading into a Polish village where we knew no one and had no place to stay and no prospects of food or work. Staring into that bleak future, I felt as if I'd walked straight through the gates of hell.

Chapter Six

The next days were hard. Poland was under strict Nazi law. Jews were required to wear white armbands with blue Stars of David at all times. They were not allowed to hold jobs or attend schools. Papa kept us moving, not staying in one place long enough to attract attention, all the while moving us closer to his family.

We made contact with the Jewish families we encountered, and each time we learned something new and more disturbing. If you were between the ages of seventeen and sixty, you never walked anywhere alone. You could be robbed, or beaten, or kidnapped and sent to a labor camp. Those taken to the camps were never heard from again. Some of the villages had already had their entire Jewish populations moved to the ghettos in the larger cities, and those who remained behind lived in misery and fear. They knew it was only a matter of time before they would be taken away. They clung to their lives and their freedom tenaciously.

In the village, after hurried and terse conversations with several men, Papa was finally directed to the home of a man who was a member of the Judenrat, a committee formed of the wealthiest and most prominent members of a town's Jewish community. Such committees were formed in all the villages and towns of Poland after the Nazi occupation. Their job was to cooperate with the Germans, to provide tributes of money, gold and jewels, and, when directed, to provide certain numbers of men and women to be sent to the work camps.

"What do you want?" the man who answered the door asked.

"We've been deported from Hungary," Papa explained. "We're trying to make our way to my sister's home in Monasterzyska. We ask only a place to rest and, if possible, food. We have very little, but we will pay if we can."

The man, whose name was Ezof, shook his head sadly. He glanced up and down the street, and I found myself doing the same. It is a habit that becomes quickly ingrained when every place you go to brings new danger and everyone you meet might rob you, kill you or turn you over to the Germans.

"Come in quickly," Ezof said, stepping aside and holding the door.

"Thank you," Papa said. We entered and the door immediately closed behind us.

"You can stay here until the sun sets," Ezof said. "After that, I will lead you to the synagogue. There you can spend the night, but you must be gone by morning."

"But we have come so far already," Irene pleaded.

"It cannot be helped," Ezof said. His eyes were awash in pain, but his expression was firm. "If you stay here, they will find you. If they find you, they will know that we allowed you to stay, and they will ask for more money. They will take you, and they will take more of my people—for their camps. I am sorry, but you must go."

"It's fine," Papa said. "We don't want to cause trouble."

Ezof relaxed slightly. "I don't have much food," he said, "but there's a little I can spare. They have taken everything. We're not allowed to work. My brother was taken last week to the camps."

We settled in against the wall of one of the back rooms of

Ezof's home. It had once been comfortable, but now it showed signs of neglect. There was no sign of Ezof's wife, and none of us asked him about her. He talked in slow, steady tones, telling us of the occupation. As he did so, Papa translated quietly as much as he could. Ezof spoke almost matter-of-factly about men losing their jobs and their businesses, about families having no food. We hadn't known in Hungary what was going on in Poland, and he let us know what we would face. When the sun began to set on the horizon, he at last fell silent.

He left us for a moment and returned with a small packet of food and an old wineskin full of water. He handed the meager gift to Papa almost apologetically.

"We must go now," he said. "I cannot risk that you will be seen here. "I will take you to the synagogue."

"We thank you for all you have done," Papa said. "May God be with you."

Ezof met Papa's gaze for a long moment and then took us out the back way, through the yards of several neighbors and onto a less-traveled path that led around the edge of the town. We met no one on the way, though we had to pull back into the shadows of an alley once to avoid a passing group of German guards who were laughing loudly and talking among themselves.

I listened to their words. They were talking about the dinner they'd just finished, and the wine. One of them was making lewd comments about a local girl he'd taken a liking to. The words seemed to come from another world as we huddled in the shadows, our hearts thudding loudly, frightened for our lives.

We reached the synagogue without further incident, and Ezof slipped us in through the back. A dark room just inside was used for the storage of cleaning supplies and tools. Ezof led us inside.

"Be gone before the sun rises and you will miss the Germans on patrol," he told Papa. "I hope that you find your family—I hope there is something to find—and that they welcome you. I wish that we had met under better circumstances."

Papa clasped the man's hand and then we were alone in the shadows.

"Rest," Papa told us. "It's only a few hours until sunrise. We have no papers for traveling, so we will need to get onto the road before sunrise and then find a place to remain out of sight while it is light out, or find another ride."

No one else spoke. There was nothing for us to say. We were exhausted, hungry and very, very alone.

Despite everything, we slept. When Papa shook me a few hours later, waking was like coming out of a deep and dark cavern. I opened my eyes and saw that the room, which had been very dark, showed signs of gray light leaking in under the door.

"We must go," Papa said.

Mama was already standing, and Irene had stirred and was gathering her things. We moved to the door and Papa opened it carefully. There was no one in sight. The synagogue was on the very edge of town, and we were able to slip out and parallel the road without actually stepping onto it. When we were far enough down the road that the town had fallen away behind us, we sat and ate a little of what Ezof had given us.

It was the first of many such days. The journey to Monasterzyska was long and filled with misery. Along the way we met many families and people who defended their possessions and one another, and daily I found new horrors to fear, new dangers to inhabit the world of my nightmares. Throughout it all, Papa held us together. He took chances, and he maintained his prayers. His faith seemed unshakable, but for me there were more questions than ever before.

Chapter Seven

Papa's sister and her husband lived in a comfortable house in the town of Monasterzyska. They had two married daughters, grandchildren and one son living at home. Though they were considered well to do and were influential in the local Jewish community, life was difficult. Since no Jewish citizens were allowed employment, their business had been closed down.

Despite the fact that she had not seen her brother for thirty-five years, this was no happy reunion. When the door opened and Papa told the woman standing in the doorway who he was, her expression barely changed. She disappeared inside and returned with her husband, who invited the rest of us in reluctantly.

There were greetings and a few old stories repeated for the sake of formality. Though we were fortunate to find family and to get in off the street, there was little welcome in that home.

"We will do what we can," Papa promised his sister. "I am a skilled carpenter. Irene and Lea can take in sewing. We will not be a burden to you."

The home was separated, and we were given some rooms of our own. We cooked and shared our meals in private—we were never made to feel part of the family. Our presence was a danger to everyone, and things were tense.

I worked hard at learning the local language. Moving about

freely was difficult, and it was even worse if you were known to be Jewish. I wanted to be able to blend in, and I took every opportunity to increase my vocabulary and improve my accent.

One day, near the outside of the village, I spotted a group of Hungarian soldiers. Hungary was fighting alongside Germany, and many Hungarian soldiers served in Poland. I heard them speak my native tongue.

I was dressed as well as could be expected for a peasant, and I approached the camp. One of the young soldiers glanced up and saw me.

"What do you want?" he asked. He mangled the local tongue even worse than I did.

"Nothing," I replied in Hungarian. "I thought maybe you needed someone to clean or to run errands."

It was a huge risk. I was young, and the soldiers could have detained me or bullied me—even killed me if they wanted. Instead, hearing my accent and that I spoke their language, a man stood and walked over to where I waited.

"You are not local," he said.

"No, sir," I replied. "I am from Satu Mare."

The man stared at me. There were a lot of questions he could have asked at that point, and I feared most of them. I didn't want to draw attention to myself or my family, but the lure of men whose language I could understand was too much.

"I suppose," he said after a moment, "that we could use someone to sweep the mess area. The men are not particularly clean, and the flies…"

I nodded, trying not to seem too eager. "I would be happy to do it," I said.

The man smiled. "Come with me," he said.

I followed, and a few moments later I was working my way between crude wooden benches, clearing the remains of the noon meal and trying to avoid the urge to pick the bits of food off the ground. When I was almost done, the young soldier I had first spoken to approached.

"What is your name, boy?" he asked.

"David."

"Well, David," the soldier said. "You've done a very good job. When you have finished, there are other things to be done."

He held out a stale crust of bread. It was about the size of his hand, and I took it gratefully. I wanted to wolf it down but forced myself to wait.

"Thank you, sir," I said.

"You seem to be a good boy. Come back in the morning. Do you know how to shine shoes?"

I nodded. I took a bite of the bread and lost control. I finished what I'd been given quickly. I was hot and thirsty, but I chewed and swallowed the dry bread as if it were the finest meal I'd had in my life. The soldier watched me. There was something like compassion in his gaze, but it was very distant, and I knew not to press it.

"I will come whenever you need me," I said. I added, "It's good to hear voices from home."

"It is at that," the soldier said, smiling.

I turned back to the work and finished sweeping. When I was done I carried several bags of garbage out of the camp and was introduced to several other soldiers who promised to keep me very busy. When I left, they gave me another chunk of bread, and as hungry as I was I carried it with me. I knew the others would be hungry as well, and I wanted Papa to know that although I'd taken a chance, it had worked out. I was afraid that they would warn me away from the soldiers.

I need not have worried. The food was welcome, and over the days and weeks to come I spent more and more time in the soldiers' camp. I ran errands, polished shoes, cleaned and swept—anything they asked of me. I never asked for anything in return, but they often gave me bits and pieces of food, and sometimes a bit more to take home with me. They also gave me *pengo,* Hungarian coins that I secreted away and saved.

Though my uncle's business had been shut down, now and then he would secretly slaughter a bull. The meat was distributed among the Jewish community, bartered and traded. Now and again my aunt slipped us a bit of food to eat; along with what Mama was able to get in trade for the work she and Irene did as seamstresses, and with what Papa and I brought home, we survived. We were often hungry, but we got by.

Unfortunately, things did not improve. Instead, food grew more and more scarce and the close quarters chipped away at our tempers and sanity. Eventually, it was too much. Papa spoke with his sister. He asked that Irene and Mama be allowed to remain and told her that he and I would move on to the next town.

It was agreed, and soon the two of us set off. Along the way Papa told me more about his childhood. The town we were traveling to was Nizniev, the town of his birth. He had a brother, and he hoped that he'd be able to locate him. The two of us were dressed as locals. I had practiced and was fairly certain that I could answer questions if confronted. It was still dangerous to travel from town to town without papers—if we were caught and found to be Jews, we could be robbed, beaten, sent to the work camps or even killed.

Despite the danger, we met no resistance and arrived at Nizniev. The streets of the village were unpaved and lined with small, one-story homes. As we walked, Papa turned to me.

"Well, David," he said. "It's been a very long time since I walked down this street. Let's see if I can still recognize the house where I was born."

We walked on in silence for a while. Papa moved slowly, taking in the decrepit state of things and scanning each home as we passed it. We had walked almost a mile from the edge of town when Papa stopped. He turned and stared at a low-slung, one-story house with a peaked roof.

I started to speak and then stopped. I saw a tear rolling down Papa's cheek. Eventually, he wiped his eyes and turned to me.

"This is it."

We stood a moment longer and then Papa stepped forward. He made his way up the walk and knocked on the door. We waited together as footsteps sounded inside. When the door opened, a man stood staring back at us. I could see the resemblance. He was older and rougher, but the resemblance was strong.

The man didn't speak at first. He stared at Papa and then, laughing, he stepped forward and caught his brother in a tight embrace. I stood and waited patiently until the two finally broke their embrace and Papa turned.

"I want you to meet my son, David."

The man hugged me tightly and then held me at arm's length, examining me.

"I see the resemblance," he said. "Come in, come in."

We followed him inside and he closed the door behind us quickly.

"They are always watching," he said. "We have to be careful. If they knew you were here? But enough of that. My God, Gabriel, I was afraid that I'd never see you again! There have been many groups of refugees. Every time they came through the town I asked after you. No one had news."

"We stopped in Monasterzyska," Papa explained. "Our sister sends her greetings."

My uncle nodded. "There has been little communication, as you probably understand. We are not allowed to travel between villages. You are fortunate to have arrived without trouble."

"We did our best to blend in," Papa said.

I scanned my surroundings. The home was small but well kept. The floors were of packed dirt. There were two small bedrooms and a larger combination living room and kitchen.

There was a large oven that seemed to double as a heater in cold weather. It was very modest compared to my aunt's home in Monasterzyska, but from the moment I had seen the genuine happiness wash over my uncle's face I'd felt more at home than I had since the day we were arrested in Satu Mare.

"You must be tired," my uncle said. "Please, rest. There are others I must tell of your arrival, and my wife will be home soon."

He left the room for a moment and then came back with a piece of bread; he broke it into halves and handed them to Papa and me.

"There is not much, but I suspect that you understand this. What we have we will share. There is work in the village. We will find a way to make do. It is good to see you again, Gabriel. It is good to have you home, even in times as dark as these."

"It is good to be here," Papa replied. "And I'm glad for David to meet more of his family. I'm sorry that I have stayed away for so long. These times—they bring new meaning to the things that matter most. They humble us."

My uncle nodded. "I will be back soon," he said. "If my wife returns before I do, introduce yourselves. She will welcome you. We all welcome you. I only wish the circumstances were different."

He turned then and left the house. Papa and I chewed on the bread he'd given us and sat quietly, resting. It was a very different homecoming from what we'd received in Monasterzyska. Like night and day.

Things were no safer in Nizniev, yet they were better. My uncle and his wife did all they could to make us feel at home. He told us, as time passed, of his first wife, who had died. His was a happy family.

After resting a few days after our journey, Papa went out with his brother to do what carpentry work they could find. They repaired windows, doorways and furniture, and in return they were given flour, vegetables and, on rare occasions, chickens. In time, I began to go out with the two men to learn and do what I could to help. Even at that young age I had begun to assume the role of breadwinner, as my work was sometimes rewarded with food.

I studied the language and mannerisms of the locals carefully. One day I pulled Papa aside.

"I want to visit Mama. It's been a long time, and we should check on them."

"It's dangerous," Papa said. "How will you make it so far? We have no travel papers."

"There's a group of locals traveling to Monasterzyska in three days," I said. "I speak their language now, and I can remain disguised. I should be able to make it even if I'm questioned."

Papa gave in eventually. He wanted word of his wife and his daughter. When the day came, the family packed what little they could spare into a bag and said their goodbyes to me as I left to meet up with the others who were traveling.

Between the two cities was a large river known as the Niester. On the journey to Nizniev, we had traveled by barge. Since that time, the bridge spanning the river had been bombed, and in warm weather it was impossible to cross unless you had a boat.

When our party reached the river, it was frozen solid. It was bitterly cold and the surface of the water was very slick, but we crossed without incident. I felt much safer than before because I was nearly fluent in the local tongue and, dressed as I was, I was able to move with relative freedom.

We reached Monasterzyska safely, and I made my way quickly to my aunt and uncle's home. When I knocked on the door, Irene answered and, seeing me, drew me inside into a tight embrace.

"What are you doing here, Dudi?" she asked. "Where is Papa?"

"Safe," I said. I smiled at the nickname—it had been some

time since I'd heard it. "We want to know how you and Mama are. Things are getting worse every day. We have some work—helping Papa's brother with his carpentry business. We've been as comfortable as you could expect."

"It's the same here," Irene said. "What is Papa's brother like? Is the village much smaller? You walked here? Surely the barge isn't running in this weather?"

I laughed. "No, the river is solid as rock. We just walked right across. The men I crossed with told me that it will stay that way for several weeks."

At that moment Mama entered the room, saw me and ran to my side. She hugged me and asked all the same questions, remarking on how much I seemed to have grown. The rest of the family was polite but not thrilled by my coming. Things had not changed, and the house was crowded. Having Irene and Mama in the house was enough of a danger. With me back, the chances of drawing attention increased.

The visit was a short one. Things were not comfortable, and I did not want to be recognized by too many in Monasterzyska after being gone for so long. I couldn't risk being questioned seriously, and I didn't want to put the family at risk.

Irene asked again and again about our uncle and Nizniev.

"I have to go back," I said. "Why don't you come and see Papa? You could meet the family."

Mama wasn't happy with the idea. The travel was dangerous, and it meant being alone with relatives she was only on polite terms with, but in the end she relented. My party was returning, and they readily agreed to the addition of another traveler. We left by night, avoiding German patrols, and returned across the Niester.

We made the return trip without incident. Irene stayed with us for a time and then returned to Mama. We did not want to leave anyone absolutely alone for any length of time. By then it had been nearly a year since our deportation, and things were desperate.

Word had spread that all the Jews in the larger cities in Poland had been removed either to the ghettos, where there was no food and no hope of survival, or to the work camps, where they worked as little more than slaves until they became too weak to be useful and then were killed. No one who went to the camps had ever returned, and though no one had witnessed the deaths, everyone knew what it meant to be taken there.

In the smaller towns, Jewish communities remained, but the Germans had stretched their influence and, slowly, like dominoes in a very long, desolate line, the homes were emptied. Families were ordered to stand in front of their homes on a particular day to be transported to the cities. The tentative safety of Monasterzyska and Nizniev faltered and faded. Word spread that within no more than two weeks, my uncle's family would be transported. There were two courses open: we could walk into certain death or take matters into our own hands and have a chance at freedom, even if the odds were against us.

One morning, Papa made his decision. He gathered our Hungarian citizenship papers, told me to wait for him, and left the house. Since our arrival in Poland, every moment had been at least partially invested in avoiding the German authorities. A Jewish man who caught their attention could be arrested on the spot and sent to the ghettos or the work camps. If things went very poorly, he could be shot on the spot. Papa had kept us as far from this particular danger as possible.

Now it was a moment of desperation, and everything changed. Jews were not allowed to travel from city to city, and no one could travel at all without authorization papers signed by the proper German authorities. Papa had never interacted with the German commander in Nizniev. He had worked with his brother and kept a low profile. This day he wore the best of the clothes that remained with him. He was cleaned up, and he carried his papers with authority.

When he neared the commander, a German soldier approached and asked his business. He presented the papers and asked to speak with the commander. The soldier looked him over, shrugged and told him to wait. A few minutes later the man returned, and Papa was escorted inside.

What happened next was never clear. The German glanced over the papers and noted Papa's Hungarian citizenship. He only gave Papa a cursory glance and then handed the papers back. When Papa turned and walked away, he held travel papers to the Hungarian border in his hand. They were good for only thirty days, but it was enough to get us out of the town. It was also enough to keep us from being taken when my uncle's home was emptied and our family was taken away forever.

Papa walked back to his brother's home, thinking all the while that he might be part of some huge joke, that at any moment they would come for him or he'd be cut down by a bullet to the back of the head. But he made the walk without incident. When he returned, he didn't hesitate.

"Pack everything of value," he said. "We will get to your mother and sister as quickly as we can. Once we are all together, we will have to hurry. We must get on the road and away from the villages. Our papers are good for only thirty days, but we can't risk the trains. Jews are not allowed on the trains. If they question the papers, we will be taken."

I nodded. I'd waited for Papa, thinking that if the Germans took him or killed him, I would run. It was nearly impossible to believe that we had been granted passage. It would be insanity to hesitate now that the opportunity had been granted.

We said our goodbyes to my uncle and his family. It was a difficult moment. It was hard to leave them behind, knowing what was to come, but we had no choice. There was one chance for us, and we had to take it.

We made the journey to Monasterzyska quickly and without incident, traveling by night and staying out of sight. We made our way to Papa's sister's home, where we broke the news to Mama and Irene. The two packed their bags quickly, and we all said our goodbyes to the family. Papa thanked his family profusely for taking us in and helping us to remain safe.

It was an odd moment. The family knew they were about to be taken from their homes—and none of them believed that Papa would lead his own family back to the Hungarian border. They said their goodbyes in a sort of shocked silence. They did not know, though they must have suspected, that we would never see one another again. Then, once again, my family and I were on our own—and on the road.

Chapter Eight

The road back to Hungary was much worse than it had been on our way out. Fear and starvation had become a way of life. The food we'd been able to pack didn't last long, despite our efforts to preserve it. Most of the journey was made on foot, though from time to time we were able to hitch rides on horse-drawn wagons.

There was no food to be had anywhere. Once or twice we were able to find remnants of the Jewish communities in the towns we passed, and we found refuge in barns or synagogues. There was no food to spare, but we bartered for what we could. After a time, we ventured into the farmers' fields and ate whatever we found there.

One afternoon we stopped by the road to rest. Irene wandered off in search of food. We often took turns looking, conserving our energy. Quite a bit of time passed without a sign of her, and eventually Mama grew worried.

"David," she said. "Go and find your sister. She has been gone too long."

I rose. I was worried as well. We had remained very close together on the road. There were too many dangers to risk separation. Our papers were only a tentative barrier preventing our arrest or being shot. The trip had already taken more than the original thirty days that the papers were good for. Papa had very carefully altered the dates on the papers, but if they were given any real scrutiny, our freedom could come to an abrupt end.

I disappeared across the road where Irene had gone. After a while, when I also didn't return, Mama came looking and then—at last—Papa. On that journey was one of few magical moments. Irene had stumbled onto a patch of wild raspberries. She had been so overjoyed, and so hungry, that she'd set to eating them and had not been able to turn back to the road, not even to tell the rest of us. We entered the berry patch one after the other, and that one time we ate our fill.

The berries were sweet and good. There were so many we could not eat them all, though we tried. We carried away as many as we could, smiling for perhaps the first time since we'd set out on our journey.

One of the towns we entered had been almost completely evacuated; everyone had gone to the ghettos. It was like a scene from Dante's *Inferno.* I walked beside Papa, staring at the dead and dying people in the streets. It was difficult to believe in the reality of what we passed through—and then, after a while, it became more difficult to believe in the rational, real world we'd left behind.

Some of the people in the streets were still alive, but they were like living skeletons. They could barely move. The skin was pulled back from their teeth, and their eyes were sunken; they were thin to the point of emaciation, except those in which the bloat had begun. There were dead bodies all over, left to rot and decompose like forgotten garbage. There seemed to be no decent burials, and there was no one left to tend the sick.

There was no food and little water. The starving and the dying lined the streets and filled the doorways. Sometimes the only way to tell the dead from those who were still alive was the amount of bloat. Those with enough life remaining begged for food as we passed through. Papa kept us moving. It was sickening and heart-wrenching at the same time. Their voices were thin and reedy, without strength or hope.

Throughout all that happened, Papa prayed twice daily without fail, and he observed the rituals whenever possible. For me, faith was becoming difficult. This town—where people were dying, alone and forgotten—went against all that I'd been taught. I'd been raised to believe that if you did good things, and you prayed and kept your faith in God, you would be rewarded, and only if you were evil or sinned would you be punished.

I could not reconcile the suffering. I could not imagine a crime sufficient to warrant the horrors surrounding me. I thought that this must have been a city such as Sodom or Gomorrah to bring such death and destruction down on itself. And I wondered about me. I tried to think of what in my life had brought me to this point—arrested and deported, sent away from my home and my friends. In my short life, my sins did not seem great. I'd stolen fruit. My friend and I had stolen candy once or twice. If I were being punished for those small transgressions and that was God's will, I could live with it. But what of Solomon? Why was my friend, who had shared in literally every mischief, spared? Could there be a God who was good and merciful and at the same time so seemingly cruel and unfair? It was a hard thing to reconcile.

We passed through as quickly as we could. There was no food to be had, and there was still the danger of being spotted and taken. Even the Germans had pulled out of the town for the most part, but we were very close to the border, and it was too much of a risk. We slept in a barn near the edge of town and, before first light, we were out and away, taking advantage of the dim morning light to put distance between ourselves and the city.

In one village we were unable to avoid the German patrols. Papa was taken to the German officer in charge. He later told us that he had remained calm, fighting back his terror, but inside he was terrified that the man would see where the papers had been doctored or find some other fault with them. Papa had stood alone and waited. After a time, someone called to the officer, and he turned, distracted.

A moment later he returned the papers to Papa and took off to deal with some problem that had arisen. He ordered Papa to return and present himself the next day to have the matter settled.

We had arranged to spend the night in the barn of one of the local Jewish families, and when Papa returned, he explained what had happened.

"It's a miracle he let you walk away," an old man said. "You must go—tonight. Do not return to him. He will have you killed. He will take you all away."

Papa knew the old man was right. That night we slipped out of town under cover of darkness, moving as quickly as we could to avoid late patrols. We traveled across fields and through patches of trees to avoid the roads. After that, we were even more careful to remain out of sight. The patrols were less frequent because most of the citizens had been removed to work camps or had died of starvation. It was a desperate, desolate time.

As we neared the Hungarian border, the danger increased. Locals warned us that we might never make it across. Anyone caught trying to cross illegally was shot. They were tightening the border and showed no mercy.

Finally, with luck and perseverance, we reached Stryy, the final village that stood between us and the Hungarian border. Similar to the previous village, Stryy was in a state of chaos and death. There was so little food that people begged in the streets, and often died there. There was no work and no hope. We had so little left to us by that time, we could barely find anything to sell or trade. We held on, talking to locals and looking for a way back to our home.

One day Papa returned with news. He'd been out, as usual, scouring the city for food.

"I met a man today who says there is another village, a small village, even closer to the border. There is a man there who has made it his business to smuggle refugees across the border."

"Can he be trusted?" Mama asked.

"We have no choice," Papa said. "If we stay here, soon we will join the others in the street. There is no food, and eventually we will all be taken away to the ghettos and the camps. I would rather be shot trying to make my way to my home and my freedom than die in the street."

None of us responded. Our lives had become a series of sudden, irreversible decisions. And if we chose wrong, our lives would end. We packed up our scant possessions and made our way by night to the village we'd been told of, and to the one man who could help.

We arrived late in the afternoon, and after only a couple of discreet inquiries made our way to a farmhouse on the outskirts of the city. The man who met us was a middle-aged Polish farmer. He asked no questions. A single look told him why we were there. He led us quickly inside and out of sight. In the rear of his home, in his kitchen, was a long table.

"Sit," he told us. "Rest."

We did as he asked, and he immediately set about putting a large kettle over his fire. He filled the pot with potatoes and left them to boil. I watched the man and the food. It was difficult to imagine so much all in one place, and soon the kitchen was heavy with the odors of cooking.

After a time, the farmer removed the potatoes from the kettle and laid them before us.

"Eat," he said. "You must be starving, and you will need your strength. When night falls we will go. We need the darkness to slip across to Hungary."

We fell on the meal ravenously. For the first time in recent memory there was hot food and enough for us to eat our fill. When we were done and could eat no more, we began to gather what we had to pay for passage. The service we were receiving was not free, and we had very little.

In the end, we handed over Mama's wedding ring and Irene's watch, which she had kept hidden since being deported. Such things were rare in Poland in those times. The payment was enough.

As darkness fell, other Jews joined us. There were a couple of families and a handful of others traveling alone. Like my family's, their clothing was threadbare, and they were thin to the point of emaciation. They were weak but determined.

The night was clear and dark. The sky was sprinkled with stars. I stared out across the fields. It was hard to believe that, after more than a year, our home was so close. The field looked like any field, and the night was like a hundred others when we'd set out without knowing what the next day would bring or where we would end up.

The food helped. Our guide was confident. He warned us to keep low and to keep quiet. There were dangers waiting. If a German or Hungarian patrol spotted us, we would be shot and killed. Despite the warnings, it was difficult not to feel a growing elation.

We walked in silence, making good time. I began to think about home, about my friends and family, and what might have changed in Hungary. I was lost in those thoughts when loud shouts broke the silence.

"What is it?" Irene cried. "Who's there?"

Before any of us could move, two large men materialized from the shadows. They held clubs, and they glared at us menacingly.

"Give us everything you have," the taller of the two said, "or we will take it."

They shouted and cracked their clubs on the palms of their hands. They moved in quickly, cuffing me and rummaging roughly through my pockets. My heart hammered, but I didn't fight back. There was nothing I could do—and I had nothing to give them.

The men searched all us but found only a single packet under Papa's jacket. It held his *tallit* and his prayer book. They threw these to the ground and grew rough.

"It's all we have," Papa said. "We are only trying to get home to our family in Hungary. We have nothing—we have been on the road a very long time. You must believe us. If we had anything to give, we would give it to you."

The men tried a few moments longer to find something worth taking, but there was nothing, and finally they quieted. They were hungry, like everyone, but they understood our family's plight. In the end, they pointed in the direction of the border, and they melted back into the night.

Papa gathered our belongings from the dirt and wrapped them carefully. We stood, alone and bewildered, in the middle of the field. We had the directions our attackers had given us but had no idea whether we had been told the truth.

"Gabriel," Mama whispered, "what will we do?"

Just then, there was another sound. It was a soft hiss. The farmer who had guided us slipped back out of the shadows.

"I am sorry," he said. "I could not risk being seen. They would send me to prison or to the camps for what I do. Come with me. We have wasted too much time already."

The man turned, and we followed him off across the shadowed fields. We crossed fences and fields of potatoes, waded through creeks and stumbled through wooded patches for what seemed an eternity. Just as I felt as if I could go no farther, our guide came to a stop and pointed off across the fields.

In the distance, dim but visible, we saw a light.

"Do you see it?" the farmer asked.

"What is it?" I asked.

"That is Hungary," the man said. "That is your home."

He continued on and, after a moment, we fell in behind him with renewed strength. It was growing close to morning, and the danger of being spotted grew with each passing moment. We heard voices once or twice, and the barking of dogs. We were approaching a small town, and the inhabitants were rising to begin their day. On the outskirts, the farmhouses were spread out. Our guide made his way through the fields behind one and knocked on the door.

My family and I stood at a distance, shielded by some trees, and waited. It was a Jewish home. We saw the *mezuzah* cover on the doorframe. Still, after the time we had spent in Poland, it was impossible to know how we would be received. Moments later our guide called us forward and we were hurried inside.

There was little talk. We were shown to a room and left to rest. We settled ourselves on the floor, absolutely exhausted but with new hope. It was hard to believe, but the freedom we'd been so long denied seemed to be in our grasp.

"Is it true, Gabriel?" Mama asked. "Are we home?"

"God has provided," Papa told her. He pulled her against him and leaned back against the wall to rest. Before long, we all slept the sleep of the dead.

Chapter Nine

The jubilation of our escape from Poland was short-lived. Early the next morning, there was a knock on the door of the room where we slept. We were accustomed to sleeping lightly, and we rose quickly.

It was our hostess. She stood in the doorway nervously. Irene rose and crossed the room to her. The traveling had been hard on Papa on this last leg of the journey, and he was not strong.

"What is it?" Irene asked.

"You must leave right away," the woman said. "I am sorry, but they will punish us. There are very strict rules about taking in refugees. We could be arrested."

Irene turned and looked at the rest of us, her expression sliding quickly toward despair.

"But we have nowhere to go yet," she told the woman. "We have to contact our family, get the money to travel. Can't we just—"

"Not here," the woman insisted. "You have to be gone before you are spotted. The risk is too great."

Irene bit her lip and turned. She seemed to be thinking for a moment and then spoke again.

"Let my parents and my brother stay just for a while. I will go for help. I will get a telegram to our relatives in Budapest and get money so we can take the train."

The woman started to shake her head and Irene stepped forward, laying a hand on her arm.

"Please," she begged.

The woman's face grew pale, but she nodded. "In the barn, then," she said. "We have cows and hay. Your family can hide in there until you return. If they are found, I will say that they must have snuck in on their own. It's the best I can do."

"Thank you," Irene said. She hurried over and helped Papa to his feet. I stood and helped Mama gather our things. I was still a little sleepy, but I knew what was happening. We were back in Hungary, but some things had not really changed. We were no more welcome there than we'd been in Poland, and until we made our way to family, we were in danger.

We moved to the barn, where we built a small shelter of hay and lay down to rest again. The woman gave us a little food, which we ate gratefully. Irene gathered her things.

"I will be back as soon as I can get a telegram to Budapest," she said. "You must stay hidden."

Papa rose unsteadily. He laid a hand on Irene's arm.

"Be careful," he said. "They are everywhere, and we are so close."

Irene nodded. She hugged Mama and then leaned down to hug me as well. When she had left, I helped my parents to get comfortable, hidden as far back in the barn as possible.

We stayed quiet and kept in the shadows, flinching at every sound we heard. After a time, I grew restless. I felt that the three of us were more likely to be discovered than only two, and that I could be of more use helping my sister than hiding in a barn.

"I have to go after her," I said at last.

Mama shook her head.

"I will be more help if I go," I insisted. "I have some money—I've saved it. I will help her reach Rachel. We'll bring help, and we'll find a way to get us all out."

I didn't wait for my parents to disagree. I rose and left the barn, following the path toward the nearest village.

I had always done what I could to present the best possible appearance. I kept my shirt tucked in, and I cleaned up at every opportunity. I had figured out early on in Poland that the less I looked like a Jewish refugee the better, and caring about my appearance was one way to set me apart.

I made my way into the first village on the road and began asking after my sister. It was simple enough to locate the family who headed up the local Jewish community. I knocked on their door, and they immediately directed me around back to their shed. I pushed the door open slowly and stepped inside.

Irene sat on a box in the corner. She had no shoes, and she looked up in surprise.

"Dudi!" she said. "Why are you here? What have you done? You are to watch Mama and Papa! I have money enough for a train ticket and I'm going to the next town to get help."

"I'm going with you," I said.

"Dudi, you can't! I have only enough money for the one ticket."

"Two of us will be more help than one," I said. "I have my own money."

"What are you talking about? Where did you get money?"

"Never mind that," I said. "I have it, and it is enough for one ticket."

I pulled out a small handful of *pengo*, the money I had gotten from the Hungarian soldiers. I'd had plenty of opportunities to spend or waste it, but I'd kept it close. Papa's lessons about never spending all that you had and always having some money to fall back on had stayed with me. There was no way I could have anticipated the need to pay for a train ticket, but now that the need had arisen, I was prepared. It was a lesson I'd never forget.

Just then a girl knocked and entered. It was a young woman

carrying Irene's shoes. They'd been ragged and worn, but now they had been repaired. They would never look new, but they would protect her feet, and they would make her look a little less like a refugee.

"My father told me that as soon as your shoes were ready I should tell you to leave," the young woman said.

"We are going," Irene told her. "Thank you, and thank your parents. We have a chance now, and it's more than we had without your help."

The girl smiled, but it was obvious that the presence of two refugees in her family's shed frightened her.

Irene turned as if she would tell me again that I had to return to our parents, but instead she said, "We must hurry, Dudi. The next town is larger and the Jewish community has more to offer. Surely we will get a message out to Rachel from there."

We slipped out of the shed and around the house, all the while watching the road in both directions. There was no one in sight, so we took off for the train station and wondered how it could be that we were home—in Hungary—and it felt so much like Poland.

Chapter Ten

We managed to buy tickets and board the train without incident. It wasn't a long ride, and we were both too nervous and excited to sleep. It took two hours, but at last the doors opened, and we found ourselves in the city of Munkach. This was a much larger town than the village we had left, and we left the train behind in high spirits, expecting that with a larger Jewish community it would be easier to find the assistance we needed.

We made inquiries and found our way to the Jewish Community Center. Irene was very optimistic, but I kept my feelings in check. I'd been disappointed and shocked so many times in the past year that it was difficult to give any credence to help we had yet to receive.

When we arrived at the community center, a man was locking it up for the night. He did not seem at all happy to see us. As Irene quickly explained our situation, the man finished locking the doors and turned to us, shaking his head and glancing furtively up and down the street.

"You should not be here," he said. "We cannot take in refugees—there are strict rules. Just by being here you risk my safety."

"But our parents are waiting. What can we do?" Irene's voice sounded lost.

"I cannot help you," the man said. He turned and hurried off without a backward glance. Irene sank down onto the steps. I sat beside her. She didn't speak, and I respected her silence, but I kept my eyes open. If what the man had said was true, we were in greater danger the longer we remained in plain sight at the community center.

Then Irene rose suddenly.

"I know what we have to do, Dudi," she said. "Remember Thal? He was one of the men we traveled across the border with."

I remembered.

"His wife and children live here in Munkach. They don't yet know that he has returned. We will find them and give them the good news. Surely they will help us."

And we were off again. It took a little time, since we didn't know where the family lived, but we were careful. It was fortunate that Irene had remembered the family's name. When we located Thal's wife, she was overjoyed by our news. The family took us in immediately and set two more places at the Shabbat table. It reminded me immediately of home with its aromas of bread and fish. I was so hungry that it was a constant pain. It was difficult for me to conceive of a table where I could sit and eat until I was full. For perhaps the first time since leaving my uncle's home in Poland, I felt as if I might be nearly home again—as if home might really still exist.

Then Irene asked the oldest of Thal's sons, a young man named Moshe, to send a telegram to our sister Rachel in Budapest. If we could get money for two train tickets, we could get back to Satu Mare, where we should have been safe. For once something worked as we had planned it. When we awoke the next morning, Moshe called to us excitedly.

"The telegram has arrived!" he said. "Your sister has sent money."

"You should go immediately," Thal's wife insisted. "It is Shabbat. They will not expect Jews to travel today—they will not be watching. If you are careful, you can pass on through to Satu Mare safely."

Though I had already begun to lose my religion and didn't worry about traveling on the Jewish Sabbath, I hesitated.

"But...what about Mama and Papa?" I asked. "They are still back by the border."

"I will take a taxi back for them," Moshe said. "I must go to find Papa, and while I am there we will pick up your parents as well. They can stay here with us until you make arrangements to get them home."

"Thank you," Irene said. "Papa isn't well after the trip. I don't think he could travel far without time to rest."

"He will be able to rest here," Thal's wife said. "You have brought my husband back from the dead. It is the least we can do."

They packed some food for us, and for the third time in as many days Irene and I were back on the road, alone and traveling into an unknown situation. We still thought of Satu Mare as home, but we hadn't been there in over a year. We didn't know what to expect when we arrived. We knew we'd have to find a way to make money there, and to survive.

We had no trouble at the train station, and soon we were rumbling down the track toward the city we'd called home for so many years. The trip took nearly eight hours but even so, it was hard to rest. We worried that someone might stop or question us, and everything since we'd returned seemed cast in gloom and despair.

When we disembarked in Satu Mare, we got away from the station as quickly as we could and made our way through the city toward our home. What we found caused our hearts to sink. The town didn't look different, but everything was turned around.

Another family had taken up residence in our home. All of our possessions were gone.

"This is our home now," the man who opened the door told us. "Nothing here is yours. Everything has been taken."

I remembered that I had hidden my violin in the attic.

"I hid something before we were sent away," I said. "Could I come in and look to see if it is still there?"

"There is nothing for you here," the man repeated. "Go, or we will report you."

He closed the door and left Irene and me standing alone in the street. We turned away in silence. A quick walk around the neighborhood confirmed that Papa's business had been closed, as had the hat shop that Rachel had opened. All trace of our family had been wiped out, and even the few people that we met—men and women we'd known all our lives—seemed more nervous than happy to see us. Some were afraid to talk to us. I felt miserable. I was homeless, without a job, no money, no parents. I couldn't have felt worse.

Along the way, I saw Solomon and a group of boys I'd gone to school with. Irene continued on, but I stopped. My friends welcomed me back as if I'd been on a vacation, and the emotions I felt were conflicting.

"Where have you been?" one boy asked. "We heard you were arrested. They said you were taken to Poland, but no one has come back from Poland."

I told them how we'd been dropped in Poland with nothing, no food or water, and left to attackers, but I could see in their eyes that they did not believe me. They thought I was making up stories. Nothing could be as bad as what I described. Men and women did not treat one another in this manner.

After a while, most of the boys dispersed, and I was alone with Solomon. My old friend listened with much more sympathy.

"It was like being in hell," I said. "There were men and women dying in the streets. Sometimes we went for days with nothing but a crust of bread to eat, and all the time avoiding the Germans. A week after we left, our family in Nizniev and Monasterzyska were to gather in front of their homes to be taken to ghettos."

"I can hardly imagine such a thing," Solomon said. "How could it happen?"

"I thought about you while I was there," I said. I knew I had to get this out, no matter how Solomon took it. "We have always been taught that for the good things we do in life we will be rewarded, and for the bad there will be punishment. I've thought back over my life, and I can only find a few things I am guilty of that stand out."

"What?" Solomon asked.

"When I was very young, I stole fruit from the orchard of a farmer who lived nearby. When I moved here to Satu Mare, you and I stole apples from a basement. Remember, we also stole candy from your father's store? When I was in Poland, I thought maybe it was these things that brought the punishment. Then I remembered all those times that you were with me and I thought, could there be a God so unfair that he would punish one of us, and not the other for identical sin? It makes no sense."

"I never thought about it that way," Solomon said. "They seemed like such small, harmless things."

"I thought so too," I said. "And now I have to tell you that it's harder and harder for me to believe in a God who would treat His chosen people in such a way. I'm forced to believe either that my family deserves what has happened to us or that we have had faith in nothing."

"You shouldn't say such a thing!" Solomon said.

"I can't help it. It's what I believe."

"Come to my house," Solomon said. "Mama and Papa will want to know you are back and that you are safe."

We returned together to Solomon's house, and his parents greeted me warmly. They invited me in to eat, and again I recounted the horrors of my time in Poland. It was hard for them to believe, but they listened politely.

Finally I addressed Solomon's father.

"I have been troubled by something for more than a year now, and I want to do what I can to make things right."

"What from the past could be troubling you after what you've been through?" Solomon's father asked.

"Before we left," I said, glancing over at Solomon, who nodded, "there were a couple of times that Solomon and I took candy from your store. We did not pay for it, and I realize now that I should have known better. It was a dishonest thing to do. I wanted you to know that I did it—but I also wanted you to know that I may have paid a great price for my transgression. I hope you will forgive me."

"My boy," the man said, laying a hand on my shoulder. "It is a very good thing to tell the truth, but you did not have to trouble yourself. You and Solomon were not as stealthy as you believed, and it was only a bit of candy. I cannot imagine what you have been through—I suspect that I'll never know—but for any wrong you have done me, you have my forgiveness."

"Thank you."

Before long, it grew dark, and it was time to depart. I had to find Irene, and we had to find shelter and food for the two of us. The whole family embraced me, and we said our goodbyes. I stepped out onto the street and felt as if another large chunk of my past had fallen away. I did not look back, and I never saw Solomon again.

The streets had become long shadows. It was even less safe

to be out alone at night. I made my way back to the home of our neighbor, the woman we had called Aunt Margarit. I stopped outside and stared into her backyard, at the trees and bushes where I'd hidden just a little over a year before.

Irene was there already, and though Margarit was less than pleased to see us, she allowed us to come in and stay. She was nervous, and it was obvious that she feared helping us.

"No one has ever come back from Poland," she said, as if the words would make Irene and me disappear.

Irene told Margarit what had happened to us and how we had struggled and suffered to return, but Margarit would not listen.

"It is not true," she said. "I don't know why you make up these stories, and I don't know where your parents are. When they arrive I will tell them what you have said, and we will find out the truth. You may stay for a few days only. You must find somewhere else to stay. If the police come, they will take us all. They will arrest me and I will lose everything."

Irene tried to calm her, but she would not listen. Finally I spoke up.

"Aunt Margarit," I said. "That day so long ago, when I hid in your yard, why did you send me back to be arrested?"

She did not meet my eyes. "I told you then that I saw your mother out in your yard. She was crying and calling your name. She was worried about you."

"Nothing that could have happened to me was as bad as what happened when I went back. Isn't it possible that my mother was crying because she was frightened, and that she called my name because the police asked her where I'd gone?"

"No." Margarit shook her head. "I know what I saw. Stop talking. Come, I have a little food, not much. You need to rest."

We fell silent and followed her to an empty room, where we

lay down with our few possessions in the darkness. After only a couple of days, we left Margarit and set out to find a way to rebuild our lives. It was the first time in my life that I had been truly alone and homeless.

Irene left Satu Mare to stay with a second cousin. I went to the home of an uncle named Shomu, who was a baker in the nearby town of Nogy'banya. He took me in and put me to work as a helper in the bakery. He also sent me out to run errands and make deliveries. It was hard work, and although I was small for my size, I worked very hard.

For a while, things were better. I had a place to sleep, and food. There was hard work to be done, and I threw myself into it. It seemed as if things might be looking up, but it was only temporary. After a time, my uncle began to berate me.

"You are too slow," he complained. "The deliveries take too long. I don't think you are concentrating on the work."

I remained respectful, but the words angered me. I worked hard every day and never shirked. I knew there was more to the complaints.

When my uncle's grumbling continued, I had to move on. I left my uncle's home and went to stay on a farm owned by relatives near a town named Porch'alma. These relatives bred and raised Angora rabbits, which were rare and valued for their fur. They sheared the rabbits regularly and made the fur into sweaters. I spent a little time there until I could get word to my brother Mendu, who was living in the city of Kluj.

Finally, I traveled to my brother's home and found my first real welcome since arriving in Satu Mare. Mendu greeted me with open arms. He made me a bed on the couch, and I immediately went to work for him running errands. Mendu built and sold baby carriages. He loaned his bicycle to me, though it was much too large. To ride it, I had to slide my leg under the bar to reach the pedal on the far side and balance the bike, but it worked.

Things were much happier for a time. Mendu shared freely with me as his brother, and I worked hard, doing anything I could to help out. I had no other way to express my appreciation for his simple gift of wanting me in his home.

Chapter Eleven

Two days after Irene and I had arrived at Satu Mare, we had received the worst news possible. My parents had gone out for a walk in the border village and were spotted by Hungarian *zandarms* and arrested. For some time I was unable to discover what had happened to them or where they had been taken. The choices were grim: they could have been sent back to Poland or handed over to the Germans. In either case, it would have meant a death sentence.

After many inquiries, my sister Rachel, who had remained in Budapest working as a seamstress, finally discovered that our parents had been taken to a prison in Hungary. They were very lucky because anyone caught crossing the border from Poland was immediately sent back to Poland—or worse.

Rachel did everything in her power to help our parents get released from prison. She wrote letters to government agencies, but nothing helped. Finally, after they'd been imprisoned for almost a year, she wrote to the Hungarian army headquarters, showing that both Moses and William were serving in the army as slave laborers and had been doing so for a long time. Based on this, our parents were finally released.

Rachel sent word, and with Papa and Mama freed the four of us—Mama, Papa, Irene and I—were reunited in Satu Mare, where we found a small apartment that we could afford to rent.

It was very different from our life before deportation, but we had survived and we were together. Papa had difficulty finding steady work. Irene worked part time as a seamstress, and I found a job as an apprentice in a print shop. It didn't pay much and was demanding, but it was interesting work and I enjoyed it.

I sat at a table that slanted back toward me. There was a large, wooden box broken up into compartments, each of which held different letters, all molded of lead. Each letter block was about an inch long, half an inch tall and an eighth of an inch wide. To create the page of a newspaper, I would take a small, metal box in my hand and place the letters, one by one, in a line. There were four lines per box. When I reached the end of a line, the print started up on the line beneath it, and as each box was filled it was placed into the printing machine until an entire page of print had been set. Then I sat with a pile of fresh paper on one side of me and placed the first sheet on the press. The mechanism worked with a foot pedal. It would print one page. I removed it, placed a fresh sheet on the press, and repeated the process.

Although the work was tedious and difficult, I enjoyed it. For one thing, there was a lot happening in Hungary and the world, and as the one who set the newsprint, I had access to news before anyone else. I read each and every article and thus had a very good idea of what was going on around me.

I was very proud of the fact that I was working and earning money. As always, I saved carefully what I made. All my life I had worn the hand-me-down clothing of my brothers. When I had worked long enough to save the money, I went to a local tailor and ordered the first brand-new suit of clothing I ever owned. The suit was salt-and-pepper gray; the jacket was tapered, with the belt sewn on in the back. It came with knickers and a cap stitched from the same material. It was the finest outfit I'd ever worn, and the fact that I had earned it myself made me very proud.

Papa was proud of me too. Though times were very hard for the family, he never lost his optimism, his hope or his faith. His dream was that his children would follow his example both in business and in life, and in his religious faith. Unfortunately, the times, and the horrors we had witnessed and been subjected to, fought against him in this. Though several of his children, me included, learned what Papa had to teach about business, faith was another thing altogether.

My birthday approached. It was not the custom in my family to give birthday gifts, and I expected nothing. Food was scarce, and money was very tight.

On the day of my fourteenth birthday, Papa entered our apartment with a package under his arm. Mama was in the kitchen, and Irene was still out working. I glanced up and Papa smiled.

"You are a year older," he said, "and a fine young man. On such an occasion, I thought something special was called for."

Papa placed the package he carried on the table in front of me.

"Go ahead," he said. "Open it."

I savored the moment. I pulled the package closer. It was the first birthday gift I'd received from Papa. When I opened it, I found a book, but it was not a prayer book. It was a book of etiquette, and it was written in Hungarian.

Papa never spoke to me, or to anyone in the family, in Hungarian. He spoke in Yiddish or Hebrew and expected us to answer in kind. This book was written in my everyday tongue. It felt like an acknowledgment of my individuality, and I knew it was not an easy gift for my father to give.

"David," he said, "I can see that you're not going to be a religious man. I hope that you will, at least, be a *mentch,* a man of dignity and honor. Maybe what you read in this book will help you along the way to leading a better life."

I felt hot tears threatening to fall from my eyes, but I forced them back. The most important things to my father were education, having a trade and religion. He saw that I wasn't going to follow the traditions, and for him to give me this book must have been a tremendous effort. It made an impression on me.

"Thank you, Papa," I said.

"Thank me with your deeds."

I took the book and carefully packed it in with my few private possessions. That was one of the last happy moments I spent in Satu Mare.

On Saturdays, I walked with Papa to the synagogue. As we went, we gathered and walked with other Jews of the city. As we walked, Papa told the others about what had happened in Poland. He told them about the ghettos and the work camps. He told them how entire cities and communities had been turned out into the streets and taken away like cattle. He told them about the starvation and the terror. Despite the fact that they that knew Papa and our family had been deported, most of the men did not believe the stories.

"Those sound like tales made up to frighten children," one man said. "Maybe such a thing is possible in Poland, though I can't see how one man could act in such a way to another, but certainly such things are not possible here."

"Yes," another said. "In Hungary, we know how to treat one another. They would never do such things here—it's unthinkable."

Papa repeated, "I was there. The guards assigned to the city where my sister lived were not Germans, and they were not Polish. They were Hungarian. Things are changing. No one is safe."

They scoffed at him, but I took it all in. I couldn't understand how they could live there, in Satu Mare, where Nazi laws increasingly removed their status, wealth and rights, and doubt

Papa's words. None of them seemed ready to outright call Papa a liar, but they couldn't bring themselves to believe his stories of Poland. They had apparently decided to pretend the problem didn't exist and wait for it to go away.

It did not. It was only a few weeks before Irene burst into the apartment one evening with news of evacuation.

"They are spreading the word for all Jewish citizens to evacuate their homes," she said. "They are relocating us."

"To where?" I asked with a sinking heart.

"They have created a ghetto." Irene's voice broke, and she fell silent. "We have only two days," she whispered.

I wondered briefly what the men who walked with us to the synagogue would say now. The world was shifting again, sending everything off balance.

Police came through the city to make sure that all the Jews were out of their homes and apartments. My family and I packed carefully and moved with the rest. There were hundreds of thousands of men, women and children forced into a single small area of the city. Families lived as many as ten to twelve in small apartments. There was very little food and water; sanitation was difficult if not impossible. Only about a year after escaping the horror of Nazi-ruled Poland, we were uprooted once again and living in fear.

I felt as if I had fallen back into the dark hole that we had clawed our way out of. It was disheartening. Not long after we were moved into the ghetto, groups were taken away. They didn't know where they were going. They were told they would receive training, that they would be put to work for the Germans, that they were being relocated to more pleasant and spacious accommodations. They were told everything but the truth.

When the deportation of the Jews to Auschwitz began, the Allies were already advancing on all fronts. They were only a year and a half from their eventual victory, but Himmler and his SS continued their operations as though they were winning the war, and no other outcome was possible.

The deportation of the Jews from Hungary was performed with lethal precision. Over 600,000 people were loaded onto the trains to Auschwitz in a matter of only a couple of months. Most of them died.

When they came for me and my family, we were told to pack one valise apiece. We were hustled out into the street and on to the train station with no time to think and no chance of escape. I wasn't sorry to leave the ghetto. In that small prison of a neighborhood, there was nothing but hunger and death. No hope.

Secrecy was Hitler's greatest weapon. If we had known where we were going and what lay ahead, we would have run. We would have fought for our lives and probably died there in Satu Mare, but we were told lie upon lie, and there was no one to tell us the truth until it was too late.

We were gathered in a large group and marched to the train station. We were not allowed time to rest or to think about what was happening. When we arrived at the station, we were forced into cattle cars, so many in each car that there was not enough room for everyone to sit on the floor at the same time. We were given no food and no water, and no form of sanitation was provided.

Once the doors were closed, they remained that way. The journey took three miserable days. There were only a couple of small, barred windows in the walls of the cattle cars for ventilation, and the heat was sweltering. There was no way to rest, no escape from the wails of the sick and starving. Those who had entered the car were, in many cases, already sick or dying. Without food and proper ventilation, there was no hope for them. There was no way to rest, and the stench was sickening.

The journey seemed to go on forever. With only the small

windows for light, it was possible only to judge the passing of the days. There were no meals, and there was no way to lie down and curl up at night. The floors were filthy, and there were too many packed in to allow anybody to lie down. Most of those who had dropped were dead, and their bodies crowded those around them even more. By the third day, the first to die had begun to decompose, and the stench of death permeated the air.

After three days, the train pulled to a stop. We waited, crushed together, holding up those who could not stand on their own, waiting. There were voices and shouts outside, dogs barking, and I heard the clanking of heavy metal sliding and groaning as other cars were opened. Then, at last, the door on our car slid open.

The train yard, the sparse camp beyond, and the waiting guards loomed like a gateway into hell. There was no retreat, nowhere to go but where we were told. In that moment, any illusions we had were shattered.

Chapter Twelve

Those nearest to the door were yanked and forced roughly from the car. All along the tracks, lines of SS storm troopers and vicious dogs stood waiting. They stretched out in a continuous line as far as the eye could see. They forced everyone from the train car without time for thought. When there was room, guards leaped up into the car and pushed from behind. The dogs were all around, snarling and snapping at our legs.

The Nazis called out to us to leave our possessions behind—to take nothing. Mama quickly dug through her bag and produced a long jacket.

"This belonged to your brother," she said. "It is too cold outside for what you are wearing. Take it."

I took the coat and slid it on. It reached all the way to the ground and was very warm.

Before I could even thank Mama, we were forced forward and rushed off of the train. In the chaos that ensued, it was impossible to stay together, though we tried. We were pushed into a long line leading off toward the gates to the camp.

As we exited the train in confusion, another group of men and women moved in behind us. I watched them jump up into the train cars one at a time and start unloading the luggage and belongings that we had left behind. I heard them talking and calling out to one another. They seemed to be Polish Jews for the most part. They were in good health, and clean.

The line moved forward toward the gates. At the head of the line, a tall man in an SS uniform stood. His uniform was crisp, the shiny death's head insignia gleaming. He held out his arm, thumb up. As each of the refugees reached the front of the line, he turned his thumb either to the right, or to the left. Sometimes he asked a question, but he seldom hesitated. Each of the thousands of prisoners was directed into one of two groups, and as I moved forward I began calculating which was the better group to be aligned with.

After watching for a while, I discovered that the people in the group on the right were aged mostly between eighteen and forty-five. The other group was comprised of the elderly, children, the handicapped and some women. My heart hammered.

My parents would surely be in the left-hand group. They were well beyond the forty-five-year mark. I couldn't see them or Irene. The line was in a constant controlled uproar. Germans with their barely contained dogs moved up and down the line. The animals snarled and snapped at the prisoners, who surged one way or the other to avoid them.

I thought back to the time I had spent in Poland, when we were deported. There had been a constant danger in those days of being kidnapped off the streets by the Nazis and sent to work camps. They had only taken a certain type of prisoner for that work, though. It had been predominantly men between the ages of eighteen and forty-five.

None of us had any real idea what to expect. I had a thought that I clung to. If the group on the right was made up of those who the Germans believed could work and might prove useful, I decided that this was the group to be in. You don't throw away a perfectly good tool; you use it at least until it wears out.

I had always been small for my age and I was not old enough

to be a part of the group on the right. My turn before the SS officer was approaching rapidly. It was hard to think, and all the while the dogs barked and people cried out. A seemingly endless line of prisoners in striped suits passed into the camp with bags and suitcases and boxes confiscated from the train.

A family of three—a young man, his father and his mother—approached the German, who indicated that the man should go to the right. The two parents had already been directed left. The man refused. The officer ordered him more sternly to the right, but the old woman—the mother—was crying out for her son. The man dropped to his knees and refused to be separated. They hauled him roughly to his feet and half pushed, half threw him to the left.

I made my decision. As the man before me stepped aside, I rose up on my toes. The jacket Mama had given me to wear dragged the ground, and it hid my deception. I was only able to raise myself a few inches, and in my weakened state, it was hard to hold the position, but I managed it. The German stared at me for a moment.

"How old are you?" he asked curtly.

"Eighteen."

The man stared at me a moment longer and then dipped his thumb to the right. Without leaving time for the decision to be reversed, I stumbled in the direction indicated. I remained on my toes until I could no longer stand the pressure. No one stopped me or questioned me and I worked my way into the center of the group, where I was least conspicuous. I stood, trying to get a glimpse of my parents or Irene.

The SS guards began moving the group on the left into the camp. I heard music and craned my neck, trying to see what was happening. Just inside the gate to the camp, a small orchestra, comprised of more of the prisoners in striped uniforms, played. The music was meant as a welcome to those entering, but to me it sounded like a dirge. There was no emotion behind it, unless it was an extension of the nervous terror rippling through both groups.

The women and children, the old and infirm, were led in a slow procession into the camp and out of sight. It wasn't until later, when we had all been taken inside the camp, that I learned the truth about what happened to them, and even then their fate seemed surreal—like something so alien and impossible that my mind couldn't process it properly.

My group was marched through the gate. As I passed through, one in a very long line of prisoners, I felt my world shifting again. Outside the gate, at least in name, I had been a free man. Once I passed through, I had no idea what I would be.

I glanced up as we passed into the camp. There was an inscription above the gate: *arbeit macht frei.* Work will make you free.

I moved slowly forward with the others, and I found my mind wandering. I couldn't shake the nagging questions. Why were we being punished? Would I see my parents again? Would I even survive?

We were marched up to a low-slung building and, one group at a time, we were taken into a large room.

"Take off your clothes," a German officer commanded. "You will keep your shoes and your belts. If you are hiding money, photographs, papers, books, anything at all, you will leave it here."

At these words, I worked quickly, using the long coat to shield me. Before leaving the train car, I had managed to stuff a little money into my wallet. There was also a thin, gold wedding ring in the wallet. I had no idea where it had come from, or whether one of my parents had slipped it in when I wasn't looking, but I knew I'd have to be quick and lucky to hold on to it. I loosened the seam on my belt where it attached to the buckle, and I slid the thin, gold band into the opening. I dropped my jacket then, and my clothes, as we were hurried toward a second room.

Before we could move from one room to the next, we were stopped.

"Wait," the officer said. He gestured for several of the prisoners in the striped suits to step forward.

"Search them," the German said.

Each prisoner in turn suffered the indignity of a search. The prisoner was made to stand naked while his body cavities were searched to make sure he had not tried to hide gold or money. Many had tried to sneak bits of money or family photographs past the guards. I had put my pictures and money in my shoes, but I quickly realized there was no use getting beaten for them. I threw the money and picture away and kept only the ring. My heart hammered. I clutched the belt and my shoes and braced myself. I stepped up near the doorway, and they searched me quickly and efficiently. They did not search my belt.

I was shoved forward into the next room. In this room I was given pants and a jacket. The material was striped blue and gray. I dressed quickly so that no one would have too much of a chance to notice my small size. I slipped my shoes back on and wrapped the belt around my waist. The ring rested there against my stomach. Everything else was gone, but I had something that felt strangely reassuring.

We dressed quickly because others were being marched in behind us, and still more had already been herded out the far end of the building. I moved with the others across the camp yard until we reached the barracks. Lines of long, ugly buildings stretched out so far I couldn't see the end of them. All of them were the same.

The Germans assigned exactly a thousand prisoners to each of these barracks. By the spring of 1944, when I arrived there, Auschwitz had been in existence for four years. When the camp first opened, the Nazis had tattooed each prisoner's number on his or her forearm. By this point they had stopped tattooing the prisoners because there were too many coming in too fast. I was issued a number: 87672. The numbers served the same purpose that the early prisoners' had, but the prisoners now had to remember them.

"Do not forget it," the German officer told me. "Here you have no name. This is your name."

The interior of the barrack was a single long passageway. To either side, along the walls, a long bench stretched for the prisoners to sleep on. There was no running water, and there were no bathrooms. Large pails were provided, and we were told that we would empty them every morning.

Each barrack was overseen by a prisoner known as a *capo*. In every barrack where you slept and got your food, somebody had to be in charge. The Germans didn't go into the barracks, so they picked prisoners to be in charge. The capos made sure everybody left in morning and came back at night. They got preferential treatment, better food and better sleeping arrangements, and they exercised a good deal of power over their fellow prisoners. Once or twice in those first days, I saw these men treating others as cruelly, or more cruelly, than the Germans did. They could do anything—beat the other prisoners, kill them even—and they would do this just to ingratiate themselves to their captors.

The routine was constant. At breakfast we were served a watery soup. There was very little substance to it, but I took my share and finished it quickly. The sooner you got your share and finished it, the lower the possibility something could go wrong. With so little to eat, there was no room for error.

In the evening, we received small loaves of bread. Each loaf of bread was to feed eight people. We developed a system to help keep the cutting of the loaves fair. Whoever was in charge of the cutting took the last remaining piece. It wasn't a perfect plan—men were starving—but it helped keep things on an even keel.

In the morning, the capo of each barrack would take a group of prisoners to the kitchen to get the soup for their barrack. After the soup had been distributed and a short amount of time was allowed for us to eat, morning roll was called. There were no names used at the roll calls. They used the numbers we had been assigned, exactly 1,000 to each barrack. There were so many prisoners, the Germans had all but given up on keeping track of us individually and had adopted the numeric system to facilitate management of the prisoners.

There was little chance of escape, in any case. The camp was surrounded by a tall, electric fence. Beyond this stretched another fence, and all around the perimeters men in guard towers maintained a vigilant watch. The towers were armed with machine guns and manned twenty-four hours a day. At night, search lights swept the perimeter.

Auschwitz was a prison to more than just the Jews. The barracks were segregated. Some held German criminals. Some held gypsies, or the handicapped, or homosexuals—any group singled out for ethnic cleansing. There was little if any mingling between different types of prisoners, though we sometimes spoke to one another in the yard.

Anyone moving too close to the fence was shot. At times, a prisoner would just turn toward the fence and start walking—those too weak, too hungry, too sick or too terrified to go on. To commit suicide, all you had to do was make a move of any sort toward that boundary. There was no warning. If these prisoners were not shot immediately, they were electrocuted by the fence and dragged away by the capos, their fellow prisoners. The fence was always there—reminding everyone that there was no hope of escape and beckoning to them as they weakened.

There was another fence at Auschwitz. I learned, after a few days in the camp, that this fence separated the male and female prisoners, preventing them from having any contact. If anyone approached too closely, or attempted to reach those on the other side, they received similar treatment to those escaping. But families and lovers were separated by that fence, and they found a way.

The prisoners on either side of the fence managed to gather small pieces of wood together without being caught. Once they had these, they took charcoal they had made from small fires and scratched their names onto the wood. On the opposite side, they scratched the name of the person they hoped to get through to. In this manner, prisoners were able to learn that their loved ones were still alive. It was so little, and at the same time it meant everything.

Word spread one morning. I heard Papa's name whispered. I stepped up to the man who was speaking.

"That is my father," I said. "What is it? What do you want?"

The man met my gaze and then handed over a small, slender scrap of wood. I had seen such messages before. My hands trembled as I read what was scratched on the small board.

On the front it said, "To Gabriel." On the reverse, it said, "Irene."

My sister was alive. I quickly found my own bit of wood and repeated the message, writing, "To Irene," on the front and "David," on the back. When no one was looking, I managed to toss the wood up and over the fence.

There was no way to know if anyone on the other side found it. The pieces of wood didn't include too much information, in case the messages were intercepted by the guards. It would be difficult to track us down by name, since only numbers were used in the camps, but it wouldn't be impossible, and no one wanted to be found out.

One morning, after I had eaten my meager breakfast of watery soup, I walked out into the yard. Because I wasn't working—I was being held with the others to see if we were sick—I milled around the camp yard. I saw an old man sitting alone on a stone and staring out through the fences to the world beyond. As I neared him, the man turned to me.

"Hello, young man," he said.

"Hello."

"I'm Hans," he said. "I'm a political prisoner, here for my crimes against the fatherland. I'm an old man, but you…you are young. Just starting your life. What is your name?"

"David."

"Are you Jewish?" he asked.

I nodded. "I was brought here from Satu Mare, with my family. My mother, my father and my sister were with me. I don't know where the rest of my family might be."

Hans turned and pointed across the camp to a gray, sooty stone chimney stretching up toward the sky. A dim haze of smoke surrounded the building, drifting up from the mouth of that chimney. The awful stench permeated the camp.

"Do you see that smoke?" Hans asked. "That is where they killed them. Your parents. All of the others. That smoke is all that remains—that and the ashes they will haul away. That smoke that you smell, that you feel coating your skin and filling your lungs—that is the dead, all of them. I have been here for four years, David. I saw when they opened the gas chambers and crematoria a year ago. The smoke has never stopped. Train after train, month after month, it always burns."

I stared at the man. I did not know what to say. It couldn't be true, that men and women were burned. For what? For being Jewish? It was not possible that this could happen, that men could do this to other men. Yet there was the smoke.

The old man, Hans, did not drop his eyes or look away. He spoke in a soft, matter-of-fact voice. "I know it is a great deal to take in," he said. "When I first came to Auschwitz, I did not believe it either—that my countrymen would be capable of...this. There is another thing I would like to tell you. It is something you will want to know, something you should keep in the front of your mind.

"There is a heaven and a hell." Hans turned and pointed a shaky finger at the smoldering chimney.

"That is hell," he said. "If you stay here long enough, that is where you are bound. There is no way around this. Whoever visits too long in Auschwitz finds his end in the flames."

Then Hans turned and pointed at the electric fence, the second fence and the land beyond. "Out there," he said, "is heaven. Freedom. Inside the fence, it is only a matter of time. The food is not enough for a man. It is not clean or healthy here. You will decline, and when you do, they will be waiting. They will take notice. Those who do not remain strong become smoke.

"If you can get outside, you have a chance. It is a big world, and there are places to hide, places to run. Here there is only one way out."

I stood in shock. The man sat there on his rock, speaking of the horrors as if they were a matter-of-fact occurrence, as if he were lecturing in school and I were his student.

"I am an old man," Hans said at last. "My time has come and gone—I will never see the other side of that fence. You, though, are young—a young man with so much ahead of you. Watch for the chance to get beyond that fence, and grab it."

I felt numb. I turned away, suddenly not wanting to hear

anything more the old German might have to say. Hans called after me.

"Good luck, my young friend."

I did not look back, but as I walked away, I felt the smoke coating my skin and filling my lungs, just as Hans had said.

Chapter Thirteen

Only a couple of days later, the German commander appeared at my barrack. He and his guards worked their way through the ranks of prisoners, and from each group they drew out the youngest men. I was among the group of young men, and although I had a bad feeling about being removed from the larger group, I did as I was told.

In the end, there were fifty of us. All of us were young and small. The German commander spoke almost kindly to us. He explained that because of our youth, we were to be transported to Germany and trained to become a part of the workforce. Each of us was to be taught a trade and put to work for the good of Germany.

I listened to the words, but they washed over me. Such promises were common and, more often than not, the more that was promised, the less was delivered. I kept all of my experiences in Poland and Hungary in mind as they explained how I would be educated and put to work in Germany, but I also kept my eyes and ears open.

One positive result of being separated with the young men was the discovery of another young man from my village. I knew Joseph, and we were able to converse in Hungarian, each catching up on what the other knew.

Many of the boys in the group were excited. They believed

the promises and thought they'd been chosen for something better. The mood was more positive than any I had experienced since coming to Auschwitz, but I didn't trust it.

I thought about the situation constantly, and no matter how I examined it, I came to the same conclusion. The Germans made a lot of promises, but thus far very few of them had been honored. The one thing that had remained true in all my experience was that those who could work were preserved. Those who were separated disappeared.

The more I thought about this, the more certain I became that I was right. I knew that if I were careful, I could slip out in the night and into one of the other barracks. The fact that they used no names would work in my favor. There would be confusion, but they might not send me back to the boys' barracks.

Finally, I spoke with Joseph about it.

"It was the same when we were deported to Poland," I said. "It was not safe to walk on the streets alone if you were between the ages of eighteen and forty-five. They took those men, and they sent them to the camps to work. The others, those left behind—they took them to the ghettos to die. When I first arrived here, the line split in two directions..."

I fell silent for a moment, then, without lifting my eyes from the ground, told Joseph what the old German, Hans, had explained to me. I told Joseph that only making the choice to stay with the line on the left had spared my own life.

Joseph shook his head and frowned.

"It can't be true," he said. "The old man was just trying to frighten you. He is miserable, and he wanted to make sure you are miserable. There is a promise here—a way out. They will train us, David, give us a trade that we can use to barter for our future."

"They promise things," I said. "It's what they do. They tell you that you are going to have something new—something better—to keep you from fighting back. They have no use for any of us who can't work. They don't believe that we are big enough or strong enough. They don't want us to know what they are doing or what they have done. It isn't safe to trust them."

"It will be okay, David. You'll see."

"No," I said. "I will not see, because I will not be here. I'm going back to the other barrack. I'm going to slip in at night. At roll call they won't know who the extra person is."

"What if the others turn you in?"

"They won't. You know they won't. I'm going back because it's safe. The Nazis keep those who are useful. They keep the ones who are old enough and strong enough and healthy enough to work. The ones they keep may not live to find their way out of this camp, but I am certain that anyone who is not immediately useful will die."

We continued like this for some time. I asked Joseph to come with me, but eventually I realized that I was not getting through. I did not want to leave my friend behind, but the longer I stayed in that barrack, the more certain I became that I needed to get back. When I could wait no longer, I went to my friend a final time.

"I have to go," I said. "I wish that you'd go with me."

"You will see," Joseph said. "It's going to be all right for both of us."

I hugged my friend and then I turned and slipped out of the barrack into the darkness beyond. I never saw Joseph again.

There were guards to avoid, but they focused their attention, for the most part, on the fences. There was nothing important that the prisoners could do from barrack to barrack, and the capos also kept watch.

I did not choose the nearest barrack, or even the second-nearest. The longer I was out in the yard, the more danger I was in, but I didn't want to be too close to the boys. At last, when

I thought I had put enough distance between myself and the other boys, I slipped into one of the dark structures and found an open spot on the bench along one wall. I slept very little, expecting that at any moment someone would find me, or that the capo would make a round or take a head count and roust me. But morning came, and no one paid any attention to me at all.

I kept my head down and shuffled out to get my soup, avoiding contact with others and staying clear of the guards. When they called the roll, as they did every morning, there were 1,001 prisoners. The guards grew rough. They pushed the capo around and screamed at the men. They ordered the extra man to take a step forward. No one moved. I didn't know if any of them would turn on me, or if they even knew for sure that I was the extra. I kept silent, and I waited.

The guards forced the entire barrack of men to their knees. They walked among them, kicking and punching prisoners, screaming in their faces. They demanded to know who the extra prisoner was, but no one spoke up. We were forced to kneel there for nearly three hours, but after that the guards lost interest. One prisoner was taken and escorted to another barrack where there was an opening. The day continued, and the issue was dropped.

Things continued as they had before for about a week. I worked my way into the new group, kept a low profile and paid as much attention to what was going on as possible. One morning, before we would normally have arisen, the barrack was rousted by the sounds of shouting guards and barking dogs.

I lifted my head groggily but was moving in seconds. I had learned on the road to sleep lightly, and I never wanted to be taken by surprise. The guards moved quickly through the barrack, waking prisoners with pokes and prods and curses and chasing us toward the doors and the early morning light beyond.

My heart hammered. I thought about bolting. The first thought that came to my mind was that we were going to be marched away to the crematorium, and that all my efforts to avoid it had been in vain. There was no time to make any sort of move. I gathered the meager things that were mine and stumbled out into the yard, surrounded by other stumbling prisoners, snarling, vicious dogs and the sharp, staccato commands of the guards.

We did not stop in the yard for roll call, nor did we receive our morning rations of soup. I was frightened by this. They would not waste food on condemned men. I watched the other barracks as we passed and wondered if they were already empty, wondering if mine was the only group chased out of sleep, and if this was the last time I would ever see a morning sunrise.

We were marched straight through the camp and out of the gate, and we didn't stop until we had reached the railroad yard. I wanted to talk to someone, to ask what was happening, but none of the other prisoners knew the answer, and I didn't want to draw the attention of any of the guards.

On the tracks, a very long train stretched off into the distance. Hundreds of cattle cars stretched out behind the puffing steam engine. Boots crunched up and down the tracks, grinding into the gravel. The sound echoed off the empty cars of the train. My companions and I were lined up and assigned to the cars.

I glanced over my shoulder. I saw the gates of Auschwitz, and I saw a black smudge of smoke rising from the chimney of the crematorium. The double fences circled the camp, and I remembered the old German, Hans, and what he'd said. I turned and looked to either side out beyond the train and the guards and the cars. I felt great relief, despite the uncertainty of my situation. I was outside that fence. I had turned my back, for the moment, on hell.

Chapter Fourteen

As each of us stepped aboard the train, we were handed the biggest surprise of an already crazy day. Each man was given a loaf of bread, some margarine and a small brick of salami. It was more food than any of us had seen in months. Some of the men fell on the food immediately and devoured it. I ate a bit and tucked the rest away.

No one knew what to expect. The cars were closed. We still heard the dogs and the guards, but we were sealed away in the cars with only a small window on either side for ventilation. The train rolled out of the station; we were on the tracks for seven days.

I had no way of knowing what was going on in the world outside the camps. There were stories and rumors, but very little real news. Three hundred thousand Jews had been taken to the extermination camp in Treblinka. Despite the incredible ability of the Nazis to hide their atrocities even from those upon whom they perpetrated them, word had leaked.

Those condemned to the ghettos of Warsaw had also learned what was to be their fate, and they had not stood still. They gathered weapons through underground channels. They met when they could, taking tremendous risks, and they organized a resistance that spread mostly through the young men and women of Warsaw. There were smaller pockets and groups in other ghettos, but in Warsaw they were a force. What started as a ragtag, desperate movement grew into an organization that came to be called *Zydowska Organizacja Bojowa*—the Jewish Fighting Force.

A young man named Mordecai Anielewicz led this resistance, and in 1943 he issued a proclamation. He called on the Jews of the Warsaw Ghetto to resist when they were ordered to go to the trains that would take them to the death camps. He called on them to fight, and in January of 1943, armed with a very small number of weapons that had been smuggled in and bought with lives and blood, members of the Jewish Fighting Force opened fire on German guards as they attempted to load one of the trains.

They won a small victory that day, and it gave courage and strength to others. Pockets of resistance rose throughout the ghetto, and for a time, there was a flicker of hope. On April 19, 1943, the Germans launched an invasion in the ghetto. Their mission was to evacuate and deport all of those remaining. The resistance rose up and fought back.

A small force of 750 poorly armed men stepped up to do battle with the well-trained, well-equipped Nazi machine. They fought, and they held. For almost a month, they kept the Nazis at bay. It was only a matter of time, though, before the sheer numbers and firepower of the Germans crushed the resistance.

More than 50,000 Jews were captured at the end of this uprising. Of those, more than 7,000 were shot immediately. All those who remained were sent to various concentration and death camps. The ghetto itself came under heavy fire and bombing. It was reduced to a heap of rubble.

All of this happened while my companions and I had been held in Auschwitz. When the doors of the train opened at last, seven days after we had departed, they opened on a desolate wasteland. As far as the eye could see was nothing but rubble and chimneys. The Warsaw ghetto had been leveled.

The city we looked out on had once been filled with beautiful homes, busy streets and thriving families. When I looked out over the city, I saw only two things: a forest of chimneys and, beyond them, rising above the rubble, the walls of Pawiak Prison, which somehow had borne the brunt of the attack against the resistance and remained standing.

We were hustled off of the train and, when we had assembled, German guards marched us along a rough path bordered on all sides by ruins. We continued on for some time, moving in toward the center of the ruins, and eventually we passed through an opening and out into a large cleared area.

There, in the center of the blasted ghetto, the Germans had constructed a camp. It consisted of many buildings, barracks and a kitchen, and it was surrounded by a high, impassable fence. I studied it as I approached. There was no dark furnace belching foul smoke, no crematorium chimney—and as we passed through the gates, I glanced up. The motto of the death camps, a*rbeit macht frei,* did not hang over the entrance.

We were taken first to the barracks. There was the next surprise. The barracks were clean and well kept. Instead of the benches we had slept on in Auschwitz, the walls were lined with bunk beds stacked three high. Each bed had a blanket and a pillow, and each of us was assigned to a berth of our own.

It was no luxury accommodation, but our mood improved immediately. It was so much more comfortable than where we had come from that it seemed as if we had moved from a ditch into a palace. We were integrated with those who had come to the camp before us. The earlier arrivals were mostly Greeks, French and some Yugoslavians. They looked much healthier and happier than the prisoners in Auschwitz had been—well fed and rested. I had the eerie sensation of stepping from one world into another.

We settled in and took stock of our surroundings. From those already in the camp, we began to piece together our purpose. The Germans were extending their railroad tracks deeper and deeper into the ruins of the ghetto. Each day, we had to scour the wreckage for bricks and steel—any sort of construction material that was still serviceable. What we salvaged we carried to the waiting trains, where we loaded the bricks and steel to be transported back to Germany. We worked long, difficult hours, but we were fed and were able to rest.

Despite the improved circumstances, the first night was a difficult one. The bunk, pillow and blanket made sleep easier, but I couldn't help but wonder what would happen the next day. There were no other boys my age in this camp. I was undersized and very likely to stand out when they got a second look. I was willing to work and to work hard, but I was not as large and strong as most of the others.

When the first roll call had been completed, one of the German officers stepped forward with a clipboard. He called out to us, ordering all carpenters, tailors, shoemakers and cooks to step forward. We were very still for a long moment. So many times over the past months our decisions to step one way or another—to answer a call or shy away from it—had been the difference between life and death.

The German waited patiently. Eventually, a tall man stepped slowly forward. I watched as others reluctantly stepped away from the crowd. My heart hammered. Should I step forward? If I separated myself, what would I tell them I could do? If I stayed behind, was it a mistake? After waiting almost too long, I took a deep breath and stepped forward, quickly taking a place in the middle of the small crowd that had already moved forward. There were eight or ten of them, and among them was the man who had been my companion for most of the journey from the death camp: a tailor named Abe.

When the last of the skilled workers had come forward and joined the group, the German officer took us away, marching us through the camp to the place where we would work with others who had the same skills.

First they dropped off the shoemakers, and our number dropped by two. I kept close beside Abe as we marched. My mind raced. I did not know which group to try to attach myself to. I had done carpentry work with my father and uncle, but I was not really skilled enough to claim it as a trade. When the last of the shoemakers had departed, the German officer, glancing up, caught sight of me.

"You!" he said. "What are you doing here?"

I tried to answer, but the words would not come. Just as I feared I'd be singled out and punished, Abe stepped forward, laid a hand on my shoulder and spoke.

"My friend David," Abe said, "works in the kitchen. They will be happy to have him."

The German officer stared at me for a long moment.

"Kindergarten is more likely where you belong," he said at last. He glanced at Abe curiously, as if trying to decide if he were being deceived in some way. I wanted to stand up on my toes again, as I had when I entered Auschwitz, but without the long coat to disguise me it would do no good. In the end, the German shook his head and made a note on his clipboard, then turned and led the group forward again.

I shot Abe a look of gratitude. Abe smiled back and patted me on the shoulder. The tailor had sat beside me on the train, and we had talked endlessly about our families, our adventures and the horrors we had been through. Abe was about thirty-five and had a wife and children to whom he was devoted. He had owned a tailor shop in the town of Siget in Romania, a business that supported him well enough. He only wanted to go back to his family.

I told stories of my family's deportation to Poland, of our return to Hungary and all that had happened in between. Throughout it all, Abe made constant reference to his family in the present tense. He worried if they were doing well, as he had been separated from them upon reaching Auschwitz.

I didn't know if Abe was just putting on a brave face or if he truly did not know all that was happening in the death camp. He seemed oblivious to the crematoria and the gas chambers, and he seemed to believe that his family was being held, waiting for the war to end so that they could all be reunited.

I thought long and hard about telling my new friend what I knew. The words of the old German, Hans, haunted me. In the end, I held my silence. If it helped Abe to have hope, it was not my place to remove that hope. I knew that anyone who gave up would die.

The group reached the kitchen, where I was told to go inside and present myself to the head chef. The group marched on and the German officer never looked back. With some trepidation, I entered the kitchen and found the man in charge.

The head chef was a man named Joshua who appeared to be in his late forties. He was a big man with a kind face. When I walked in and reported, Joshua looked me up and down.

"What are we going to do with you?" he asked.

"I've come to help in the kitchen."

"Well, there's no way you could be a cook," he said. "You haven't been alive long enough to have learned that skill! And if you can't cook, what will we have you do?"

One of the chef's helpers over in the corner glanced up and grinned. "He can peel potatoes," the man called out. "No one else wants to do it. You can do that, can't you, boy? Work a peeler?"

I nodded without hesitation. I was taken to a corner and

given a huge bag of potatoes and a knife, and after a very short bit of instruction, I was launched into my next career: potato peeling. It was a lifesaver. Working in the kitchen was much easier than loading train cars and carrying bricks. There was plenty of food to be had and, though we were watched carefully, I still got more to eat than I would have at any other post. The work was long and monotonous, but I was able to do it easily. Being the youngest prisoner in the camp, and one of the smallest, the work helped to keep me alive and safe.

Over the days and weeks that followed I learned a great deal about the camp, and about the ruined ghetto beyond. The Pawiak Prison that loomed up from the rubble was still in use. It was not a standard death camp like Auschwitz but was kept open for the incarceration of political prisoners. Those imprisoned there were mostly gentiles, men and women who had refused to cooperate with the Nazis, or those who, for one reason or another, had fallen foul of the invaders. These prisoners were not added to any work force. Almost without exception, they were executed. From where I worked in the camp, we heard the shots of rifles from the prison walls and knew when the executions were taking place.

The trains moved in and out of the ruins like clockwork. Every morning after roll call, I marched with those who had special duties in the camp while the larger mass of the prisoners went to work. They carried and loaded brick and steel from sunup to sundown and watched as the long lines of cars rolled in and out of the jungle of ruins, carrying salvaged material back to Germany and then returning for more.

When the workers moved into new areas they were accompanied by groups of specially trained Nazi guards. As they worked their way through the fallen homes and buildings, they often found hidden or closed-off rooms and chambers intact beneath the rubble. Some of these were empty, just pockets in the stone and silt. Others contained bodies. When a new pocket was discovered, the prisoners were ordered back.

First, the dogs were taken to the openings. Their job was to sniff out bodies and living refugees. Some survivors of the uprising and the carnage that followed remained hidden beneath their homes. Some were trapped. The dogs and then the guards cleared each of the recesses before the prisoners were allowed to move in and begin removing the rubble.

If the dogs found a sealed chamber with survivors, the Germans opened the entrances, often blowing them open with dynamite. Once the way was clear they ordered those inside to climb out. If a few came while others stayed back, the soldiers promised those who emerged that if they cooperated, nothing bad would happen. Then they were sent back in to bring out those who had hesitated.

When refugees refused to exit their hideaways, the Germans used gas and grenades to flush them out. The Germans were careful to be certain that every living soul had been removed from each hideaway. When they were all cleared, the refugees were gunned down on the spot with automatic rifle fire. They were not put to work with my group but made into examples for their participation in the uprising.

I could hear the shots from where I worked, peeling endless piles of potatoes in the kitchen. I knew what it meant each time there was the explosion of a grenade or the rapid fire of a machine gun: more people had died. I could hear the executions in the prison as well, and they served as a reminder that, no matter how much better it was in the work camp, it was still far from safe.

I was the only boy near my age in the camp, and though the others made me feel at home and included me in their conversations, I always felt somewhat isolated.

Joshua, the head chef, talked in a seemingly endless stream

as he worked. He was Greek, and he was fond of telling stories about the large family he had left behind. In his hometown there had been a large and thriving Jewish community, and he never tired of sharing his memories. He taught me a few words in Greek and entertained me for hours. It made the passing of the time in that lonely place more bearable, and I shared my own stories as well.

The man in the bunk just above mine was named Gustav. Besides me, he was one of the youngest in the camp, only twenty years old. Gustav worked with the crews that left the camp each morning to load the trains and returned at night. He and I began telling one another our stories and our dreams. We talked through the long evenings and late into the night, only falling silent, at times, when the other prisoners cursed us and told us to be quiet so everyone could sleep.

In the kitchen I heard stories about the ruined Warsaw Ghetto and what took place beyond the fences, but when Gustav told the stories they were firsthand. As the darkness fell, the young man's voice cut through the shadows.

"There are bunkers out there still, David," he said. "I've seen them. It's been nearly a year since the Germans bombed the ghetto and executed the resistance, but the city has not given up all its secrets.

"There are survivors. They have carved deep holes, chambers in the ruins where they hide out like trapped rats. At night they slip out and make their way out of the ghetto into the city, looking for food. They beg or steal what they can and before the sun begins to rise, in the darkest part of morning, they slip back through the ruins. They are like shadows, hurrying to get back underground before there is enough light for them to be seen, and careful not to leave any sort of trail to follow.

"They are as quiet as ghosts, David, but it doesn't matter. One home at a time, one pile of rubble after another, we move through the ruins. The dogs miss nothing. If they find a sealed room or a hidden passageway, they bark and dig and howl. The Germans move forward and they call down to whoever is below.

"'Come out,' they say. 'Come out and we will not hurt you. We have a camp, we have work for you, we can help.' The survivors don't always come. When some do, the Germans tell them everything is okay, and they send them back in to bring out their friends, their families and their comrades.

"If the survivors don't come out, the Germans throw grenades in after them, or gas canisters. One way or another, everyone crawls to the surface, some coughing, some screaming, some smiling and believing that everything is going to be okay for them."

"I have never seen any of them come back to the camp," I said. "I watch when I can. All I ever see are the guards and the work crews."

"They shoot them," Gustav said softly. "As they stand there, trembling in terror, they are gunned down in the street. All of them. There are no exceptions. After it is done, we continue the work as if nothing has happened. We load the train, and they carry the rubble of the ghetto back to Germany to be rebuilt into—what? Castles? Forts?"

"Hey!" a prisoner across the room called out. "Shut up with that. We have to sleep. Tomorrow you'll see it all again."

Gustav fell silent for a moment. Then, before he rolled over and drifted off to sleep, he said, "They kill them all, David. All of them. The survivors hide themselves away for more than a year, and then they are gunned down in the streets."

I fell asleep trying to banish the images from my mind, but it was impossible because I had heard the guns myself.

Chapter Fifteen

Gustav and I became as close as brothers. We shared our secrets and talked whenever we could. He kept me current on everything that happened beyond the gates of the camp. He brought back stories from the ghetto, tales of the prison beyond the camp, and anything he heard or learned that someone could not learn in the camp.

In turn, I snuck food back when I could and gave it to my friend. I listened as I worked and I learned things in the kitchens, though it was difficult, as it always was with the Germans, to know what I should believe and what I should ignore.

The German officers frequented the kitchens. They came for snacks or for special occasions. They ordered meals and while they waited, they talked with the help. Sometimes they brought news of the war, battles that were happening on various fronts or at least their versions of what was happening. It was the only source we had of news of the world beyond the work camp and the progress of the war. The news was tainted, of course, but it was news, and bits and pieces of it, at least were born in fact.

Other officers had different messages. They would sit in the kitchen, waiting for the chef to finish, or eating their food, and they would talk. They would tell the Jewish workers that they had better hope that it was Germany who won the war. Certainly, they said, things were bad, but if Germany won, there would be work, and they would survive. If the Germans lost, though, the Jews were going to die for certain. No one would be allowed to carry the things they knew back to the world. No one would be left to tell tales.

I told all of this to Gustav as we sat in the barrack in the evenings, sharing food I had sneaked from the kitchen, or as we lay in our bunks, awaiting sleep. We discussed what we believed was true and what was a lie.

Over time we came to some conclusions about life in the camps and in the war. Food was very important to our existence. The lack of food at Auschwitz, and the better accommodations in the work camp, drove home the importance of having enough food to keep our bodies healthy and strong.

Beyond this, though, there was one thing more important. food for the soul. Belief. No matter what happened, no matter how bad the situation got, the most important thing was the belief that if we were strong and smart and we worked our way through each trial that was placed before us, we would survive. We had to believe that there was an end to it, that we would get through it, and that there would be another life waiting for us in a place where the world had not gone insane. That was what mattered the most. If we lost our belief or our strength, we might as well walk out toward the nearest fence and let the guards shoot us down.

We vowed to keep this faith alive and to help one another to believe. Without belief, our fates were sealed. We would end up just two more forgotten skeletons buried in a mass grave or piles of ashes blowing in the wind.

And so, time passed. After a few weeks, a new sound intruded on the camp. In the far distance were explosions. Artillery fire was close enough to shake the walls and keep us awake at night. I learned, through the rumors in the kitchen, that it was the Russians. They were advancing on Warsaw, and the Germans were retreating. Of course there was no talk of losing among our guards, but the message was clear enough.

We listened to the approaching destruction with mixed feelings. It was obvious from the proximity of the sound that the Germans were being pressed hard. This meant that the Allies, specifically the Russians, were nearing Warsaw. This was good, except that we all remembered the words of the German officers.

"If the Allies win the war, you will certainly die."

Every day we wondered what our fate would be. We worked and we loaded the trains, but there was an expectancy in the air—a sensation that something was about to change. A couple of weeks after we first heard the sounds of battle, we learned what that change would be. The Germans were evacuating the city and the work camp.

Preparation for the evacuation was completed swiftly and with brutal efficiency. The day before they were to leave the city, the Germans took the prisoners to the warehouses and opened the doors.

"Take what you want," the German officer said. "Take as much as you can carry. Nothing will be left behind, and we will not be transporting this food. Carry what you can. The rest will be burned."

Gustav and I worked together. We found two long poles and manufactured a sling between us made from an old blanket. We loaded this with the best of the canned goods we could find and with bread, sugar and meat. We knew that, whatever was to come, we would have to eat, and we knew that if the Germans said to take what we could and what we wanted, it was likely to be a long journey during which food would be scarce.

When we had gathered what we could and made our preparations, the Germans gathered us again. The commander stepped forward.

"We are about to embark on a very long and arduous journey," he said. "If you do not believe you can make such a march, if you are sick or injured, step out of ranks now. You will be transported by the trains carrying supplies out of the city. We cannot afford your slowing us down, so if you have such a problem or fear that you might have such a problem, step out now."

At first no one moved. We all knew by this point that no one was going to be transported on a train. If we were too weak or sick to make the journey, it was the end of the line for us. We knew that to break ranks and step forward would seal our doom.

Still, after a time, men began to move to the front. Some were sick. Some were just tired or beaten. It was an end to the suffering and the pain. They probably all knew that they were walking forward to meet their deaths, but still they went. All of those who stepped forward were led away. After they were led away, they were shot, and then burned along with the camp.

The evacuation began with about 4,000 prisoners. The Germans ordered us into groups of about 200 each. Gustav and I shouldered our stretcher full of food with a mixture of fear and hope. We had no idea where we were going, how long we would be marching or what the journey would bring, but the food we had between us was the most we'd had in a very long time, and we kept our hopes alive.

The Russian artillery we had heard outside the city had been no real threat. Russian troops had hovered near Warsaw for months but had not entered the city or truly engaged the Germans. They sat back and watched as the great city fell, not allowing the United States or Great Britain to fly in supplies, weapons or troops. They allowed Germany to bomb the city into dust, apparently planning on annexing this part of Poland into their own empire once the dust settled.

The Germans were taking no chances, and the camp was evacuated. Even as we left, Gustav and I believed that Russian troops could not be far behind. We talked in hushed tones of finding a way to slip out of the lines. If we could escape, we thought, we could hide out in the city, as the refugees had done. If we managed to get clear of the Germans and into one of the well-camouflaged bunkers, we could wait it out. When the Russians rolled through, we would be taken to safety and new lives beyond all the horror. We had no idea that no one was following.

We started out early in the morning. It was a sunny day, and at first things didn't go too badly. Gustav and I carried our makeshift stretcher, loaded with the canned foods and other supplies we had taken from the open warehouse. Each prisoner carried the food he had gathered and a blanket; we were each issued one before we started. We walked straight through the day.

Our spirits were high that first day. We were outside the camp. We had the most food we'd had in months—years for some of us. Even though we were still under guard, we believed the Germans were retreating from the Allies, and though this brought us the fear that our own lives were in danger, it also brought hope. The hope, even more than the food, kept us moving. It gave us strength.

After the first day of carrying our burden, Gustav and I were tired. It was heavy, and we had covered a lot of miles with very little rest. After the camps, where we'd had bunks and pillows, sleeping out in the chilly night was difficult, and the strangeness of the situation kept us from sound sleep.

The second day was much worse. We were still tired, and we were stiff from the unfamiliar labor. The Germans kept us moving. Each group of prisoners was assigned to a certain number of guards who watched them night and day. Despite the physical condition of those marching, the Nazis apparently expected us to try to escape. They walked us until we were about to drop and allowed no one to stray from the ranks.

Before the second day had ended we began to realize our error in carrying so much food. Gustav and I began pruning some of the heavier food from our stretcher. Others discarded heavy cans and packages of sugar—anything they could to lighten their loads and make the marching easier.

As the days progressed, our situation worsened. More and more of the food carried out of the camp was left along the roadside. Gustav and I abandoned our stretcher completely and left most of our food behind. Those who had been weaker at the beginning of the march had begun to lag behind. Some were so desperate that they eventually dropped their blankets—anything to lessen the weight they carried from sunrise to sundown and allow them to keep the pace that the guards set.

The nights were cold, and those without blankets lay freezing, huddled together and trying to find any way to rest. Men started to fall out of the ranks. They were moved to the side of the road and ignored. The rest of the prisoners marched on past, leaving them behind. At first I thought they were just being left to starve on their own, too weak and sick to move on or to help themselves.

A final group of guards brought up the rear of the huge company's ranks. When they came upon those who were unable to go on, they stepped to the side and shot them. The first day men dropped out, the shots rang out and echoed back up the ranks. I flinched and closed my eyes. I had heard the shots in the ghetto and the shots from the prison. I knew what they were. We all knew. That sound gave even the weakest among us a temporary burst of strength.

Gustav and I walked with Abe, the tailor who had ridden into the camp with me from Auschwitz and helped me get my job in the kitchen. Talking was all we had, stories that matched the cadence of our stumbling march and carried us slowly along. After miles and miles of forced marching, your mind goes on a sort of autopilot. You walk, but sometimes you sleep. The three of us took turns watching out for one another, two of us supporting the third when he dozed. We couldn't afford to lag behind or to stumble, and so we talked and told our stories over and over, leaning on the words and the memories for support.

As we traveled we passed through and near many villages. The locals could not help us. If they tried to come out and draw near to those marching, they were shot and killed. They lived in fear of the Nazis, but still, at times, they tried to help.

Sometimes they would come into the road ahead of those marching and leave pails or baskets of raw potatoes or fruit. Other times they left them on their porches or near the side of the trail. This was a dangerous practice both for those leaving the food and for the prisoners, who by this time were crazed with hunger and thirst. If the prisoners broke ranks to run out after the food, they were beaten or shot on the spot.

My friends and I stayed as close to the edge as possible and kept our eyes open. Our two foremost rules had not changed. You had to have food to keep your body strong enough to survive, and you had to keep hope. Without those two things you were done—a dead man walking among the living.

Suddenly, I spotted a bucket of potatoes near the edge of the road. I nudged Gustav.

"I see it," he said.

Abe was walking on the far side and Gustav drew him closer. The tailor saw the food.

"It's too far to the side" he said. "If we try to get it, they'll kill us. That's why no one else has gone after it."

"It's not too far," Gustav replied. "We have to try. It's been two days since we've eaten."

I kept silent. I knew that Abe was probably right: the bucket was too far away. But the food was too tempting to ignore. We would have to go after it whatever the price. To survive, we had to eat.

Before any of us could make a move, a man in front of us broke from the ranks and stumbled toward the bucket. One of the guards, about twenty yards back, saw him and called out sharply for him to return to the ranks. A second man followed, and then a third. Before the guard could hurry his steps and force the man back into ranks, there were half a dozen others pouncing on the bucket.

They clawed at the food frantically. All the time this was happening, the ranks marched forward without hesitation, and the guard, running up beside us, grew closer. As the three of us drew parallel to the bucket, Gustav hissed.

"Now."

At that moment, the guard reached those struggling to grab potatoes from the bucket. He drew back and cracked the butt of his rifle across the back of a man's skull, sending him sprawling. As the man fell, the bucket toppled and the potatoes rolled out across the road. Gustav and I lunged. Gustav managed to grab two, and I got one. We ducked back into the ranks and kept moving. Behind us, panicked prisoners trying to get morsels of food mobbed the place where the bucket had spilled. Moments later, rifle fire opened up and we knew the fight for food had ended.

Gustav gave one of his two raw potatoes to Abe, who took it gratefully. The three of us did not speak for a while. We ate slowly, trying to make the meager ration last and to keep our feet moving forward one step at a time. Many of those who had made moves for the food were not so lucky. Some were shot. Others were beaten and left for the cleanup squad. Still others made the effort and came away empty-handed or were trampled by other prisoners, left unable to rise and continue on. Those who made it back into the ranks without any of the food began again to watch feverishly for the next opportunity.

As the days passed and our journey continued, more and more prisoners fell by the wayside. The lack of food and the long, forced marches of the day took their toll. The Germans paid no attention to this attrition. It was their system. The fewer who continued the march, the fewer they had to feed, guard or deal with at the far end of the march. They killed all who failed to keep the pace, leaving them dead beside the road, untended. After a while I learned to keep my eyes focused ahead and to use what energy and concentration I had to put one foot in front of the next and move forward.

The roadside tempted too many others. They saw an end to the pain and the hunger, and they took it. They gave up and lay down in the dirt, and when the final squad passed through, they gave up their lives. The only way to survive was to keep moving. You had to ignore everything else or you would be drawn in and fall away.

After days without anything to drink, I glanced up and gave a low cry. I thought I was seeing things, but when the image did not fade, I turned to Gustav and Abe.

"We are coming to a river."

Even more than the pain of our hunger was the pain of our thirst. It withered us, parching our throats and making conversation all but impossible. The idea that there was water nearby—an entire river full of water—was maddening.

The Germans brought us all within sight of the water and then stopped the march. They broke the prisoners into groups. They explained that one group would be allowed to go forward to the water at a time. When a group had gotten enough to drink, it would return to the ranks and the next group would move forward.

We were in no condition to run. We were emaciated and starved, weak and barely able to force our tortured bodies forward. Still, the Germans sensed that there were those among us who might make bids for freedom. They very carefully led the first group toward the water, watching them to see that they didn't stray. When those men reached the river, plunged their faces into the cold water and drank, the others were in full view. They saw the water, and it was too much.

In a single, ragged surge they rushed forward to the river. My companions and I were caught up in it, racing for the river with strength we would not have believed we possessed. We hit the water and fell to our knees, drawing in long gulps, soaking our clothing.

At the first sign of trouble, the guards began shouting for order. They waded in and beat at the prisoners, dragging them back from the river viciously. I saw a guard drawing near. I took a last long drink, gripped Gustav by his shirt and dragged him up.

"Get back or they will kill us," I said.

We moved back away from the water, running toward the ranks we had left behind. At our backs, the sound of gunfire erupted, and we ran faster still, not able to take the time to glance over our shoulders and see the danger.

The guards rained death upon those remaining near the river. They forced them back, firing at them ruthlessly, beating and herding them back and away from the river. Some managed, as my companions and I had, to get water, but many others were turned away from the river and back onto the road with no relief for their thirst.

The river, which had run clear and fresh, was awash in dead, floating bodies. I stared at it as we moved away—the water that had now grown muddy with the blood of the fallen prisoners.

Where it washed onto the shore it left a red, rusty bloodstain; the water glittered crimson in the fading sunlight.

It had become a death march. Men dropped away behind us like flies. More than a third of the 4,000 men we had begun the march with were dead, and another huge percentage was as good as dead on their feet. We marched until, at last, we came to a train yard and a set of tracks. The tracks were lined with the familiar cattle cars that had brought me to Auschwitz so many months before.

Though we did not know the reason at the time, we were loaded into these cattle cars, packed in without food or water and closed away. We were taken by train so that we would not be marched across German soil in the condition and manner in which we had been brought from Warsaw. As much as they worked to keep the secrets of their atrocities from the Allies, the Nazis worked equally hard to keep the truth from their own people. They made up stories, published lies and performed the most evil of their deeds behind curtains of secrecy that few had the courage to press aside.

When they finally opened the doors of the cattle cars we traveled in, we had not eaten or had anything to drink for days. Some of the people had drunk their own urine out of desperation. There was no room to lie down, and we were very lucky to find room to sit. The cars were so cramped that when we finally disembarked less than half of the prisoners managed to stumble off the train. The balance, those still in the cattle cars, was mostly dead, or close to death. Of the 4,000 prisoners who left Warsaw, barely 1,200 survived the journey to Dachau.

Chapter Sixteen

Once inside Dachau, with its motto of *arbeit mach frei* on the iron gates, my fellow prisoners and I were led to a separate set of barracks, away from the longer-term inmates of the camp. Dachau had been organized by SS Officer Theodor Eicke, and though neither my fellow prisoners nor I knew it, it had been intended as a model for future concentration camps.

It was designed as a forced labor camp with 123 subcamps or external *kommandos* that supplied labor to industries in nearby Munich, including BMW, Messerschmitt and Photo Agfa.

We were too starved and weak to be fully integrated. If we had been put to work, we would certainly have died almost immediately, so we were moved into the barracks, provided minimal food rations, and left to recover, as much as was possible, on a starvation diet. The workers in Dachau lived in a series of wooden huts with very tightly packed bunks.

The camp had a different feel from others where I had been imprisoned. I stood at the door of the barracks and stared out beyond the fences and walls. The camp was surrounded on all sides by munitions factories. It was bleak and desolate, but at least one change brought hope, however small.

Every day, around noon, air raid sirens sounded. When the Germans heard them, they went into a panic. There were bunkers beneath the camp and beneath the city. They scurried into them like frightened rats, but the prisoners did not run. When the sirens wailed, we stepped into the yard surrounding our bunkers and we turned our faces to the sky.

Each day, hundreds of US bombers roared over the city. Bombs fell, smashing through the walls of the factories and pounding the city of Dachau to rubble. They never hit the camp. The bombs hit their targets and we watched, our fists raised to the sky, and cheered. For us, it was like a celebration.

As the bombers flew over, they dropped huge, fluttering masses of tinfoil that whirled and flipped through the air, dropping to the ground as the bombers passed. At the time, I had no idea that the purpose of this was to interfere with Nazi radars. I stood and watched, and I smiled at the falling bits of foil, wondering as always if the end of the war would bring freedom or if, to keep their dirty secrets and save themselves from prosecution, the Germans would exterminate us all and destroy us as if we had never existed.

The days in Dachau passed slowly. As the other new prisoners and I began to regain our strength, we worried about our futures. Abe was the old man among us. He was the one who had been in the most camps, seen the most places and had the most experiences. One day I pulled him aside.

"How long do you think they will keep us here, feeding us but not making us work?" I asked.

Abe thought about it for only a moment.

"Not much longer," he said. "They can't afford for us to be idle, and they wouldn't march us all the way here and give us time to recover if they just intended to kill us. Either we'll end up working in those factories soon, or they'll be moving us to another camp."

I knew from experience that if there were two groups, one

that was working and one that was not, the working group was the most likely to survive. I didn't like sitting idle.

"I hope you're right," I said.

Abe smiled. "I'm right. You'll see."

Two weeks later, we were formed up outside our barracks and marched back to the train yard, where once again we were loaded onto the cattle cars.

As we leaned on interior wall of the train car and the doors were closed, Abe turned to me.

"They're taking us by train because they don't want their own people to see. There can be no death marches inside Germany. What happens inside the gates of these camps—they pretend it isn't true. The war is nearly over now, and they know they aren't going to win. We are their dirty little secret. The fewer who know the truth, the more confusing it will be when it's over."

The train rolled out of the station and away, and we waited to find where we would be taken next. Our destination turned out to be a group of seven camps near Munich at a place called Landsberg. The camp where we disembarked was the newest of the seven, just opened. My companions and I were the first prisoners to arrive.

The general layout of the camp was pretty much like that of the other camps in which I had spent time. There were two layers of barbed-wire fencing around the camp. Along the perimeters of these, guard towers had been set up, though in the middle of Germany, escape was even less likely to succeed than it had been in other camps. Even if a prisoner were to somehow find his way beyond the fences and the fields, where would he go? Who in the middle of Germany would be willing to risk life and family to help a Jew?

The barracks in Landsberg were different. Each was formed first by digging a trench or pit. Each was about five feet deep and a hundred feet wide, covered by a peaked, wooden roof. The roof was covered by dirt and then grass was planted atop it. This served as insulation against heat and cold, and it concealed the nature of the structures from an aerial view. There were a small number of vents in the ceiling to allow for the circulation of fresh air. At the front of each barrack, a couple of windows and a door faced out onto the courtyard beyond.

The interiors of the buildings were very plain. Down the center of each barrack was a walkway that measured four feet high at its lowest along the sides, and eight feet high at its tallest along the center. Six-foot-deep wooden shelves ran along the walls on either side of the walk; that was where the prisoners slept. There were about eighty of us to each barrack.

In the center of the camp, separated from the barracks, was a small group of buildings necessary for the management of the camp and its operations. These buildings housed the kitchen, shops for tailors and carpenters, and more-comfortable quarters for the German guards and officers.

The entire camp was clean and new. There were two medical clinics. The German clinic was operated by German doctors and surgeons. It was equipped for treatment and minor surgery. There was a smaller clinic for the prisoners. The doctor was Jewish, and there were no medicines or treatments available. If a prisoner went there to be seen, the best he could hope for was to be told what he suffered from.

Beyond the fences, though, things were different. Unlike Dachau, which had been hemmed in on all sides by factories and filth, Landsberg was surrounded by farms and fields. Many of the prisoners were employed in cultivating and maintaining those fields. The air was cleaner. In just about every way, it was superior to the crowded, dirty conditions of Dachau.

In the Landsberg camp, I made a decision. There were certain prisoners who performed the duty of running messages, along with whatever other chores the German officers came up with. It was a preferred job, and I determined that in this camp, it was the job that I wanted. These runners were called *läufers.*

After roll had been called on the first morning, I screwed up my nerve, stepped out of the ranks and approached the German guard who was in charge.

"Pardon me, sir," I said quietly. "I would like to perform the duties of *läufer* for the camp."

It was a horrible chance to take. Speaking to a German officer without having been spoken to first was a dangerous proposition. I might have been beaten severely or even shot. Before the officer could reply, several more young men, emboldened by my actions, stepped up beside me, proclaiming that they, too, would like to be considered for the job.

The German scanned the group critically. He walked around us and took our measures, and then he began to question us. He asked a few questions of each of us but did not really appear to listen to our answers. The man was tall. He looked to be in his late forties and he wore a stern expression as he studied us.

Eventually, he pointed at me.

"You," he said, "follow me."

In that moment, my time in Landsberg took an extreme shift. I became the camp *läufer,* and my position was set.

When our barracks had been assigned, each of the prisoners had been given a blanket and a metal dish. The dishes were shaped like cups, and they were for the distribution of the daily ration of watery soup. Then we were assigned to the various work details.

Gustav, Abe and I were split during the initial roll call, and at first I couldn't find out what had happened to them. Some prisoners were sent to work at the other six camps nearby. Eventually, when I found Abe, I learned that Gustav was out working in the fields.

Gustav and a large group of others were assigned to a team responsible for fertilizing the fields. The fertilizer they used was human excrement. It was pumped out from the various camps to the fields and spread by hand over the soil.

Once we were settled in, I managed to find Abe again one day after work. It was the first chance we'd had since arriving to really talk.

"Another camp, but very different this time," I observed. "When we were in Dachau, I asked you how long you thought we'd stay there, and your answer was right. What about this time? How long do you think they'll keep us here?"

"Things have changed for us," Abe said. "They have changed for the Nazis too. It's much more difficult and dangerous for them to move us now. They can't march us from camp to camp because they don't want anyone to see us. We make quite the picture, you know. There are no other countries to send us to now—we're in the heart of Germany. The work that they most need done is here. I believe we'll be in this camp for a while.

"Everyone knows that the war is as good as lost," he said. "They're still fighting, but it's only a matter of time. We'll be here until they can't keep us any longer. Then..."

We stood in silence for a few minutes. We both knew that while we were prisoners and laborers now, when the war ended we would be marked men. We had seen far too much to be allowed just to walk away. Though we still hoped, we knew the situation would be dangerous.

Then, slowly shifting our thoughts from what seemed all too inevitable, we began to discuss other things. We considered what we would find if we survived. We talked about our families, the chances that those we knew might have survived, and where they had ended up. Escape was always on our minds, but the idea was remote and seemed unattainable. Instead we talked about survival, trading stories of what we dreamed about and hoped for. It passed the time.

After a few months of good weather and work in the fields, summer gave way to fall and then to the beginning of winter. Eventually, the first snow fell. Things continued as they had in warmer weather except that it grew much harder on the prisoners. We were already hungry to the point of starvation, tired and weak from long hours of work, and depressed. The encroaching cold seeped into our bones and ate away at our health. As it grew still colder, the harsh weather began to take its toll.

There was already a high death rate in the camp, but the cold increased this dramatically. After a while it seemed that more than twenty men a day never rose from the benches for morning roll call. The method for determining this death rate was grisly and very simple.

Each block or barrack had a prisoner assigned as the block *eldester*—the leader. It was the *eldester's* duty to rise earlier in the morning than the other prisoners and roust them for roll call. When they were gathered and the roll had been taken, two prisoners were chosen. I watched again and again as these men reentered the barracks.

Those who had remained behind, the dead, and those too weak to rise and make it out to roll were carried from the barracks one at a time. In front of the building, crusted in snow, the bodies were piled like oddly shaped five-foot logs. These men were so thin and undernourished that there was no substance to their bodies. Many of them weighed only fifty or sixty pounds. Once they'd been stacked for a day or so, snow and ice formed over and around the piles and the features lost detail, becoming shapeless masses. As the piles grew, you could count the rows and the heights and guess the number of the dead.

There were no gas chambers or crematoria at Landsberg. The dead in these camps were kept in piles until it became cumbersome. Prisoners were then assigned to dig through the frozen ground until mass graves had been opened. The bodies were dropped into these and covered without thought, prayer or respect, in the same fashion that the Germans disposed of their garbage.

The winter brought another hardship. Food, which was already too scarce, became even harder to come by. Rations were short, and with the end of the harvest season we could no longer supplement what we were given by picking greens or crops during the day. The frigid weather, reduced rations and brutal conditions wore away at our immune systems.

And then it happened.

Some prisoners began to grow weak and feverish. Spots appeared on their skin. The first of them were taken to the prisoners' clinic, and the Jewish doctor pronounced them infected with typhoid fever. Their bodies were too weak to resist the infection, and they were unable to walk or work.

Those who were infected became feverish. They were unable to keep down food or water. If they survived, the fever broke after about three days. This was just the beginning of their trouble. If they survived, their bodies were even weaker. They returned to consciousness parched, starving and too weak to rise and return to work. The meager rations available were not adequate for recovery, and not many were able to pull through it.

The Germans reacted quickly to try to stem the epidemic. One of the barracks was cleared of healthy prisoners and set aside for those who were sick. If anyone showed symptoms of typhus, he was immediately removed from whatever barrack he had been staying in and moved in with the others who were ill.

For a while this seemed to work. A smaller number of new

prisoners contracted the fever. Unfortunately, it was only temporary. The barracks were overrun with lice. The lice were perfect carriers of the fever, and all it took was the transfer of one of these to a new host to spread the sickness. As the days passed, the barrack housing the ill grew too full. There were too many to be housed in a single space, and the epidemic had regained its momentum. When it spread to the adjoining camps, the Germans took further action.

The camp where my barrack was located was chosen for quarantine. Any prisoner in the surrounding camps who showed symptoms or who was diagnosed by one of the camp physicians as having typhus was moved to that camp. The Germans removed themselves from the camp immediately. They took a select group of prisoners with them—those considered essential. These were the carpenters, tailors, cooks and other skilled laborers. I was among those who were removed, being the camp runner.

Those who were removed from the sick camp were to be assigned to new barracks outside the gates. These barracks were very well guarded, but they were much nicer than those the prisoners had vacated. These were similar to those that housed the guards. Each prisoner was assigned a comfortable bed with a pillow. There were running water and heat. It was very strange walking from the hellhole we had lived in for so long into this relative luxury. It eliminated part of the dread—the knowledge of the piled bodies freezing in the snow out front, and the constant fear that you would be the next to grow sick and weak, that you'd fall into the fever and never return.

In the old barrack from where we had moved, a rule had been instituted regarding the rationing of food. Each prisoner in that camp had an allotment of food each day. If a prisoner were to be away from the camp for any reason—including those who moved to cleaner and better quarters outside the gates—he could assign his food allotment to another prisoner. I knew only two people in the camp; one was Abe, who had already been taken out to work as a tailor, and the other was a middle-aged man named Mendel.

Mendel was from my hometown of Satu Mare. I had no memories of the man, but Mendel claimed to remember my father fondly. I told him that when I was gone, he could accept the daily food ration assigned to me.

Mendel was overcome with gratitude. He thanked me profusely, claiming that there was no way to express how grateful he was.

"You've saved my life," he said. "May God bless and watch over you. If I ever find my way out of this hell and back to freedom, I will not forget this. I will find your parents, and I will tell them what you have done for me. I will tell anyone who asks that you were a real mensch."

I shook Mendel's hand and then gathered my things. When the time came, the others and I were marched through the gates of the camp. I wondered what it meant even as I passed into the outer camp. Was it the first step back to my life? Would I be any closer to freedom?

Apparently not. Once we arrived at our new barrack, one of the German guards grabbed me by the back of the neck, dragged me to the doorway and flung me inside with contempt.

The prisoners were separated for work and assignment by specialty. Those who were carpenters were grouped with the other carpenters, cooks and tailors with their fellows and so on. I was assigned as orderly, houseboy and messenger to a German officer named Lieutenant Werner. Lieutenant Werner was not SS but a member of the old-guard German army, the Wehrmacht. He was in his mid-forties, of average height and build with a dark-black mustache. Compared to his Nazi counterparts in the camp, the lieutenant was friendly and easygoing. His face held a kindly, understanding expression that I caught right away. I was immediately happy to be assigned this duty and knew I would work as hard as I could to do a good job.

Lieutenant Werner's duties in the camp were strictly in a management capacity. He had nothing to do with the prisoners, how they were assigned or treated. He oversaw the bureaucratic affairs, and it was in these duties that I was assigned to assist.

When I reported, the lieutenant questioned me.

"So," Werner said, "what is your name?"

"David."

"How old are you, David?"

I kept to the story I had been telling since the day I'd stepped from the train in Auschwitz. "I'm eighteen, sir."

Werner examined me skeptically and then nodded slowly.

"Where are you from? You speak German very well."

"I'm Hungarian," I said. "I grew up in the town of Satu Mare. My father insisted that we learn to speak German, and I began studying the language when I was very young."

"Well, David," he said, "I believe that things are going to work out very well between us. If you do exactly as I tell you to and work hard, we will get along just fine. Do you understand?"

"Yes, sir."

The lieutenant's voice was soft and even, and his eyes were kind. I found that I believed what he told me and, despite the deeply ingrained lessons I had learned about dealing with German officers, felt something like trust.

Lieutenant Werner then did something totally unexpected. He held out his hand, as if to shake mine.

I was petrified. I had no idea what to do. Was it a trick? Was I being tested? To touch one of the German guards would have meant, at the least, a beating, and as often as not was cause enough for a prisoner to be shot. I stared at the lieutenant's outstretched hand but didn't move. I was paralyzed.

Lieutenant Werner watched me for a while, studying me. He must have seen that I was afraid, because eventually he withdrew his hand.

"It is okay, David. I understand."

My heartbeat slowed. Eventually I said, "Thank you, sir."

That is how I began the best of the many jobs and times I spent while locked away in the Nazi camps. My daily routine quickly became set and fairly comfortable. I rose early and reported to make the lieutenant's bed. I cleaned the rooms, polished the lieutenant's boots and generally cared for the man's needs. After preparing and bringing breakfast, I spent the remainder of the morning running messages and errands about the camp.

At noon I brought the lieutenant's lunch, and the afternoon consisted of more errands. I worked hard, trying to meet or exceed what was expected of me.

The officers were served much finer food than the prisoners. It was my job to carry Lieutenant Werner's food back and forth from the mess hall. Sometimes the scent of the food was too much for me. There was actual meat on the plate, and it had been so long since I had smelled or tasted anything so fine that I could barely believe it existed.

From time to time I took small bites of the food. I was very careful not to take enough that it would be noticed. I felt guilty and feared that I might be caught, but I was careful because being caught would likely have meant banishment to one of the other camps, or being shot on the spot. I didn't really believe Lieutenant Werner would kill me, but the others—the SS officers—would not hesitate, and they had no love for the officers of the Wehrmacht.

Lieutenant Werner appreciated my close attention to his needs and my hard work, and as time passed he grew friendlier and closer. I began to feel more comfortable in the man's presence.

On weekends, Lieutenant Werner traveled outside the camp and into the city beyond. He had family there, and he often went to visit, share a meal and see his nephews and nieces. When he went on these trips, he seldom came back empty-handed. He brought parcels of food, baked goods and treats. When he did, he often shared bits of the food with me.

In sharing his food, Lieutenant Werner reminded me that I was a human being. In the camps, outside the quarters where I served the lieutenant, I was a faceless, nameless prisoner. Number 87672. To Lieutenant Werner I was more than that; I was a person worthy of talking to and interacting with.

"Where is your family?" he asked me one day. "I know your mother, father and sister were with you in Auschwitz, but...your brothers? Your aunts and uncles?"

"I have relatives in Budapest," I said. "I'm sure there are still some there. There are others in Hungary—we are a big family."

Lieutenant Werner countered, "I have a wife," and his expression grew empty and far away. "I have not seen her in a very long time. I have two sons. Both of them are in the army now, serving in places very far from here. I hear from them from time to time, but it's been many months since I have seen them or talked with them. I also have a daughter. She is a nurse. I have not talked with her for a very long time either. I miss them."

We talked quite a lot about our homes, our lives and our families. The lieutenant showed me pictures of his wife and children. He genuinely cared for them and missed them. He wanted the war to come to an end and often commented that he hoped both of us would be free to return to our families soon.

"I have family in Landsberg," Werner said one day. "You know that I visit them as often as I can. I have talked to them about you. Did you know that, David?"

I shook my head. I did not know where this was going, and I didn't want to say anything that was out of line.

"They are very interested in your stories. They tell me that they would like to speak with you, to meet you and get to know you. What do you think about that?"

I felt a return of the fear I had felt on the day I'd met the lieutenant, when the older man had held out his hand to shake mine. Was this a joke?

"No prisoners are allowed beyond the camp, even with an escort," I said. "Surely it would never be allowed for me to meet your family."

The lieutenant smiled.

"Don't worry about what is and is not allowed," he said. "I will see to it. The next time that I go out to visit my family, you will go with me."

I didn't know what to say. I still thought it might be a joke, and if it were not a joke, it frightened me.

"Thank you," I said at last.

For the moment, the subject was dropped, but it stuck in the back of my mind. The city—even a German city where Jews were hated and scorned—seemed like a miracle of freedom. The fact that the lieutenant would suggest such a visit pleased me greatly.

Chapter Seventeen

The prisoners in my barrack were given clothing that was shipped in from Auschwitz. What they got were the remnants of the belongings gathered from the trains and from those who had died. Among the prisoners these were things of value that could be bartered.

There was food—always the food. The rules that Gustav and I had set for survival had not changed. The two most important things were enough food and the will to survive, but the outer camp provided new layers of barter and a slightly changed dynamic for survival.

I saw that there were three types of prisoners. Some were willing to trade anything for food. Some were willing to trade food or clothing for cigarettes. The last thing you might trade for was clothing.

I had always been careful about my appearance. No matter how bad things got, I tried to look my best, to keep myself as clean as possible and to dress as well as possible. I watched the others in the camp. Those who traded what they had and what they could get their hands on for food survived fairly well. Those who were willing to trade what their bodies needed for cigarettes did not last as long. They grew weak, and the cigarettes didn't help.

My position allowed me to eat well. I did not smoke, and I

was able to trade for what clothing arrived that would fit me. I was still small for my size, and there were few others my age in the camps. It was sometimes difficult to find anything that would fit, but I did what I could and picked up the best that I could manage.

I believed that a man's appearance was important. Part of doing a good job and working to the best of my abilities was taking care of myself. Looking as good as possible under whatever circumstances was a part of the attitude that helped me to survive. When I found something that fit better than what I had, I traded food for it. Even my cap fit better than most.

Many of the prisoners had long given up on caring about their clothing or their appearances. They had wasted away to the point that their frames barely supported their clothing. It hung on them limply, the caps sliding down over their heads to their ears. They resembled stumbling skeletons. I didn't want to see myself that way or for others to see me that way. A part of my will to survive was based on self-esteem—what was left of it.

One Friday when I reported for work, Lieutenant Werner pulled me aside.

"Tomorrow," he said, "I want you to look your best. Make sure you are clean and that you wear the best clothing that you own. Wash carefully, and shine your shoes. It is important that you look as little like a prisoner as you possibly can."

"Why, sir?" I asked.

"Tomorrow I will visit my family in Landsberg," he said. "You will accompany me on that trip, and we can't have you walking into town looking like a prisoner."

My heart raced, but I fought to hold back any outburst. I was afraid, even after so long in the lieutenant's company, that it was a joke. I didn't want to show my enthusiasm.

"Yes, sir," I said.

That day passed in a blur. I went about my normal tasks, but it was almost impossible to concentrate. When I returned to the barrack I carefully went through my clothing, choosing the best jacket and pants that I had. I had kept just enough polish from what I used on the lieutenant's shoes to shine my own shoes. I was done with everything I could possibly do to prepare long before it was time for sleep, and when that time came I lay awake into the night. I still could not quite bring myself to believe that I was leaving the camp, and I was terrified. If it were true, if the lieutenant intended to take me outside the camp, we would both be in great danger. I couldn't believe the man would risk so much for me. I got very little sleep.

When I reported on Saturday, I was more presentable than I had been in years. My clothing was clean, and I had folded it so that the worst of the wrinkles were ironed out. I had buffed my shoes to a shine and set my cap firmly on my head. I had been eating better since working for Lieutenant Werner, and my frame was not quite as thin. I could have passed for a local boy except for the yellow stars of David on my chest and on the back of my jacket.

"So, David," Lieutenant Werner said when he saw me. "I see that you have done as I asked."

The lieutenant walked in a slow circle around me, inspecting me closely. I stood very still, heart pounding, certain that at any moment Werner would change his mind or tell me it was a joke of some kind and that I should get to work. Eventually, he stopped and nodded.

"It is good," he said.

Turning, Lieutenant Werner pointed to a rucksack in the corner.

"Put that on, David. Make sure that you wear it so that it covers the mark on your back, and that one on your chest. Whatever you do, don't take it off unless we are safely inside the home of my relatives or back here in my office. Is that clear? At no time can anyone know that you are a prisoner."

I nodded. My throat was dry, and I didn't trust myself to speak. I picked up the rucksack and strapped it on, carefully adjusting it. The telltale symbols were completely hidden. When we set out from the office I looked, for the entire world, like a young man out for a walk with his father or his uncle.

Lieutenant Werner walked with confidence, and I followed. A driver was waiting, and we climbed into the back of the car, which pulled away from the curb and wound its way through the camp and out the main gate. We rode in silence through the outlying fields and down rural roads. When we reached town, the driver pulled over to the curb. I stepped out and held the door for Lieutenant Werner. He leaned back in and spoke to the driver, who laughed at whatever he heard. Then Werner closed the door and the car rolled slowly away, leaving us on the side of the street.

The sensation was overwhelming. For a moment, I couldn't speak and could hardly breathe. The air was cleaner. There were no fences, no barbed-wire rings with their razor teeth, no guard towers or dogs.

I smelled food and heard voices raised in laughter. There were open shops and people wandering among them, talking, eating and drinking. It was a world so alien to the one I had been trapped in that it was nearly impossible to reconcile it with reality.

Lieutenant Werner gave me just a moment to gather myself.

"Come, David," he said. The man's voice was kindly, and when I met his gaze we both smiled.

As I followed the lieutenant, I looked at each new thing we passed in wonder. At first I watched carefully to see if everyone was staring at me, but when I realized no one was paying any attention, I relaxed. It was a happy time, watching children playing and men and women going about their daily business as if nothing had happened—as if the war were not raging all about us. As if there were still sanity left in the world.

It gave me hope. It strengthened my belief that there might come a time when I could walk down such a street as a free man. It was a magical moment in the midst of a living hell, and I soaked up every sensation as if it might be my last.

We reached Lieutenant Werner's family's home. It was a nice two-story home with a well-kept lawn. We were invited inside, and the moment we had cleared the door, the lieutenant's family greeted him warmly. There were two children and several adults, all clean and happy and well-dressed.

I felt out of place and stood very still by the door. I wasn't sure what was going to happen or what was expected of me, so I waited. Eventually, Lieutenant Werner turned to me and smiled.

"I almost forgot," he said. "This is David. He takes care of my needs at the camp. He is not a German soldier, but he is almost as good. I hope you'll all welcome him."

I met them all then: Werner's cousin Joseph, and his wife Gertrude, the children, ages ten and twelve, and the rest of the family who had gathered for the meal. They were all very polite, but I still felt uncomfortable. The children stared at me, not knowing what to say. Soon it was time to eat, and the tension eased.

The table was set and they were all seated. If felt very strange, but soon they brought in the food and, as everyone began to eat, my anxiety slowly eased. They served a three-course meal, and I sat in amazement as dish after dish was served. I smelled and tasted things I had not seen in years. There was bread and meat, and there was wine to drink. The lieutenant did not treat me any differently from the others at the table.

As the meal progressed and the food slowly disappeared,

conversation picked up around the table. At first, the lieutenant caught up on what was happening with the family. He listened attentively as the children told their stories and smiled at news from other branches of the family.

I paid strict attention to what was said, but I kept eating. I controlled my hunger and ate slowly, but I continued to eat. I was still chewing when one of the girls turned to me, wide-eyed.

"David," she said. "What did you do? Why have they locked you away?"

The table fell silent. I swallowed the food in my mouth, which had suddenly gone dry. I opened my mouth as if to speak, but no sound came out. The girl's father came to my rescue with a nervous laugh.

"Tell us, David," he said, "about your family. Where do you come from? You speak German very well, but you have an accent. Is it Hungarian?"

My heart skipped a single beat and I felt blood rushing to my face, but my voice returned to me and I nodded gratefully, ignoring the stare of the girl whose question I did not answer.

"Yes," I said. "I was born in Hungary. I grew up in the town of Satu Mare."

I told them about my father and my mother, my sisters and brothers. I told them what life had been like before our deportation to Poland. This time, when the questions came around to where I had been imprisoned, I was able to continue.

They wanted to know where I had seen my family last, where they'd been taken and where I had been kept. They listened as I explained about the work camp in Warsaw and my journeys on the trains. I avoided any mention of the slaughter, the crematoria or the gas chambers. I didn't know what they knew or suspected, and despite the lieutenant's goodwill I didn't know what would happen if I told them everything. I didn't even know how I would explain such things to someone who had not seen or experienced them for themselves.

I didn't want to do anything that might hurt Lieutenant Werner. Without him, there would have been no food, no freedom, and I would not have been sitting there talking to them as if I were some long-lost member of their family. After hearing me out, my hostess smiled at me.

"I hope that one day you will have the chance to return to your family," she said. "I believe that someday soon this terrible war will be over. When it is, everyone who has lost someone will be able find them, and those who have been away from their loved ones can return to where they belong."

"I hope that you are right," Lieutenant Werner said softly. "I hope that we will all be home soon. But for now, David and I must return to the camp. Our day of freedom is at an end."

They cleared the table and our hostess put together a package of food for Werner and a package for me as well. They all shook my hand and wished me well. They invited me to return and visit again, and the lieutenant promised that, if it were possible, we would indeed both return.

When all our goodbyes had been said, we stepped back onto the street and headed back toward town, where we would meet our driver. Lieutenant Werner walked in silence, enjoying the evening, and I followed a little more slowly. My mind wandered, and I found myself in turmoil.

I thought about the family I had just visited, and I thought about my own family. I had lost my mother and my father, my sisters and my brothers. The home I had grown up in had been taken, and everything we had ever owned was gone. I thought about the deportation to Poland and the second arrest in Satu Mare, and the train to the death camps.

All of it had been at the hands of the Germans. I tried to

think of them as a single entity—the SS guards, the soldiers and the people we passed as we walked down this street. It was difficult. I should have hated them. I knew that I should have hated them all, but I found that I did not, and this realization bothered me as well. I was very confused. The lieutenant had done a great deal for me. He had treated me fairly and with respect, and he had risked his own career and possibly his life to take me out of the camp for something as intimate as a meal shared with his family. How was I to hate such a man?

Lieutenant Werner was as good as his word. Over the weeks to come, I often accompanied him to his relatives' home. Over time I grew less tense in their presence and more comfortable with the small glimpses of freedom. They gave me hope and strength. The times that I spent with them were the happiest of any since I had first stepped off the train at Auschwitz.

Chapter Eighteen

I did my work for the lieutenant every day, working as hard as I could to do a good job and to make him comfortable. Werner was a wine drinker. At first, when I'd gone to work with him, the drinking was a casual thing—moderate and well-controlled. As time wore on, though, more and more stories of the war reached the camp. Lieutenant Werner took to drinking more, and earlier in the day. Rumors of the war coming to an end reached us from time to time, but there was never anything certain.

As time passed, Lieutenant Werner began talking to me more and more often as if I were an equal and not a prisoner at all. When he'd had some wine, he would start discussing the war. He saw it as an unending hell. He told me stories of the Wehrmacht. It was the real German army, not the Nazis and their SS. He had stories from before Hitler, and it was obvious he'd once been proud of his job but now felt differently.

He complained about the miserable conditions of the camp and the way the prisoners were treated. He talked about his sons, how far away they'd been stationed and how they were growing up and living their lives and he had no chance even to be part of them. He missed his wife, and he missed the career he had left behind.

He said he had been an engineer. He had given that up to join the Wehrmacht—and for what? To be taken from his wife and his children and put into a position where he was overseeing a death camp, doing Himmler's dirty work for him?

I knew that I should have hated the lieutenant. I knew that the personal kindnesses that he had shown me did not make up for the atrocities. The sharing of a few meals and the fair treatment at this man's hand did not erase the loss of my own family, the starvation or sickness. Still, I felt that Lieutenant Werner was, in his heart, a good man. Despite the disparity of our positions, I found myself feeling badly for him.

As the days and weeks passed, the drinking increased. One day I arrived to find the lieutenant standing in front of his mirror, staring at his reflection. He'd been drinking, though it was very early in the day. I stepped up close and stood, waiting for his instructions. Instead of telling me what to do, he put a hand on my shoulder. He didn't turn to face me but continued staring at himself in the mirror and sipping from the glass in his other hand.

"David," he said, "I'm afraid that this war is coming to an end. It's a matter of time, you know? They are closing in on us, and soon it will end. If the Allies come here and take me and put me on trial, would you testify on my behalf?"

In that moment, I didn't see a war criminal. I didn't see an evil monster. I saw a middle-aged man full of sorrow, standing drunk in a fancy uniform. The lieutenant was obviously in pain. The fact that he would ask me such a question, that he cared what I thought, touched me deeply, and I hoped that when the war did end, Werner would not be made to suffer.

"Lieutenant Werner," I said. "You have no part in the atrocities here. You have harmed no one and, when possible, you have helped. You will not be put on trial. You are one of the only decent human beings I have met since being taken from Satu Mare. If it came to a trial, I would gladly testify to that effect, and so would many others."

Lieutenant Werner nodded, but he looked unconvinced. I hoped that my words would help to ease his guilt, but it seemed as though he could not be reached. I continued about my work, but the mood was continually more somber. As the days passed, he would not be calmed. He drank, and he worried over what was to come.

Lieutenant Werner was the most decent human being of all the German officers I met. He was kind and considerate toward me, almost like a surrogate father. He did all that he could to make me feel like a normal boy instead of a prisoner. I always believed that was why he took me out of the camp to visit his family. I was very grateful for all he did.

As the months went by, the lieutenant drank more and in larger quantities. He tried to bury his sorrow in liquor. I saw the suffering in his eyes. Like all German officers who guarded the concentration camps, he was afraid that at the end of the war he would be sentenced to a long prison term or executed and never see his family again. Even though he was not involved with the treatment of the prisoners, I tried to do anything I could to help him. I would have testified on the man's behalf, given the chance.

In addition to my work for the lieutenant, I sometimes joined the other prisoners for extra hours of manual labor. With prisoners locked away in the sick camp, there was a lot that needed to be done, and it fell to the prisoners who were still healthy.

One day during a work detail unloading coal, after working for about two hours I began to feel weak. I tried to work through it, hoping it was just a dizzy spell and that it would pass, but it didn't. I knew what it meant, and my heart sank.

One of the others in the working party was a carpenter named Saul. I turned to him. "I'm very tired," I said, choosing my words carefully. "Do you think I could sit down just for a minute? If I could rest..."

Saul's eyes grew wide. He knew what the weakness meant, and he leaned in close. "Are you crazy? Don't sit down. You can't get sick. If they think you have the fever, they will send us all back to the camp. All of us!"

I knew it was true. I turned back to the work and did my best, but only a short time later my legs lost their strength and I collapsed in the dirt. The guards saw me and ordered other prisoners to lift me to my feet. I was dragged away from the work detail and taken to the prisoners' physician.

The examination was swift, and the diagnosis was no surprise: typhoid fever. The guards took me next to the German doctor to have the diagnosis confirmed. They did not want to lose workers, but the fever was carried by lice and if one prisoner had it, those who roomed with him were suspect as well. They couldn't take a chance on sending just the one man back to the sick camp. They had to send them all.

Within one day I recovered my strength. I examined myself but found none of the spots that I knew had appeared on the others who were sick. They had red spots and high fever, couldn't eat and, after three or four days, recovered or died. In my case, I never knew if I had typhoid fever because I never saw the red spots. Maybe I just had a mild case because both the German and Jewish doctors had diagnosed me. I suspected that the doctors were just not taking chances. I wasn't sick now, but I knew that when they sent me back to the sick camp, I soon would be.

The others and I were sent back. It was a horrible, infested place. The prisoners and the barracks were infested with lice, and the lice carried the fever. The prisoners—those with the energy for a sense of humor—joked that you should never lay your blanket down unattended. If you did, the lice might have carried it away.

I entered that camp with failing courage. Even Lieutenant

Werner was powerless to do anything to help me. Two days after collapsing during the coal detail, I walked out into the yard as if I had never been sick at all. I didn't know if I had somehow gotten a very mild dose or if I had never really been infected at all. It didn't matter. We were all sent back, and there was nothing anyone could do to stop it.

Once back inside the gates of the sick camp, I went immediately in search of Mendel, the man I had given my food ration to when I had left. I knew that I was going to have to adjust my world again. Inside the gate, I was just another prisoner. Lieutenant Werner could not reach me or help me, and I had to look out for myself.

I found Mendel sitting alone along the outer wall of his barrack. I greeted the man, who glanced up in confusion.

"They believe I have the fever," I said, "and so, I am back. I will have to have my food ration back. I'm very sorry to have to tell you that, but without it, I won't be able to live."

Mendel's eyes took on a pained, glazed look. I wished that there were another way. The small extra bit of food was a great advantage in the camp.

"It's okay, David," he said at last. "You are a good boy, and you have helped me. I would be dead now, I think, if it had not been for the extra food. You did not have to do that for me but you did, and I will never forget it."

I wanted to lift his hopes. "Maybe it won't matter so much," I said. "I've heard rumors—even the Germans are talking about the end of the war. They believe that it will be soon. Before you know it, it will all be over, and the two of us will walk out of here as free men."

Mendel nodded, but even as he did he grew distracted, and his motion slowed. I could see no emotion, no light or hope in the older man's eyes. He didn't seem to share my belief that we could regain our freedom. I left him sitting as I had found him and went about settling back into the small corner of hell to which I had been returned.

It was a couple of weeks before I made my way back around to Mendel's barrack. I was saddened by what I found. Mendel had grown thinner, and he stood hunched, as if years had passed since we had last spoken.

All of the prisoners received the same bad food, slept under the same roofs in the same lice-infested blankets. All of their circumstances were the same, and yet it affected them differently. Mendel received the same rations as others, but the older man was wasting away.

"Mendel," I said, "what has happened to you?"

He glanced up at me with empty, haunted eyes. His clothes draped over him as though he were made of walking bones.

"What's the use?" he asked. "Why go on living like animals, starving, sick and cold, beaten and treated as if we are not men at all? This is only going to end one of two ways. Either we will die here from the lack of food or the fever, or the war will end like you say—and they will shoot us like dogs. There's no point in living."

I didn't know what to say. I wanted to comfort Mendel, but the man was beyond comforting. He was no longer really a man. I had seen it many times before—it was like talking to a walking corpse. Mendel was as good as dead and it left a sick feeling in my gut as I walked away again, leaving him alone.

The next time that I returned to that barrack, my fears proved true. I saw Mendel, or what was left of him, with the other dead, stacked in front of the barrack.

I knew it took more than luck to get by. Mendel had the same physical circumstances as everyone else; the only thing that was different was what was inside—what he thought and believed. I believed it was the will to survive that kept me alive when others dropped and died. It was the thought that if I could stand up against it all, deal with the starvation, mistreatment, beatings and humiliation, I would come out the other end of the tunnel. And it was the thought of walking away from it all a free man, and being able to look back and to realize that I had survived, that kept me healthy. It was not giving in but instead depending on my strength of will. I had to believe I was strong enough to endure anything.

Not long after I found Mendel's body, the typhoid camp received word from the German guards that the entire camp was being evacuated. This time the move was even more sudden and confusing than it had been in the past. We were gathered together, set in ranks and started out marching before we knew what was happening. No one knew where we were going or why, but everyone knew that it must have been important—and different—if we were to be force-marched through Germany, where German citizens might have seen us passing.

I tried to spot Lieutenant Werner as we passed through the gates. I wanted to know that the man was safe, but there was no sign of him. As had been the case with so many faces and places, the lieutenant disappeared from my world. I never found out what happened to him, whether he faced the trial he had feared or had escaped with his life intact and found his way back to his family. I never saw or heard of him again.

We kept to side roads, avoiding as much interaction with those in the towns and cities as possible. The formation was similar to what I remembered from the Warsaw evacuation—the prisoners marching, flanked by guards and dogs. There was no time to take stock of our situation. The camp, along with everything and everyone associated with it, fell away behind us quickly, as if we were awakening from one nightmare into another.

The company moved with more stealth than any earlier march. We marched night and day, but it was impossible to get a fix on where we were heading. The guards shifted directions in a seemingly random pattern. At night we were allowed to sleep for a few hours. The guards stopped at locations that provided valleys or lower grounds for us, with higher vantage points from which they could watch closely for deserters or runners.

As we marched, I often heard gunfire, sometimes very close to our position. Each time, the guards shifted their direction yet again, steering us away from whatever conflict we drew too close to. It grew apparent in time that, as long as they had the prisoners to watch over, the guards could use that responsibility to avoid the direct fighting. It was better to guard in the dark than to fight and maybe be shot down as the front lines of the war advanced on them.

One morning the German officer in charge of the detail stood before us all.

"The war is over," he said. "We will not move out until I have received further instructions. Germany has...surrendered. Until we have more information, we will remain here."

I stood quietly with the others. We were too stunned and confused by the news to work up much excitement. We were allowed to return to our makeshift beds and sleep, and we remained there in that same valley for over half the day. Then, as suddenly as our respite had begun, it ended.

"Get up!" the guards cried. "Get up, get moving. The information was incorrect. We are moving out now!"

Just like that, we were back in line and moving. Now the Germans moved much more quickly, forcing us to march most of the day and night, allowing us very little sleep. As we moved out, I fell in beside a young Yugoslavian man I had befriended during the wait in the valley. The man, named Manny, was about nineteen.

We helped one another along, preventing sudden spills and falls. After too many hours of walking, our bodies began to fail us. We could have fallen asleep as we walked and been shot down, but instead we told stories, each helping to distract the other from the starvation, pain and weariness, and reaching out to offer support when sleep threatened to overwhelm another.

The guards were spaced out at about fifty-foot intervals. This meant that while we were constantly under surveillance, we could talk about anything we wanted without fear of being overheard. Manny and I talked about escape.

"There are a lot of turns," Manny said, seeming to concentrate on keeping his feet moving and not tripping. "Some of them are very sharp."

I glanced up. The men ahead of us rounded a corner in the road, and the guard marching beside them moved around the bend and out of sight. We continued until we hit that point in the road, and when we made our own turn we realized that the guard behind us could no longer see us. We kept our eyes on the Germans in front. The guards seldom if ever glanced back, keeping their eyes tight on the prisoners marching directly in front and beside them and leaving the next block to the guards behind.

"That is the time," I said.

Manny nodded. We watched around several more bends in the road, and the pattern repeated. Only the guards to our rear were watching. When we first rounded a corner, there was a window of opportunity.

"I think it could work," Manny said finally. "If we can still run, and if we can get far enough away from the others before the guards to the rear reach the corner, we can do this. If we could just get away and out into the countryside, we could hide. All we would need to do would be to find food and a place to rest. We could wait until the Germans are overrun or their enemies push the battle lines far enough into the country for us to surrender ourselves."

"Anything is better than waiting to die," I said.

Neither of us liked talking about it, but what we had heard time and again was ingrained in our minds. The Germans had told us that if they lost the war, they would remove all witnesses to their atrocities. I didn't know if the guards would follow through on that promise or not. In the face of their own capture, would they slaughter a group of innocent prisoners and risk being caught doing the deed? Or would they consider it a greater risk that those same prisoners, given a chance to speak to the Allied forces, would expose them for the monsters they were?

We talked over our plan through the march, and got as much rest as we were allowed that night. The next day we kept watch, trying to gauge the exact amount of time we would be in the guard's blind spot, and how far out we would have to get to either side to be out of danger. When the day faded and night fell, we started watching for our chance.

"Next turn," Manny said. "I'll go to the right. You take off to the left as fast as you can go. Whatever you do, don't slow down or stop. If they catch us…"

"They will kill us," I finished.

We continued on in silence, and finally, just ahead, the road took a hard turn to the left. We watched the guards disappear around that bend, then glanced at each other. Impulsively, I reached over and took Manny's arm in a tight grip.

"Be careful," I said. "I will see you after they have passed, if I can. If you don't see me, keep going. The important thing is to get far enough away that we are out of reach of the guards."

Manny nodded. We had talked through every possible detail, but really, once we were committed there was only one thing left to do: run. I felt reasonably strong, but I knew that this could have been deceptive. It was a very different thing to run all out than to walk in a shuffling line of weak, starving prisoners. I knew I had to push myself and get beyond the range of the guards' peripheral vision or it might have been my last steps in life.

Hearts pounding, we stayed in step with the others, edging closer and closer to either side of the ranks. I shifted left. We reached the corner, and the minute we were sure we were out of sight of the guards coming up from behind, Manny whispered, "Go!"

I broke away from the ranks and scrambled off the left side of the road. There was a narrow ditch, and I clambered across it, hit the edge of the field beyond and began to run. Almost immediately, though too late to change the plan, I realized my mistake: the field I had run into had been freshly plowed. Long furrows of overturned earth ran the length of the field. I had no choice but to run against the grain of the rows. My shoes caught in the furrows and the soft, loose soil refused to support me as I struggled to sprint away from the marching prisoners.

Every second the line moved forward, and I knew I had only a few moments before the guards would round that corner and I would be visible to anyone glancing out in my direction. Running through the furrows was much harder than running on flat ground would have been, and I was weakened from the march and from the lack of food. I fought for more speed, but it wasn't possible. Again and again I was afraid I would lose my balance, but somehow I managed to remain upright and moving.

A loud engine sounded behind me. I kept running, but a moment later the beam of a single headlight swept around the corner where I had bolted. As it turned, the headlight beam cut a swath of light across the dark field and came to rest directly on me. My heart leapt in my chest.

It was the camp commander on one of the squat, low-slung motorcycles that the German army used. He rolled up and down the line, checking in with the guards and relaying instructions. Manny and I had chosen the worst possible moment, and for me the mistake had doubled. I was on the side where the commander appeared.

"Halt!" he cried. "You there, halt!"

I froze in place. My legs lost all their strength. I could have tried to keep running, but he would have shot me on the spot. I was paralyzed with fear. The commander climbed off his motorcycle and left the headlight beam slicing the night. He walked slowly out across the field to where I stood, trembling.

The man casually drew his gun as he approached. When he reached me, it was pointed directly at my chest. He didn't speak. He circled, looking me up and down disdainfully. I didn't know what to do. I was afraid if I moved I would be shot, and I knew it was likely that I would be shot even if I didn't move. I concentrated on breathing.

"Run!" the German commanded. He waved his arm toward the retreating ranks of prisoners. "Run!"

I walked as fast as I could back toward the ranks. I passed the officer and kept on going. The minute I passed him, I felt as if a bullet were about to fly after me, aimed at my back or my neck. It was the Germans' style. They would catch a fleeing prisoner, tell him to run back and then cut him down. Shooting a prisoner in the back was almost a sport for the Germans. I did not expect to live another minute.

But the shot never came. I could barely breathe from the fear and the exertion. I thought each and every step would be my last, and I had exerted myself nearly as far as my weakened body could take, but I made it back to the line of prisoners and, gratefully, sank back into their ranks and began to march. The commander watched for a few moments, then returned to his motorcycle and rolled on.

David's parents, Lea and Gabriel.

David, age four.

David, Germany, 1946.

Left to right: William, Moshe (Moses), David (center bottom), Mother.

Sisters Irene, Ilana, Rachel, 1943.

Brother Armin, 1950.

Mendu in Israel.

David, third from left, in an Israeli orphanage.

The Three Musketeers: Jacob, Kostik and David in the orphanage, 1947.

In the orphanage, 1948.

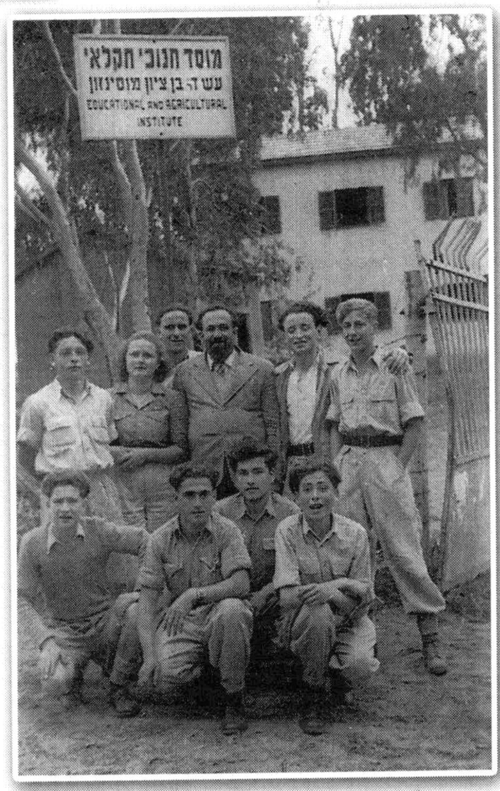

David, standing second from right. Class saying goodbye to teacher and school, entering the army, 1948.

David, first week in the army, 1948.

In the Israeli army, 1949.

David on the left, arriving for seargent major's course, 1948.

David in Italy before leaving for Palestine, 1946.

A Syrian tank penetrated the Daganya Kibbutz, which was destroyed by Israeli troops, 1948.

David and Ariel Sharon at the Israel Bond Conference. In the orphanage, Sharon was David's instructor and taught him the use of different weapons. Sharon took David's unit on night patrols where they exchanged fire with Arab infiltrators. He also made David a member of Haganah.

Left to right: Glenn, Cora, Emily, David, Lauren, Jessica and Kimberly.

The following are samples of some of the commercial and residential buildings developed by David Karmi in New York City.

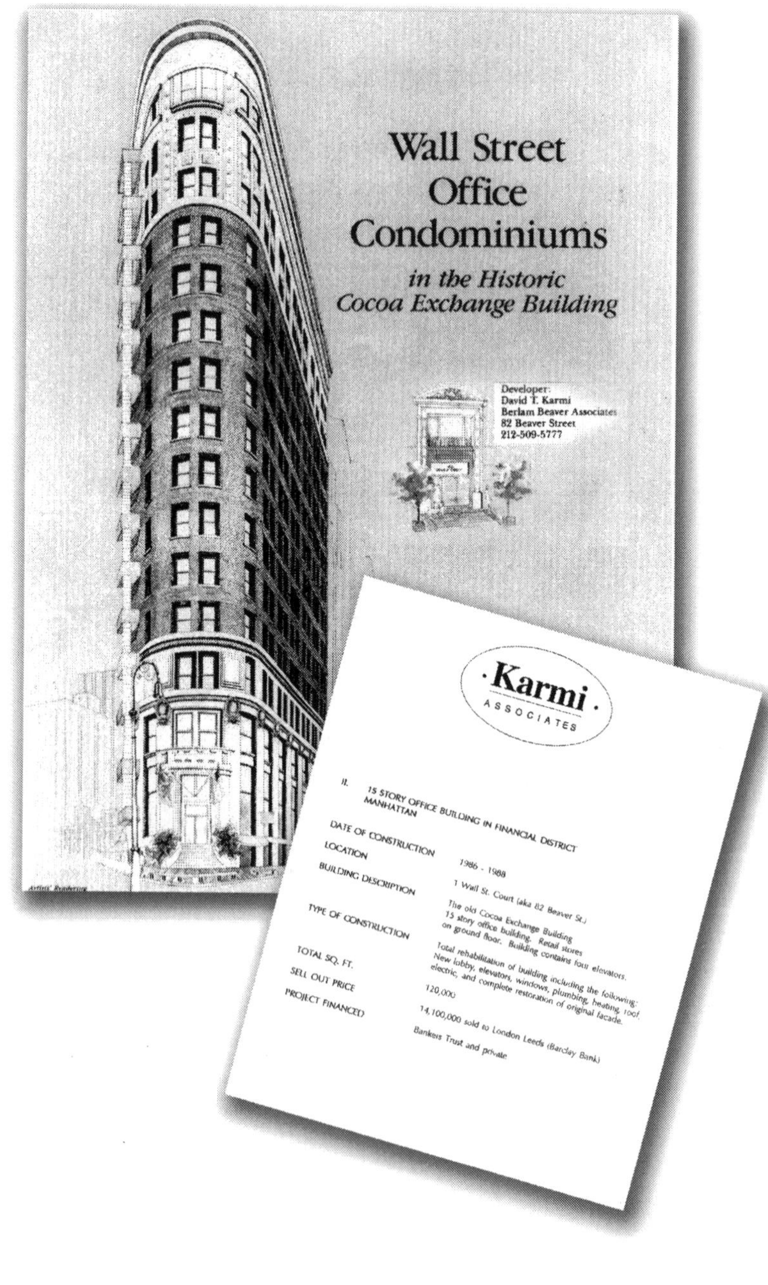

Wall Street
Office
Condominiums
in the Historic
Cocoa Exchange Building
Developer:
David T. Karmi
Berlam Beaver Associates
82 Beaver Street
212-509-5777

·Karmi·
ASSOCIATES

II. 15 STORY OFFICE BUILDING IN FINANCIAL DISTRICT MANHATTAN

DATE OF CONSTRUCTION	1986 - 1988
LOCATION	1 Wall St. Court (aka 82 Beaver St.)
BUILDING DESCRIPTION	The old Cocoa Exchange Building 15 story office building. Retail stores on ground floor. Building contains four elevators.
TYPE OF CONSTRUCTION	Total rehabilitation of building including the following: New lobby, elevators, windows, plumbing, heating, roof, electric, and complete restoration of original facade.
TOTAL SQ. FT.	120,000
SELL OUT PRICE	14,100,000 sold to London Leeds (Barclay Bank)
PROJECT FINANCED	Bankers Trust and private

"The New 321 Broadway"
A Condominium
Located directly opposite 26 Federal Plaza

321 Broadway

III. 7 STORY OFFICE AND RETAIL CONDOMINIUM
MANHATTAN

LOCATION	321 Broadway, N.Y.C.
BUILDING DESCRIPTION	7 story office condominium. 6 upper floors occupied as office condominiums. Ground floor is a retail condominium. Mr. Karmi retained the ground floor.
TYPE OF CONSTRUCTION	Total rehabilitation of building including: plumbing, heating, electric, roof, lobby and facade.
TOTAL NUMBER OF SQ. FT.	33,000
TOTAL SELL OUT PRICE	2,800,000 excluding ground floor retail condominium
FINANCED BY	Citibank

22 Perry
All the charm of the Village.
Karmi
ASSOCIATES
RESIDENTIAL AND COMMERCIAL CONDOMINIUM
GREENWICH VILLAGE, N.Y.C.
DATE OF CONSTRUCTION
LOCATION
BUILDING DESCRIPTION
TYPE OF CONSTRUCTION
TOTAL NUMBER OF SQUARE FEET
TOTAL SELL OUT PRICE
FINANCED BY
Manhattan
Landmark Design
New Construction
Square Feet

Chapter Nineteen

As I marched, I ran over and over in my mind what had happened. I could not understand why I hadn't been shot. I glanced through the ranks, tried to search the others, but there was no sign of Manny. I wondered if my friend had made it or if he'd been less lucky. Was he hiding in the trees, or had he been shot in the back and left to die in the dirt?

It took a very long time to regain my breath. Even as we moved onward I had a hard time believing someone wasn't about to yank me out of the ranks, pull me to the side of the road and execute me to make me an example for the others. I had seen so many others try to escape, and they'd all been shot.

Eventually I fell back into the rhythm of it. For a long time I was energized by the fear and the adrenalin. Then, as those wore off, I paid the price for the exertion. It was everything I could do that night to keep on my feet and to keep moving, but I did it. We continued on down the road, and when we finally stopped for the night to rest, we slept the sleep of the dead.

Our meandering trail finally stabilized soon after my failed escape attempt. We continued in a straight line, and in the distance we could make out the Trilo Mountains, near the border of Italy. We still didn't know for certain why we were evacuating or where we were heading.

Along the roadside, I saw small bundles and piles of clothing.

I scrutinized them as carefully as I could and finally realized what I was seeing. They were uniforms. German uniforms. Word spread through the prisoners, and we worked out the possibilities as we marched.

If the Germans were ditching their uniforms, it had to mean that—regardless of what we had been told about a false alarm—the war was going badly. The men who had shed those uniforms were trying to blend in and leave their military status behind. They didn't want to be caught, killed or taken prisoner. Whatever was going on, the end was near, and still the guards and the commander kept us moving forward at a crazed pace.

As we neared the mountains, it grew colder. A crust of snow covered the ground, and the nights were bitter. We weren't able to continue quite as long by day, and when it came time to rest at night we were hustled, as usual, down into a valley. We were surrounded by pine trees. To protect ourselves against the night, we cut branches from the pines. We created layers of pine boughs on the ground and then grouped together, huddling three or four in a group, and covered ourselves with all our blankets at once, sharing the warmth. Those who could not keep warm did not survive.

We continued for a few days more. One night we bedded down in another valley, and when the guards should have come to wake us the next morning, they did not. We woke, confused and frightened. We were alone in the valley; there was no sign of the guards. We rose and prepared ourselves for the day's march as if what was happening was no different from any other day of the march.

We were used to having the guards surround us from above. It was the perfect way to keep us from escaping, but now it took on more ominous implications. From above, out of sight, the Germans could fire into the small dish of the valley. There was no place to hide and there was no way up that provided enough cover. We could be picked off at will, mowed down with automatic-weapon fire and left in that snowy valley as our mass grave.

We kept ourselves ready and waited to see what would happen. The longer we stood there with no idea where the guards were or what was going to happen, the more anxious we became. After an hour passed with no sign of our captors, we knew we had to act.

"I'll climb up there," one man said.

Another, the man's closest friend, stepped up beside him. "I'll go with you."

No one else moved. I watched the two turn and begin to climb, and suddenly time seemed to slow. I knew that whatever happened next, it was going to be a moment of truth. It seemed unlikely, after such a long delay, that we would suddenly be called back to the road and continue our journey. That left the possibility that we would stand at the bottom of the valley, gunfire raining down on us, and we would fall and die, exterminated as our captors had promised us so many times, unable to tell stories of the monstrous treatment, torture and madness we had endured.

Despite the quiet from above, most of the prisoners stood as if they were condemned. It was almost impossible to find hope after so long and after so many losses and lies. The two men who had disappeared up the hill did not return. The remaining prisoners began to mill about.

"What was that?" one called out.

"What?" I asked.

"Gunfire. I think I heard gunfire."

Even though no one else had heard anything, panic rose in the group, but we still didn't know what to do, where to turn. And then we heard it.

A roar rose, distant at first—a grinding, tearing sound. We

couldn't run, and no one knew what it could be. It wasn't the sound of the commander's motorcycle or any other sound with which we were familiar. It sounded like some giant, dangerous animal crashing through the trees, and a moment later the trees actually bent and broke, leaning down over the edge of the valley and snapping in a wide swath.

At that moment, I was sure that the end had arrived. I didn't know if it would be the end of my prison life or the end of my life altogether. Different thoughts ran through my mind. Was Mendel, my fellow prisoner, right when he said, "What is the use of living through slave labor, sickness, starvation, when at the end we will either die of starvation—or, if you are lucky and live to the end of the war, you will be shot?"

I could not bear the thought that this might be what was really happening after all I had been through—the years in the camps, the deportations, the sickness and starvation. I had survived two death marches and Auschwitz by sheer inner strength, will power and hope, all for one purpose: to make it to the day when I would be a free man. Now I found myself in a forest in the Tirol Mountains bordering Italy, in a deep valley, knee-deep in snow. My body was nothing more than a skeleton covered with skin. I was shivering from cold, fatigue and fear. The old man with the scythe—Death—had always walked five steps behind me. Was this the place where he would finally catch up? Would I be shot and left to die in this valley like an animal?

A moment later, the gun barrel of a tank crested the ridge. It halted at the top, and we looked up at it in shock. A few tried to run for the sides of the valley, though they didn't get far.

There was a creaking sound, and a moment later the hatch on top of the turret began to swing slowly upward. We stared as a helmeted head rose cautiously from the tank's interior. The man inside, his head fully raised, glanced down, and when he saw us he seemed startled.

We pointed, and a few laughed out loud. In that moment we knew the truth: that it was an American tank, that we had been rescued, that the guards would not return and that we would—against all the odds and everything we had believed—be free.

The man who climbed slowly up and out of the tank was a black man—a black soldier. An American, and he was the finest sight to meet our eyes in so long that we didn't have words to express it. Some fell to their knees; others sat down, unable to support their weight on legs gone to rubber. When he called down to us, no one answered at first. It was our first precious moment of freedom.

When other soldiers made their way down into the valley accompanied by a couple of officers, they mingled with the survivors, who were still nearly too stunned to speak. A soldier, speaking broken Yiddish with a heavy American accent, approached me.

"Are you Jewish?" he asked.

I nodded, and then found my voice. "Yes, I am Jewish."

"You were in the camps?"

Again, I nodded. "We were marched from Landsberg," I said. I had to repeat some of my words more slowly so the man understood.

"Why were you in prison?" he wanted to know. "What did you do?"

I stared at the man for a moment before answering.

"I am Jewish," I repeated.

The soldier's expression grew frustrated, and he repeated his question, obviously believing that I had not understood.

"That is all there is to my answer," I said. "I was in the camp because I am Jewish. I committed no crime."

The blank stare that greeted my words helped me to understand. These American soldiers, who had come out of nowhere to save us, did not understand what they had found. They did not know about the camps, the killing, the furnaces. They had probably heard rumors but believed them to be just that—stories made up to frighten people. In the end, the soldier walked on and asked his question of others.

One of the officers climbed up onto a stump and called to us to listen. He explained that we needed to remain where we were. He said that he and his men would be back shortly, and then they disappeared back up the hill. The tank pulled back and away. Within only a few moments, we were alone again, and the encounter began to take on a surreal aspect. It was hard to believe—even though we had just spoken with them—that rescuers had come and that we were free.

Later, several trucks pulled up near the rim of the valley. We were led up and carefully loaded. When everyone was accounted for, three trucks rolled away. It still didn't feel real, but as each moment passed it began to feel more possible.

None of the German guards were seen again. They had disappeared, having discarded their uniforms, done what they could to blend in with the civilians or run off across the country to try to find some remnant of their own forces with which to band together. It was as if they had been swallowed by the shadows.

The trucks rolled eventually into a small German village near the Italian border. There was a school there, almost brand new. It had been constructed for the Hitler Youth, but as the Allies approached the building had been abandoned. We were brought to the school, and given rooms with clean bathrooms and comfortable beds. We were also issued private lockers, though very few of us had any belongings.

We were left to acclimate ourselves to our new quarters while our liberators prepared food. I wandered around the room, examined my locker and eventually made my way into the bathroom. It was clean and new. There were no commodes, but instead there were holes in the floor with stone footpads on either side.

It was an odd thing, but the opportunity to use the toilet safely, and in private, was something that had been denied me for so long that it was a novelty. I stepped inside. My clothing was dirty and old—I had worn it for so long now that I couldn't recall when I had last changed. My belt was cinched tightly against my hungry stomach. Other than loosening it to relieve myself, I hadn't taken it off for a very, very long time. As I stood there alone, I suddenly felt that this was something I needed to do.

I stood beside the toilet and loosened the belt and tugged it free of the tattered loops holding it to the waistband of my pants. As I did so, the worn, cracked leather twisted. I caught a glint of something bright and gold. There was a clink of metal on stone, and I glanced down in surprise.

The gold wedding band that my mother had given me so long ago when we arrived at the first camp bounced once and spun on the floor, then rolled into the hole. I had no time to react. It was there only long enough for me to realize what it was, and then it was gone.

I started to lean down and try to retrieve it. All those months it had rested there against my skin. It had been a talisman of sorts. As long as I'd had it, I'd had—something. If I had been starving, I could have traded it for food. If I had been in danger, I might have used it to buy my way out. As I stood staring down now, a new sensation stole over me.

Maybe the ring had served its purpose. Maybe its magic was no longer needed. I was free. I could begin a new life and accumulate other things. I could have food and clothing. It still didn't exactly feel real, but now the time I had just lived through was beginning to seem surreal as the reality of liberation solidified in my mind.

I finished in the bathroom, cleaned myself, cinched up my belt and left the ring—and its memories—behind me. It felt like saying goodbye.

Chapter Twenty

The Americans fed us three meals a day, the same food that they themselves ate. Many of us got into the habit of going back through the line more than once. I would go through, get my meal, eat it and then go through again. The second helpings that I received I carried back to my room. I packed the extra rations in my locker, keeping it carefully locked. The others did the same. We couldn't help it.

All through the past years, food had been uncertain. The urge to keep rations against an emergency was too strong to resist. Eventually, the Americans serving the food began to notice that the same men were coming through more than one time. There was plenty of food, but not enough to squander, so they began issuing meal vouchers to the survivors to be certain that they only took their fair share of the food.

As time passed, it became easier to believe that the next meal would appear on schedule, and that we would not be suddenly starved. Like the ring I'd left behind, eventually I was able to let go of the feeling that there was some sort of trick behind each meal. The freedom was real.

Some of the prisoners were not so lucky. Compared to the weak soup and bread they'd eaten for so long, the American rations were very rich. Many of the prisoners had grown too weak to digest anything but what they'd become accustomed to. They ate too much too quickly and developed diarrhea and stomach cramps. Many of them died after having survived so much and coming so close to the freedom they sought. They got their freedom, but the chance to enjoy it—the chance to return to the world—was denied them.

Eventually, as things began to settle, I made my way out of the school and into the town. I hadn't seen civilians out living their lives since the trips with Lieutenant Werner, and even then I had been afraid at every turn that something would go wrong, that someone would realize who I was—what I was—and that even the lieutenant wouldn't be able to help.

Here it was different. People were just living their lives. The war had come and gone, and they were trying to put their world back together. I didn't know how to react. I had thought about this time for so long—the time when I would be free and the Germans would hold no power over my life. It was strange, but now that it had come to pass, there was no great sense of exaltation.

Nor was there an urge for revenge. I walked the streets. I saw men and women walking, children playing, and it seemed very much like my own hometown back in Hungary. I knew I should have been bent on revenge, but it was not there. I was tired of hatred—far too tired of it to become a mirror image of my captors.

The only group of prisoners that had been released and felt differently was the Russians. The Russian soldiers were hungry for revenge. They terrorized the citizens of the village, stealing from them, beating them, attacking their women and, in some cases, killing them.

Eventually the local families began to reach out to the Jewish survivors. They invited us into their homes because houses where survivors stayed were left intact by the Russians. On one of my trips into town, I was approached.

"Excuse me," a man said to me on the street, "are you one of the Jewish survivors?"

I stopped, met the man's gaze and said, "Yes."

The man offered his hand almost shyly. "My family and I," he said, "are so very glad that the war has ended. It has been horrifying, and the things we've been told about our own army—our leaders—it is too much. I wonder, would you come to our home? We have food. We don't have much, but what we do have, we would like to share. It is all we have to offer..."

I was touched, and I agreed to join the man and his family for a meal. Soon after that, I moved out of the Hitler Youth school and in with the family. We shared stories. I enjoyed talking with the children, watching them play and telling them about my childhood in Hungary.

I avoided the stories that would hurt. I did not tell them how I had been ripped from my home. When they asked about the camps and the years I had been imprisoned, I said as little as possible and changed the subject. It was wonderful to feel the normalcy of their family and to know that they accepted me in the same way. While I stayed with them, the Russians stayed away, and though there were moments when I felt pangs of...something, not exactly guilt but maybe doubt, I stayed with them until it was finally time for me to move on and leave the city.

For years after, I received letters from them. They told me about the children, about the family. They told me of life in the city, and when I could, I answered. They were people, just people—men and women who wanted the same things that I did. They wanted to live their lives. They wanted to educate themselves, to love, to build their businesses and their families, and to leave a legacy for their descendants.

For the most part, the survivors and the villagers got along. The only sign of revenge-seeking, other than that of the Russians, was directed toward the capos. When they were discovered—these men who had collaborated with the Germans, as often as not treating prisoners with as much or more viciousness than the Germans—they were dragged out. Often the former capos were beaten and, in a few cases, killed. Somehow the betrayal, the turning on your own people for personal gain, was worse than the actual incarceration and torture.

In the end, what drew me from the town was the need to tie up my own loose ends. I needed to go back. I needed to know what had happened to my family, to my brothers and sisters, who had not been taken to the camps, and to those who had. I needed to talk to my siblings about our parents.

Eventually, many of the other Jewish prisoners and I were transferred from the town to a different refugee camp. The new camp was named Feldafing, and by the time I was taken there it was almost exclusively maintained for Hungarian Jews who had been liberated from the death camps.

Feldafing had come into being through the courageous acts of several members of the Wehrmacht. When the war ended, thousands of Jewish survivors had been loaded into cattle cars and had been on the track to be transported to a remote area. Once they arrived, they were to be slaughtered by SS troops waiting for them to prevent the survivors from testifying against the guards and the Nazi hierarchy.

The Wehrmacht officer in charge of the train did not carry out his orders as they had been given. He delayed the train several times, guarding the prisoners from any who would set it in motion toward its goal. He allowed enough time for the Allied forces to arrive and take over the town. The prisoners were liberated, and those who were identified as helping them were also allowed their freedom.

There was a very large Hitler Youth school in Feldafing, and this was used to house the refugees, much as the smaller school had been used at the first liberation camp. At first there was an area of the camp that housed liberated Russian soldiers, but they were too much of a risk; they looted and killed civilians. They were transported from the camp and returned to Russia as soon as it was possible.

Meanwhile, Jewish refugees, primarily Hungarian, were transported in from all over because the facility was large and had a hospital. It was easier to provide them with the aid they needed in a single place than to create camps all over the German countryside.

I settled in and began to work on making something of my chance at a new life and freedom. I was able to make a little money by buying and selling cigarettes. I worked hard at this, saving every penny I managed to earn, and eventually I was able to buy myself a new pair of boots, a jacket and matching cap. This was one of the only signs of affluence available to the refugees—to be rid of the sometimes worn and ragged clothing that we had been provided with after the liberation and to become presentable. Owning the clothing was strangely fulfilling; it gave me hope.

Not far from the Feldafing camp a special unit of the British forces was camped. The unit was called the Jewish Infantry Brigade. It was mostly made up of Palestinian Jewish volunteers. They had their own insignia, a Star of David emblazoned over blue and white stripes. They had fought with distinction on the side of the Allies, and now they were working as quickly as they could on their own agenda.

Not far over the border in Italy was a town named Modena. The Jewish Brigade soldiers transported as many of the Jewish camp survivors as they could to Modena to await the chance to immigrate to Palestine.

One day I was standing outside my quarters when several trucks bearing the Jewish Brigade emblem rolled into town.

They stopped and the soldiers inside climbed out. They gathered for a moment and then dispersed into the camp. As I watched, one of the men crossed to my building.

"What are you doing?" I asked.

The soldier stopped. "You haven't heard? We are helping to pave the way for those who want to reach Palestine. We will be taking a load of survivors to Italy to prepare for the journey."

"I would like to see Palestine," I said. I thought that it would be a marvelous thing to see a place—a country—where I might find a real home.

"You'd better get your things, then," the soldier said. "We'll be leaving in less than an hour."

I hurried to my room. I had managed to earn some money, and I had a few things to pack. I gathered it all and returned to the sidewalk, where I asked another of the soldiers where I should go. Moments later I had a seat on one of the covered trucks waiting to depart for Italy.

When the caravan rolled out there was a line of covered trucks, each carrying a cargo of twenty to thirty Jewish survivors. We were packed in fairly tightly, but not uncomfortably. The trucks were escorted by a few jeeps and some motorcycles. As we traveled toward the Italian border, brigade soldiers told us that no matter what happened, we had to remain silent. All would be taken care of.

When we reached the border, we slowly rolled to a stop. I kept my head down as Italian border guards jumped up into the back of the truck. They shone lights over the interior of the truck. They called out questions loudly, to which the Jewish Brigade members responded.

After only a very short time, the trucks rolled forward again.

I leaned close to the man sitting beside me.

"Why do you think they let us through?"

"I don't know," he answered. "Perhaps they were fooled, or perhaps they were bribed. Does it matter?"

I leaned back. We continued on into Italy and arrived at last in the city of Modena. We were taken to a DP camp run by the United Nations. I settled in with the others hoping to reach Palestine. As I had in the Feldafing camp, I set about finding a way to improve my situation.

One morning I saw several young men getting ready to leave the camp. I had spoken with one of them earlier and now stopped him. I asked him where they were going.

"Naples," the young man replied.

"Why?" I asked.

"To buy uniforms. The US soldiers leave from Naples to return home. Before they go, they sell their extra uniforms, boots, jackets, caps. They let them go for almost nothing."

"What do you do with them?"

"In Milan or Rome, they bring a higher price," he said. I soon learned that right after the war, clothing was impossible to get in Italy. It was expensive, so people were wearing the American uniforms. The pants, for example, were good compared to what the Italians could get in stores.

"Can I come with you?" I asked, excited about the chance to get out of the camp.

"You can't go like that," he said. "You'll need to get yourself a British uniform. It doesn't matter if it's in good shape. As long as they think you're a British soldier, you can travel on the trains for free."

"What do you give them if they ask for papers?" I asked.

The young man reached into his jacket and pulled out a small stack of folded papers. He handed them to me and I unfolded them, then glanced up in surprise.

"But—"

"I know," he said with a grin. "I tore them from an old

Hebrew prayer book. The conductors don't know the difference. They can't read it. They just know it's a foreign language, and when they see the British uniforms they assume we're legitimate. It almost always works."

"What if it doesn't?"

The young man shrugged. "Then you pay. The less you pay, the more lucrative the trip is. The profits are good, but not spectacular. It's business."

I nodded. "When will you be back again? Where will you go next?"

"We'll go first to Milan to get rid of what we have. Then we'll be back through here for a rest and head back to Naples. It won't last forever, you know. The soldiers are slowly clearing out, and eventually they will be gone."

Shortly after that, the group left, and I began planning my own venture. I needed to earn some money. I had some left from the cigarette sales, and I thought that the uniform sales made sense. I bartered and traded for bits of a British uniform as a disguise and did what I could to accumulate a stake with which to buy.

Within a week I made my first trip to Naples. I found it was just as the young man had told me—the US soldiers were anxious to get rid of their old uniforms. They could only carry so much back with them. Many of them had souvenirs from the war or things they'd bought for themselves and their families. They kept only enough uniform items to get them through the trip home. I was there for a day and bought the uniforms from the locals in a kind of open-air market. The locals bought direct from the soldiers because they knew when the soldiers were going to sail.

I grabbed up the American soldiers' cast-offs for a very good price, packed them up and boarded the train for Milan, where such items fetched much higher prices.

On one trip to Milan, after making a particularly good sale, I stopped to get a bite to eat in one of the market stalls. While I was there, a young Italian girl caught my eye. She saw me watching her and smiled. When I had my food, she walked over.

"You aren't Italian," she said.

My Italian was very basic. I managed to answer, slightly embarrassed. I had always picked up languages quickly but had not yet had a chance to study Italian. It made my trade business more difficult, and at that particular moment, it seemed even more of a handicap.

The girl, whose name was Jenny, was patient with me. The two of us spent the afternoon together, walking and talking. She taught me Italian. The language was not so distant from the pronunciations and constructions of Romanian, which I knew. I picked up Italian quickly, and before I knew it, I had my first girlfriend.

What followed was one of the most pleasant periods of my teen years. After a very short time with Jenny, my Italian was fluent. She lived outside Milan, and she owned a motorbike that the two of us rode together. We traveled between Naples, Milan and Rome, bartering cigarettes and American uniforms. For the most part, business was good and profitable.

We made the trip to Naples a couple of times a week and we slowly built our business. It was a good time, but finally the past called out to me, and I began to wonder about home.

I had not heard from any of my family since my liberation. On the street in Naples I ran into one of my cousins from my father's family in Poland. We sat and ate together and talked, but there was no news of my siblings. I knew that I couldn't really move on with my life without knowing what had happened to them, so I slowly began to put my affairs in order and to look toward returning to Hungary.

Besides Jenny, I had developed a business relationship with a partner named Jack. When I started to close out my business, it was at a time when the paper currency was of little or no value. Instead of holding the worthless paper, we kept our money in bullion. My plan was to take my share and cash it in, but before I did, Jack learned something interesting. He had friends who had just returned from Poland. The exchange rate there was a great deal higher than it was in Italy.

Jack planned to head across the border and exchange his share of the money. He offered to do the same for me and bring back my share before I departed for Hungary. I was a smart businessman, but at that young age I was too trusting. I agreed and handed over almost all I had to Jack.

Jack did not return from Poland. The money from all the months of hard work was gone. I was hurt, but I was not discouraged. I concentrated on finding a way to get out of Italy and back home to Hungary. I filed the lesson away with so many others and filled my mind with thoughts of home.

Postwar Europe was a nightmare for those trying to travel, particularly in and out of the communist countries. There were no trains available for the journey from Italy back to Hungary. It was, in fact, illegal to cross the border into Austria. At first I was discouraged, but I made inquiries and eventually located a group of men smuggling cigarettes across the border.

I approached one of the older smugglers late in the afternoon in the market.

"I need to get to Hungary," I said.

The man ignored me. He was packing his goods in order to close his stand for the day.

"I am told that you might have a reason to cross the border," I continued. "I want to come with you."

The man glanced up at me. "No one may cross the border. It is against the law."

"Friends told me that you carry cigarettes over the border,"

I insisted. "They say you are leaving on such a journey tonight. I will help you to carry whatever you need. I have to get over the border. I have to get back to my home and find my family."

The man turned away. "I cannot help you. You are too young, and it is a rough climb through the mountains. Even if I knew people making such a journey, you would slow them down."

I thought of the death marches and the miles I had struggled to cover with no food and little rest. "I can make the climb," I said. "I will do anything you need me to do."

"I'm sorry," the man repeated. He started up the street.

I hesitated, but when the man was almost out of sight, I followed him at a discreet distance, keeping him in sight until he disappeared into a small home on the outskirts of the town. I marked the doorway in my mind. I hurried to my rooms and packed my things. Along my way back to his home I picked up food and water for my journey.

Then I settled in and watched. Before dark, several other men arrived. I chewed on some bread and cheese and waited. The darkness deepened, and eventually the group of men exited the home. They were dressed for travel, and as they slipped off down the street toward the edge of town, I followed.

As long as they were in town, I did my best to stay out of sight. Once they were in the wilderness, though, I moved in closer. I stayed about a hundred yards back from the group, traveling at the same speed and keeping them in sight. They saw me. More than once they tried to wave me away, but I ignored them and kept my distance. The group traveled up into the mountains toward the Austrian border, and as they left Italy farther and farther behind, I moved in closer.

Finally, the man I had spoken to on the street called out to me.

"Get up here, then," he said. "If you're going to be with us, at least get close enough so we can keep an eye on you."

I joined the group at that point, grateful for the companionship and for their small fires. I had no trouble keeping up and eventually earned their grudging acceptance. We crossed over into Austria without incident. I thanked the smugglers and took my leave of them, moving on in search of a way to cross into Czechoslovakia. That border was equally closed to travel and watched carefully.

I made contact with the local Jewish community in Austria and found that the Haganah was active in the area. This group, which was involved in everything from anti-British operations in Palestine to the training and gathering of Jewish troops for transport to the Holy Land, was running an underground operation helping Jewish refugees out of Czechoslovakia and transporting them to Italy.

After several inquiries, I found one of the officers in charge of the operation.

"I am trying to get back to Hungary," I said. "I have not seen my family since we were separated in the camps. I want to find them—to know if they are alive and to let them know that I am alive. If possible, I want to find out what happened to my parents."

"I am sorry," the man said. "We are here to help our people out of the country. You should be traveling in the other direction, to Palestine. You are needed there."

"I am going to Palestine," I explained. "I only need to know about my family before I go. I do not want to return and live in Hungary. That country drove me out twice already—I could never trust the Hungarians again. But I can't turn my back on my family without at least trying to make contact. Will you help me?"

The man shook his head. "I can't. It is not my purpose here, and I have to follow orders. My suggestion to you is to wait for the next group coming back through and join them. Return to

Italy and get on one of the boats. Make your way to Palestine. You are needed there."

I didn't argue. I accepted the advice he offered, packed away some food and remained ready. I kept a close eye on the Haganah. Eventually, I caught a group heading off on foot toward the border at night. As I had done with the smugglers coming into Austria, I followed. I remained out of sight for longer this time. The Haganah members were military and very serious about their job. Eventually I slipped closer, and when the group crossed over the border into Czechoslovakia, I was with them. I thanked the officer in charge, though the man was still not happy about my leaving.

I traveled to Prague, where finally things became easier. There was a Romanian consulate in the city, and they were actively helping expatriated Romanian and Hungarian citizens back across the border to their homes. They were helpful, and after only a couple of days I had a train ticket to Budapest and then on to Satu Mare.

Before taking me to the train, some members of the consulate gave me some food to tuck into my pocket.

"Be careful," one man told me. "On the train, there are a lot of soldiers coming back from Russia. They are a rough bunch, and they have caused trouble in the past. They have stolen money and clothing. You are dressed well, and you may have trouble with them."

"Thank you," I said.

I took the warning to heart. Before boarding the train, I carefully packed away my good clothing and the new boots I had bought. I wore the oldest and most ragged things that I owned. I kept my food tucked away in a pocket, and what little money I had I kept well hidden.

When I climbed onto the train, I sat near one of the railway officers. I had no idea if the man would interfere on my behalf, or if the soldiers would pay any attention to him, but I felt a bit safer next to him. I sat quietly, making myself as insignificant as possible. In the end, I made the journey to Budapest without incident.

There was a holdover in Budapest. My train for Satu Mare didn't leave until the next day, and so I settled into a large room. There were a great number of soldiers there returning from the war. Many were dirty and injured, infested with lice, suffering from amputated limbs. I felt sympathy for them and shared some of the food I had been given. Eventually, I settled in and slept.

When I awoke, I discovered that the remainder of my food had been stolen. I still had my bags, and so I hadn't lost the good clothing I had packed away. While in Budapest, I located a group that was trying to help out Jewish survivors returning home by giving them a little money. I had to prove that I was Hungarian, and once I did they handed me 45,000 *pengo,* the local currency. It had been a long time since I had been home, and I had no idea what the value of currency would be, but it seemed like a fair amount.

I exited the station to the street beyond and was immediately assaulted by an amazing scent. Roasted chestnuts. I was hungry, and with my food gone I was unable to resist. I stepped up and asked how much.

The chestnuts cost me half of the 45,000 *pengo,* which put the financial situation in Hungary in immediate perspective. I ate the rich, warm food and pocketed my change. I stayed in the station until my train boarded for Satu Mare and made the journey without further mishap.

Chapter Twenty-One

In Satu Mare itself, I found no friends or family. I eventually got word that Mendu was living in the Transylvanian capital city of Kluj, and that my sister Irene, who I had not seen since we were deported to the death camps, had returned and settled there. My sister Ilana and my brothers William and Armin were alive as well and living in Bucharest.

Mendu had served in the Hungarian army along with William. The Hungarian army, which went with Germany, had drafted all Jewish men who were of age and forced them into slave labor; they did things like dig ditches. My brother Moses had died while serving in the army. My sister Rachel had been shot by the Danube River. There was no word of my parents, but I knew in my heart that they never survived the death camps.

I managed to piece together the money to travel to my brother Mendu's home, where I was reunited with the remnants of my family. It was a bittersweet time. We shared stories of what we knew and didn't know about other relatives and friends. We shared experiences too painful to dwell on and too recent to ignore. Mendu asked me to remain and live with or near them, but I refused.

"I can't stay," I said. "I've been driven out of this country twice, and now I'm afraid that if I don't go, I won't be allowed to leave. I want to go as soon as possible."

Again, there were problems with travel. There was a months-long waiting list for legal tickets from Kluj to Bucharest. My sister Irene had been waiting for some time and had received her tickets. She had planned to visit our sister Ilana, but she gave up her tickets so that I could be on my way.

There was no way to communicate with Ilana or her family, to let them know of the change of plans. She was expecting Irene. When the train arrived in Bucharest, I waited until I was the last person to debark. I was afraid that after so much time my relatives wouldn't recognize me, and I didn't want to miss them.

I found my brothers, who recognized me after a few moments, and we embraced. I explained how Irene had given me her ticket, and they all determined to play a joke on Ilana. When we arrived home, William went to Ilana and told her that Irene had not come. Instead, she had sent a boy to bring her regards in person.

I walked over to Ilana, who smiled at me. I stood there for a moment, and then could stand it no longer.

"Don't you recognize me?" I asked. "I'm your brother, David!"

When I spoke, Ilana realized it was me, and we embraced. She was very happy to see me, and all of my siblings and their families were filled with questions. I stayed with them for a while, but I kept my focus on getting out of the country and making my way to Palestine.

My brother Armin was involved with an organization that was gathering groups of Jewish refugees to take to Italy and then on to Palestine. I knew by then that this was what I wanted. After a couple of weeks spent with my sister and brothers and their families, I joined up with those preparing to leave.

My group was made up of thirty to forty people departing Bucharest as Greek refugees trying to make their way back to

Greece. We were taken onto the train and ordered not to speak. None of us knew exactly how we made it past the border. I assumed that the leaders of the organization had created false papers, or that they had bribed the guards at the border. Perhaps it was a combination of both those things. In any case, a couple of days later, we were in Yugoslavia.

During this time, the British were supervising searches at all the borders. The train we were on was stopped and searched by British guards. We were discovered, and the entire group was turned away from the border, but the men in charge were undeterred. They had other ways of crossing the border on foot and by truck, and eventually we crossed into Greece. A short time later, after a very circuitous route through Europe, I was back in Italy, where I had started out.

The port city of Genoa, on the coast of Italy, was the launch port for a great many ships carrying Jewish survivors and refugees. The British did all they could to prevent the boats from leaving port. They patrolled the air and sent destroyers to crisscross sea lanes in search of ships transporting survivors.

The ships were bought with money from groups in the United States and commanded by Jewish agents out of Palestine. They were fishing ships, converted and gutted to hold 700 to 1,200 passengers. It was a tightly run, systematic operation.

A delegation out of Palestine had rented a large villa overlooking Genoa. We were fed and housed there, and we studied Palestine and its history and worked on our Hebrew. Those who came to the villa remained there from six months to a year. It was all very clandestine. Anyone coming near or flying over would see nothing but a quiet, slow-moving settlement. Behind the scenes the operation was in constant motion.

I joined a group that had arrived before me. I counted somewhere between fifty and eighty people in all. There were no luxuries in the villa. It was very crowded, but there was food and it wasn't bad. We studied hard at our lessons in Hebrew during the week, but on weekends we traveled into Genoa. All in all it was a pleasant time.

For a Jew to travel legally from Italy to Palestine required a certificate from the British Mandate. This was a certificate granting future citizenship. Only a couple hundred of these were issued a year, and there were literally thousands of applicants. If an illegal ship that made landfall in Palestine was captured or detained by the British, the refugees were marched into camps in Palestine. When the British became overwhelmed, they decided to discourage people from coming by creating camps in Cyprus where the refugees were kept and made to wait—sometimes for years—for their legal paperwork.

The Haganah, a word meaning "defense," became the underground Jewish army. They organized escapes from the camps, and it was their men who traveled on the boats outfitted by Americans that transported the survivors to Palestine. They arranged a very intricate labyrinth of routes to avoid the British destroyers and planes. If the ships were stopped before they reached Palestine, they were boarded and diverted to Cyprus. The Haganah fought to avoid this at all costs and to make landfall where their passengers could escape and be hidden. They didn't always make it.

I waited in the villa for about six months. One night, a caravan of trucks pulled into the villa. Working under cover of darkness, the group I had been staying with was loaded into the trucks and driven to a small, remote fishing village. The village consisted of a group of small tents gathered closely in a forest near the coast. When we arrived and debarked, we found that the camp was empty. We dispersed into the tents, and the trucks rolled off into the darkness.

"What does it mean?" a man asked me. We sat, staring out through the flap of our tent into the darkness. The camp was quiet, as it had been when we'd arrived.

"I don't know," I admitted. "It is strange that the camp is empty, but they will tell us what we need to know. We'd better get some rest."

We made our beds and he slowly dropped off to sleep. I lay awake, listening. In the distance I heard the steady chug of diesel engines as boats traveled up and down the coast. The engines ran steadily, providing a backdrop to the night, and eventually the monotony of the sound helped me to relax and sleep. I wondered, as I drifted off, why they ran all night without stopping.

The first morning we awoke, lit fires and cooked, and moved about the camp as if we had been there all along. After a couple of days at the camp, the Haganah came in the middle of the night and took us away in small groups, fifteen to twenty at a time. We slipped onto the small, diesel-powered boats and were ferried slowly out across the bay to one of the modified fishing boats. As I was led away, I glanced back at the empty tent we had left behind, and I understood.

I grabbed the arm of the man I had talked with before. "The trucks," I said.

"What?" he asked.

"They will bring the trucks again later tonight. Others will be in the tents before morning. It will be as if no one ever left."

The man looked startled for a moment, then smiled.

"And the boats," he said. "They run constantly so that when they are carrying us to the ship, it will seem part of the regularly scheduled run."

The operation was smooth and efficient. The camp was always alive with people. The boats chugged up and down the coast and out through the bay. It was like a giant, living clock, and in the middle of all of it, people moved in and out, making their way out to sea and on to Palestine.

The locals near the camp were completely in the dark. The transfer of trucks in and boats out always happened late at night, and the camp always appeared the same. Though they probably suspected that something odd was going on, if questioned, they could provide no useful information. It was an amazingly complex plan that worked.

The boat I was taken to was a gutted fishing boat. The craft had been refitted to carry up to 700 passengers. The bunks along the sides were stacked six high. There was barely enough room between us to sleep, but none of the refugees complained. We were ushered below as quickly as possible and instructed to remain there.

The British knew the boats were transporting refugees. They did all they could to track them and stop them, flying numerous reconnaissance flights to search for boats carrying suspicious crews or passengers. Only the boat's regular crew was topside by day, to prevent the British from spotting the refugees. At night the passengers were allowed topside for fresh air and the chance to stand and watch the stars.

During the day it was hot and stuffy in the boat's hold. There were men, women and children all packed into a very small space. We told stories, and we speculated about what life would be like when we arrived in Palestine. Despite the cramped conditions, spirits were high.

The crew worked methodically. More than once they painted the ship, changing its colors so that the aircraft overhead would be confused or lose track of what ship had departed from what port. They changed the flags often, practicing naval deception in a constant stream to cloak our true purpose.

We were fed regularly. There wasn't a lot but there was enough, and it was good. The journey normally should have taken only a week or so by sea. It wasn't possible for the boat to take a direct route, however. We crisscrossed shipping lanes and wound our way slowly. It took more time, but it kept us from drawing unwanted attention.

Once the ship was underway, the captain descended the

ladder to speak with us. He was Italian, as was most of the crew. We gathered around to listen as he spoke.

"I am Giuseppe Martoni," he said. "If there is trouble, you are to remember my name and that I am the captain of this ship. My men and I will do what we can to keep the ship moving and to prevent our being discovered or boarded. For all else, I would like to introduce you to Captain Rosenberg. He was trained in the United States Navy and he's here to help train you and see us all through to Palestine."

I watched with interest as a thin, dark man stepped forward. There were several others with him. They were Haganah, along to help in case of any trouble and to assist with the training of the refugees.

"As Captain Martoni has told you, I am Captain Rosenberg," he said. "My men and I are equipped to get you through any trouble we might encounter, but you will have to listen to us carefully.

"If all goes as planned, we will reach Palestine and you will debark and be escorted away before the British can detain you. You will be taken to a kibbutz inland to merge with the locals. The important thing is to reach Palestine and get off this ship. If the British detain you, you will be taken to camps where you will be kept either until they deport you or until you are able to obtain papers. There is not enough time in most of your lives to wait for those papers, but if you get into the camps, you are still in Palestine.

"If we should be discovered before we are able to make port in Palestine, the British will attempt to prevent our landing. They will try to take you from the ship. You must refuse."

I looked around at those with whom I traveled. I saw children, pregnant women, boys and men. It was a varied group and not well-suited to any sort of revolt.

"What can we do?" one man called out. "They will be armed."

"They will not board the ship to kill you. They only want to prevent your reaching Palestine," Rosenberg said. "They will try to get you up to the main deck, where they will transfer you to one of their own ships and divert you—possibly to a camp. We must prevent this. If they board the ship, you must pull down the ladders."

Two of the Haganah members went to the nearest of the ladders and demonstrated how it could be loosened and lowered into the hold. With the ladders down, there was no way for anyone to get down without climbing, and certainly no way that many of the refugees could make their way out.

"When the ladders are down, you must not listen to the British. They will tell you many things. They will threaten you and promise you anything they think might get you to acquiesce to their demands. Instead, you must drown them out. Scream at them. Yell, 'Palestine, only Palestine.' You have to wear them down and make them understand.

"There are those ashore who will help if they can. There will be protestors. If we can slip you out and ashore, we will do that, and you have to run. Keep in mind, all of this is in case things go wrong. We do not anticipate that they will. We are on schedule, and though we are taking a very roundabout route we are on track toward the shores of Palestine. I welcome you all aboard."

We asked a few questions and more introductions were made. The Haganah agents moved among us, offering suggestions and encouragement. I hung back and watched. When the sun had dropped below the horizon, I was one of the first to make my way up to the deck and the fresh air. The stars were bright, and the salty air felt fresh and cool on my face. I glanced back in the direction of the Italian shore that fell away behind us and then turned toward the east. I did not look back.

The first week of the journey was an almost magical time. We came together like a small community, reading, telling tales of our families and dreaming of our arrival in Palestine. There was singing and laughter.

For me it was an awakening of sorts. We were traveling to the land of our ancestors. Soon we would come to a place where, like all the other people of the world, we would be citizens. Though most of us had never seen Palestine, it felt very much as if we were going home.

Things began to grow slightly more strained as we entered our second week at sea. There was no land in sight, nor had there been any since we had left Italy behind. As the time stretched, I found myself spending more time with another young man named Chaim. The two of us sat together on the deck under the stars and talked late into the night.

"It seems as though we should already have arrived in Palestine," I said one night. "I have seen the maps, and the journey should take only a little more than a week."

Chaim thought before he answered. "It doesn't feel to me as if we are following a straight course. I think they must be zigzagging. It will confuse the British if they are watching our progress."

"I've heard planes," I said. "Never at night, but in the day, when we are below."

Chaim nodded. "I've heard them too."

"Do you ever think about what will happen when we get to Palestine?" I asked. "I know that we will get off the ship and hide, and that we will try to remain out of sight of the British, but…"

"Of course I worry," Chaim said. "What if we get caught? If the British find us out on the open ocean, will they turn us back? Will they take the ship back to Europe? If they do, what will they do with us then? Will we be arrested?"

"I don't know," I said, "but we probably worry too much. If the British knew we were here on this boat, they would have tried to board it by now. I think we just have to be patient. Soon we'll be off the coast of Palestine and then free."

"I wonder what a kibbutz will be like," Chaim said.

We went on like that night after night, talking our way through the hours as the boat plowed on tirelessly. Soon the second and the third week had come and gone, and there was still no sign of the journey's end. The food rations grew steadily smaller. I was frustrated by not being able to get on deck by day. Without a good view of the sun it was difficult to tell in what direction we were headed. I had the sinking feeling that we were no longer heading east but were moving on a westerly course instead.

The refugees grew more and more restless as the days passed. The food was running out, and the water was stale and tepid. The good spirits we had begun our journey with had faded. Soon our discouragement grew to anger and boiled over into outright revolt.

I woke to the sound of loud voices.

"Palestine!" someone cried. "Take us to Palestine now!" Other voices chimed in: "There is no more food!" "Take us to Palestine and we will face what comes!"

All around me, the frustration and fear rose in waves. I felt caught up in it. Many of my fellow refugees were running about and screaming up at the Haganah and the Italian crew. Some cried. Things were falling apart, and it was frightening. We were caught in the middle of the ocean without any real control over our own fate.

Finally, the American captain, Rosenberg, was able to silence us. He came among the refugees, speaking to us openly for the first time since being introduced.

"I understand your fear," he said. "I left my home, my family, everything that was mine, to come here and bring you to your new home. And it wasn't just for this boat or this group, but for all survivors who hope to find a new life in Palestine. There are others, and they all require our help.

"There is another ship out here as well, and they are in trouble. Their engines are no longer operating properly. We have diverted from our course to try to help. We are going to intersect their course, and it is my duty to help—it is the duty of all of us. I hope that you will bear with me a little longer."

The man's Yiddish was stilted and rusty, but his meaning was clear. For the moment, the crowd quieted, but we were skeptical. We had been told a great number of things in the past few years. We were not easily fooled, and it was hard to trust what we were being told after being kept in the dark until we threatened revolt.

"What do you think, Chaim?" I asked later that night. "Is there another boat? Will they bring more people onboard?"

"There is barely any food or water," he replied. "What will we eat? Where will we sleep? The bunks are nearly full now."

I was thinking the same thing. "I don't know what they are going to do if there is a ship or no ship, but I think that whatever happens, we aren't going to be on this ship for many more days. People will begin to starve and to grow sick. Then they will rebel."

The situation continued to worsen. As we entered the fourth week, the water was almost gone. People were unable to eat the small rations available and grew sick. Tempers simmered just below the boiling point, and revolt was near the surface all the time, charging the air with tension.

One night Chaim and I could stand it no longer. It was hot below the deck, and the air was thick and difficult to breathe. People were angry and sick. We slipped up to the deck above. We talked the situation over in the clear, clean air beneath the stars. There was still no land in sight, and we both knew by that point that we should have arrived somewhere if nothing were wrong. We didn't know where we were being taken.

"Anywhere would be better than here," Chaim said. "The food and water are almost gone. If the others revolt I don't think they can pilot the ship to land. We will be stranded."

"There has to be a good reason why they haven't taken us into port," I said. "Captain Rosenberg and the Haganah are here too. They would not risk their own lives just to—what? Sail around the middle of the ocean?"

"I don't know," Chaim said, "but I know I'm not going back below."

We had brought up our blankets. We slipped under them and drifted off to sleep in the dim moonlight.

Chapter Twenty-Two

I woke very suddenly to loud voices amplified over a speaker. The sun was out, and I sat up, confused. Chaim was beside me, clutching his blanket and looking around in alarm.

The boat was flanked by two British destroyers. Lines bound the ships one to the other, and orders sounded over the speakers. We were being told to follow the two ships into port. A third ship pulled in behind us.

My heart pounded. We were trapped without any way of escaping. Being under the control of the British after having suffered so much was a sickening sensation. There was no way to make a run for it, nothing at all we could do but follow as directed and wait to see what would happen.

We sailed on through the coming night and part of the next morning. Then a cry went up. Land had been spotted to the east. We knew it was the east because the sun rose directly over the shoreline.

I turned to Chaim, but before I could speak, my friend said, "Palestine."

I heard a tremor in his voice. We went among the others, and many had tears streaming down their faces. The ship was brought to a halt and anchored off the port of Haifa. Everyone moved below as our captors boarded the ship. The Haganah agents and the crew disguised themselves as well as they could, blending in with their passengers. Those coming aboard intended to arrest them first.

The Haganah agents acted quickly, releasing the ladders and dropping them into the hold to prevent those boarding the ship from accessing the hold. They drew everyone back as far from the openings as possible. Word spread among us, passed from the crew, that there were protestors gathered on shore, perhaps a thousand of them. They were demanding that the refugees be allowed to debark in Palestine.

When it became obvious that we would not put the ladders up or surrender, those on shore were allowed to send out food and supplies. First a boatload of fruit was sent. The Haganah refused it. They wanted to use the hunger of the prisoners to force the British to take us all ashore.

Later that day members of the Jewish community came in barges filled with grapes and bananas. They came onboard and negotiated with the Haganah agents to convince them that the Jewish community could handle the situation through diplomacy.

"Let us protest," the members of the community said. "You don't have to starve yourselves—it won't work. Accept the food." The Haganah agreed, and the fruit was passed down into the hold.

Nothing changed. We were in a standoff with the British. They had no way to get a ladder down into the hold safely, and they could not force the refugees to come up. On shore, the protests continued. The Jewish community put all the pressure at their command on the British to bring the refugees ashore, but there was no progress.

About three or four days later, the boat pulled alongside, as it always did, to deliver the fruit. When the boat's crew handed it up to the main deck, the guards watched them carefully to prevent prisoners from going over the side to the boat, or to keep people on the boat from trying to rush the ship. This day, things were different.

I saw one of the Haganah who had traveled with us slipping up to the main deck. When a second followed, I stepped closer.

"What are you going to do?" I asked.

The man shook his head and held a finger to his lips. I waited a few moments and then followed him up, poking my head through the doorway to the hold. The two Haganah had sneaked onto the deck and were headed to the far end, where the fruit was delivered.

Suddenly, one of the two ran toward the guards near the gangway to the British ship. He cried out loudly, and the guards spun around to see what the disturbance was. The second Haganah joined the fracas, and guards ran from all over the deck to assist their comrades.

In that moment, four men who had been waiting down on the fruit boat leaped up onto the deck. Before they could be stopped, they ran for the hold. I dropped away from the opening just as they dove through.

"Stop!" the guards above cried.

It was no use. When the guards tried to stop the newcomers, the four who had started the diversion also dropped back through the hole. The Haganah blended in with the refugees. The ladders were pulled away again, and despite orders and demands from above, no one spoke up. The newcomers were dressed to match the refugees as closely as possible, and those above had no way to get them out. They tried for a while and then gave it up. Meanwhile, the Haganah, who had slipped onboard, conferred with those already there. News was spread, though there was little to tell.

After a few days, when things had quieted again, the Haganah made their move. A group made its way quietly to the deck of the ship. They rushed the guards near the British destroyer and engaged them in a quick, brutal battle. As some fought, others managed to sever the lines tying off the two ships. As the guards screamed for help from the ship, the two vessels floated apart. Cheers broke out down in the hold as the big ship began to drift slowly toward shore.

Refugees poured out of the hold, and a number of them leaped over the side, making for the shore. Boats were sent after them, and many were caught, but others escaped, made it to shore and were assisted by those waiting. They disappeared.

The British guards were very angry by that point. The Haganah had destroyed the engines on our boat to keep it from being used to convey the refugees to Cyprus. On the shore, protestors continued to fight for the refugees' freedom, and the continued efforts of the Haganah both on shore and on the boat were wearing down the patience of the guards.

After a week of tense standoff, a huge, old British freighter was brought alongside and tied off. Once it was in place, the British began screaming over the loudspeaker. They started in Yiddish and then continued in Italian, English and Hebrew. The message was always the same:

"You will climb to the main deck and move slowly to the freighter. You will do so now, and without a struggle. If you do, you will not be harmed. You must climb up now and depart this ship."

The Haganah had moved at the first sign of new trouble. All ladders had been pulled away from the hatches leading to the deck above.

"Palestine," they cried. "We will only go to Palestine. Take us ashore!"

The refugees took up the cry.

"This is your final warning," the voice droned on. "Exit the cargo hold without a struggle and you will not be harmed."

The refugees continued to scream their defiance. I was

yelling as loudly as anyone, but despite our cries, loud thumping sounds from above could be heard clearly. Something was happening, but it was impossible to tell what it might have been. We were pulling back into the hold as far as possible, getting out of sight.

Then fire hoses opened up through the hatch. They caught the front row of refugees and pounded them back. The water struck like a giant hammer blow. It drove those in front into the others behind them and pressed us all toward the wall. People were screaming and panicking, stumbling back and away from the water. There was nowhere to go. The hoses were strong and relentless.

The British continued to pound us with water for what seemed like an eternity, and then the flow of water weakened and stopped.

The voice on the loudspeaker returned.

"You must come up. Climb up to the main deck and make your way to the freighter and no one will be harmed."

We pulled back as far as we could from the openings.

"Palestine!" we cried.

After this went on for a while, the hoses returned. At odd intervals the British tried the loudspeaker again, but though the water in the hold grew deeper, reaching waist-level, we held our ground. It went on through that night and the next day and into the next night, but we did not give in. Finally the hoses were pulled from the hold and did not return.

"Will they let us go?" Chaim asked.

I shook my head. "I don't think so."

We all waited, huddled in the dark, doing our best to protect the women and children and the sick. It was wet and miserable, and our captors had grown silent.

The speakers crackled and then the voice returned.

"You will exit the cargo hold and climb to the main deck or

we will be forced to use gas to remove you. I repeat, we will gas you if you do not come up without a struggle."

The message was repeated several times, then new ladders were dropped in through the hatches. Before they could be secured, refugees, led by the Haganah agents, rushed forward and cut them away, dropping them to the wet floor below.

After that, the deck above grew very silent. We began talking softly among ourselves, wondering what would come next. The stronger among us supported the weaker, but all were cold and wet and shivering.

Then the night was suddenly filled with explosions. Gas billowed and filled the hold. It sounded as if the explosions came from every direction at once. People screamed and coughed; they gagged and were unable to breathe. We stumbled about in panic, but there was nowhere to go. The ladders had been cut away. I held my throat and fought for air. I thought that after all I had been through, this was where I would die. I did all that I could to resist the gas, but without a ladder or some other way out, there was nothing to be gained from fighting.

Though I had struggled past so many obstacles and survived so many horrifying moments and journeys, I believed it had come to an end. I stumbled about the hold. I couldn't find Chaim, and it was nearly impossible to make out the forms of the others.

We didn't know that the gas was not fatal. Most of us had spent time in the camps, and we had been exposed to what the Nazis had done. The gas terrified us in ways that other things could not.

Eventually, as the air cleared slightly, the British began hauling the refugees out. At first they used ropes, then they got ladders down into the hold and descended, helping the rest. There were children and pregnant women, and sick people in need of medical attention. All were escorted up and out of the hold. All our fight was gone.

We were led between long lines of soldiers who created a pathway to the freighter. There was no way to escape, nowhere to run.

"Wait," I said, stumbling over to one of the guards. "My things are over there on the deck. Let me get them first."

The guard pushed me back. "Keep moving," he said.

I wanted to protest, but we were kept together in a group and herded across the gangway to the old freighter. Onboard we were body searched and given new clothing, and as we passed through this, we were moved to another part of the ship. There was a lot of talk among the prisoners about what would happen next. We wondered where we would be taken and what would happen to us.

Several people said they believed we would be taken to Haifa, but the Haganah went among us quickly and explained. The British had begun taking all refugees who did not have the proper paperwork and diverting them to Cyprus. They were not going to allow the boat ashore.

We were kept under guard on the ship for some time, but the British made no sign that they intended to bring the boat to shore. When rumors spread that we might sail soon for Cyprus, the Haganah gathered about ten of the refugees around them in a circle. When they were hidden from view, they opened a trap door, about two feet by two feet. It was only large enough to allow one man access at a time. They tied a rope around the first man's waist and he dropped out of sight. A second and then a third followed. They were gone for some time and then they reappeared and returned the cover to the trap door. No one spoke about what had happened, and though I wondered what they had done, I had to go to sleep without learning a thing.

As I lay in my bed, trying to drift off, the hull of the ship shook with a tremendous boom. The explosion nearly forced us from our bunks, and acrid smoke rose from below. The Haganah had set off explosives to destroy the engines.

When I asked one of them why, the answer was short:

"They can't take this boat to Cyprus now—they can't take it anywhere."

The ship was damaged too badly to sail. The British were very angry. They brought another freighter, a newer one, alongside. The refugees were hustled across yet another gangway, and subjected to yet another body search. Again we were not allowed to bring anything with us, and we were issued new sets of clothing. This time, however, there was no hesitating. The ship set sail immediately after the refugees had been transferred aboard.

We stood on the decks and watched as Haifa disappeared from the horizon. Men, women and children stood crying—so close to what we had worked for, the place we had dreamed of reaching, only to have it yanked away from us.

Shortly after we were underway, secrets that had been kept from us throughout our journey began to surface. I listened as someone explained why we had been at sea for so long after leaving Italy.

The boats that carried the refugees were financed and outfitted with money from America and groups in Europe. The boats weren't cheap, and they took time to modify. The reason we had spent so much time sailing in zigzags and circles was that we had been waiting to rendezvous with a second boat. We had been told that there was another boat out there with engine trouble and that we needed to help, but the truth was, we were to meet with that second boat and move all the people to one boat so that the other could head back to Italy. That way, if we were diverted to Cyprus or captured, we would lose only one boat.

The problem was that the second boat had never appeared.

No one knew for sure what had happened. It might already have been captured or diverted. There was no way to know. Whatever the reason, our orders had been to rendezvous, and the rendezvous had not happened. The plan all along had been to get one boat near Haifa and scuttle its engines. The Haganah already knew that all refugees were being diverted to Cyprus. Despite all of the efforts of the Haganah both in Haifa and on the boat, this was the fate that befell my companions and me.

Before long we came in sight of land again. Our boat moored off the coast of Cyprus near the port city of Nikosia, which was the largest port city on the island. When the ship pulled in, it was a nice, sunny morning, but it was difficult to maintain a positive attitude after all we had been through.

It was finally time to depart the boat. We were taken from the ship to a large camp. As we approached it, my heart sank. From where we approached, we saw hundreds of square, drab army tents. The perimeter of the camp was circled with fences topped by barbed wire. I had a horrible moment of déjà vu. I thought of Auschwitz and what it had been like to enter that horrible place. Along the fences were watchtowers. Machine guns were planted in those towers and powerful floodlights were also mounted, to watch for escapees. Even without the oven and the gas chambers, the camp at Nikosia resembled Auschwitz all too much.

As I was brought into that place, all the horrible things I had endured, all the pain and agony, the hunger and the loss, suddenly became real again. In only a few moments I experienced again being thrown out of my home, banished to Poland nearly to starve, only to make my way home to be sent to the death camps. I felt the loss of my parents, the agony of the prolonged marches, the hunger and the sickness. I wondered if I would ever find my freedom and live as a human being.

They took me to a tent that I would share with four other prisoners, one of them Chaim. We were left there, alone in the dark. We huddled and spoke little, trying to take in what had happened to us and to recover enough to figure out what to do next.

In the middle of that first night, we heard a huge explosion out in the bay. Word spread through the camp, and eventually I learned that the Haganah had managed to slip men out onto the boat that had brought us from Haifa and scuttle it. It was meant to prevent the boat from being taken back to transport more refugees to Cyprus.

We had been brought to the island without our belongings. I was surprised when, a few days later, what we'd had on the boat was brought to us. I had an old rucksack with my clothes and a little money. I had purchased several Doxa watches before leaving for Palestine because I had been told that they were better than currency, and that I could sell them for a good profit when I arrived. The British had taken my watches, leaving me with almost nothing.

It took about a week for me to start to come to terms with this new existence. I spent the time with my three tentmates. We were given new clothes and attended daily lectures where we studied Hebrew and Jewish history. Our teacher assured us that if we were patient, sooner or later we would reach Palestine, and we would be free men despite the efforts of the British.

As we had done on the ship, Chaim and I spent our time trying to figure things out.

"How much of it do you believe?" he asked me one day. "They say we will make it to Palestine, but we've heard this all before."

"I believe them," I said, "but how long will it take? So many times we've been told 'soon'—and here we sit."

For a moment Chaim was lost in thought. "What will happen to us when we finally get there?" he asked. "Where will we live? What will we do?"

"I think we will be taken to a kibbutz. That is what the

Haganah on the boat told us, and it makes sense. We will work alongside others and make our own way eventually."

"I don't know," Chaim said. "We are young still. There are orphanages there. I think, since we are both without parents, that they will take us to one of those."

I wasn't sure we would get the chance. "If things continue to get worse," I told him, "there will be a war. We know what the British think and what they will try to do. They do not want us there, or any of our people. If it comes to war, we may be taken straight into the army. We're old enough to fight."

At that time, the British had been granted a mandate by the United Nations to manage affairs in Palestine. It was not a country—no one owned it. The British mandate was set to end in 1948. The United Nations was looking for a solution to the problem that would be amicable to both Arabs and Jews. What remained to be seen was what would happen when the nations of the world began to take sides. It wasn't so much a matter of whether there would be trouble but how long it would be before it started.

The Jewish Committee from America and the Palestinian Jews lobbied the United States and the world to have the United Nations force the British to allow a greater number of immigrants into Palestine. The Arab and British sectors attempted to thwart these efforts and extend British control. The British gave control of the police force to the Arabs. The problem slowly escalated until it was out of control. There were over 100,000 Jewish immigrants waiting to be allowed into Palestine with nowhere else to go.

In the midst of this, Chaim and I attended classes, studied and waited. Finally, stating humanitarian reasons, a group of teenagers was allowed to proceed to Palestine. I was one of them. As I walked out of that camp, free again, and about to board a boat for Haifa, I began to hope.

Chapter Twenty-Three

We reached Palestine without incident and were transferred by bus to a camp in Atlit, a suburb of Haifa. It was close enough to the port that it was similar to a suburb. We had to remain in the camp while we awaited the certification papers from the British that would allow us to enter Palestine fully legally.

When we reached the camp, we stepped off the bus and looked around carefully. The camp, like so many others we had seen over the past few years, was surrounded by barbed wire, but there were no watchtowers and no machine guns. It felt very different and had none of the sense of dread of the other camps.

I felt much less isolated in this camp. At Atlit we were cared for by local Jewish families. The food and accommodations were tolerable, and we were allowed some contact with the outside world. Visitors came to the fence around the camp, and though the visitors could not enter and we could not leave, we were able to interact and make friends through the fence.

During one of my early days in camp, I was standing by the fence when a girl waved to me from the far side. I stepped closer.

"Hello," I said.

She smiled at me and came up to the fence. "Hello, I'm Shoshana."

I smiled back. It was a pretty name, and I knew from my studies that it meant *flower* in Hebrew.

"I'm David," I said. "I hope we won't be in here too much longer."

"I'm sure it won't be long. Until then, I could come back to visit."

She was a very pretty girl, and the thought of seeing her again made me happy. "I'd like that very much."

I made many friends during this time, but I spent as much time as possible talking to Shoshana. We talked about life, the British rule over Palestine and how it favored the Arabs, and many other things. I learned that there were about 600,000 Jews in Palestine but millions of Arabs. The problem was that the Arabs controlled all the oil fields, and that gave them leverage with the British. Throughout my time in the camp, I remained close to Shoshana, and after I left we exchanged letters for a while and visited one another from time to time. But once I joined the army, the letters I wrote to Shoshana never reached her.

The time in the camp passed quickly, and almost before I knew it the other boys from Cyprus and I were directed to pack our few belongings. We were sent out from the camp to a variety of places. I was separated from Chaim and others I knew. My group was relocated to an orphanage in Magdiel, near Tel Aviv.

The orphanage, which also served as a high school, was a far cry from the camps, even the one I had just left. It was surrounded on all sides by green fields as far as the eye could see. There were orange orchards surrounding the fields. We arrived at the school via a long, narrow country road that wound through thousands and thousands of trees. When we rounded the last corner, we came to the gates of the school, which was an agricultural-based learning facility.

We entered the gates and pulled up to find that there was a very large group of people waiting to greet us. There were students, teachers and locals gathered for our arrival. Refreshments had been set out, and it was a very happy moment. We were made to feel at home, and that was something I had not felt in a very long time.

We mingled with those who were gathered, ate fruit and had something to drink. Eventually we were told what our daily routine would be at the school. From 6:30 to 7:00 a.m. we would eat breakfast. From 8:00 a.m. until 1:00 p.m. we would be in classes and then break for lunch. At 2:00 we would take our shifts in the various areas of the agricultural complex.

"There are a lot of different jobs to be performed on a farm," the man who was instructing us said. "We have broken the work into different areas, such as the vegetable farm, the citrus orchards, the melon fields, the cattle and livestock, the mules, the fields that need plowing. You will get your chance to work in each area, shifting once every two months."

After the orientation, we were issued clothing and supplies. We were given pajamas, khaki pants, shorts, white shirts, toothpaste and other necessities. We were shown to our rooms and assigned in groups of three or four to a room. I found myself rooming with three boys who had been at the school longer than I had.

The school grounds consisted of several small dorms where approximately 200 boys and girls—all of them Holocaust survivors—lived. There were several classrooms, the agricultural fields and one large main building that housed the kitchens, the dining hall and a large area that was used for parties, shows and dances. We often gathered there for square dancing and small theater productions. Curfew was 10:30 p.m.

Saturday was the day of rest. The food that day was special. We had gefilte fish, chicken soup and some chicken or beef.

Saturdays were the happiest at the school, except for those students whose turn it was to serve in the kitchens. These duties fell to each of us once every couple of months.

Ephraim, the man who taught us Hebrew, had a goatee and a huge pot belly. He spoke a number of languages, but when we came into the classroom to study he spoke only Hebrew and required us to do the same. If he needed to explain to us what a word meant, he would use sign language to get his point across. He was a funny man with a great personality and a gift for teaching. All the students liked him and looked forward to his class.

I found in the school something that had been missing far too long in my life: a place to belong. It was a caring place that offered an education and a trade—a future to look forward to. It was a place I could call home. And it brought about a surprising change in my life.

In public school, I hadn't been a particularly good student. Now I found that I wanted to learn, and I worked very hard at my lessons. When it was necessary, I would sneak into the bathrooms after the 10:30 p.m. curfew to read and study. It was the only place we were allowed to have a light burning after hours.

It didn't happen overnight, but after a while my grades improved. Suddenly it mattered to me that I learned and learned well. I participated in class, library, choir and drama and even wrote poetry occasionally—often doing so for boys with less ability who wanted to express themselves to a special someone in a letter. The school, the students and faculty became my home and my family. I got along very well with my fellow students, and the counselors and teachers were like surrogate fathers. I did my best and enjoyed every minute of my studies.

The whole experience had a positive effect on me emotionally. I received respect for my work. My self-esteem began to grow, and I took pride in all that I accomplished. Life had taken on new meaning. I came to believe for the first time in my life that the days I was living—the things I was doing and the experiences I found in that place—would be the best in my life.

There was a certain social honor code among the boys and girls in the school. We had dances and parties, but if a girl had a steady boyfriend, she was off limits. The problem was that there were a small number of pretty girls, and they were all taken. Despite this, I took notice of a dark-haired girl with blue eyes. We met each Friday night at the square dance and sat together. When no one was looking, I held her hand. We continued our flirtations throughout my time in the school. When I could, I sat behind her and played footsie beneath the bench or the desks. We could only really talk when the class took trips together. We dreamed and planned for the time when we would be finished with school and with the war that we knew would follow.

During this time, I also grew very close to my roommates. There was Jacob, a roly-poly Polish boy with a big smile and a love of life that was infectious. There was the blue-eyed, blond-haired Kostik, a talented artist who painted many of the background-scene panels for the drama club's productions. Of our group, he was the ladies' man. For him, the fun and the girls came first, school a very distant second. He was always ready for a good time and never seemed to worry about anything—not even the future.

My roommates and I were inseparable. If we had been brothers, we couldn't have been closer. We covered for one another whenever we could. On Shabbat we were all required to wear nicer clothes—short pants and clean, white shirts with six-inch Vs at the neck. Most of the boys who had girlfriends had embroidered blue borders around their collars. We were expected to be clean and to look nice.

If we could sneak off the school grounds on Saturday, we could work for the farmers in the orchards surrounding the school. It wasn't allowed, but if we were careful and our friends covered for us, we could make some money.

The work was hard and dirty, and the pay was not good, but if we could, we did it because it was one of the only ways to earn something. Out in the orchards, the farmers needed to have ditches dug around the trees. These were about four feet wide and twelve inches deep around each tree. Each ditch connected to a larger ditch that led to the water. Water would be released into the ditch. When the ditch filled with water, dirt was removed to allow it to flow in around one tree, then sealed off again and so on. The work was all done in a hunched position, and was hard on the legs and back.

Like many of the other boys, I slipped out as often as I could on Saturdays. I would dress in my Sabbath clothing and crawl beneath the barbed-wire fence surrounding the school. I carried work clothes under my arm and slipped away as quickly and quietly as possible. I worked six-hour days and saved every penny I earned. When the work was done, I put my Sabbath clothing on and climbed back under the fence. While I was gone, my friends covered for me, and when they slipped away to work, I did the same for them. This went on for a long time and began to be almost routine.

Then, one day, everything changed. Like so many other Saturdays, I got away from the school grounds, shifted into my work clothes and hit the orchards. The work was hard, and the farmers were demanding. By the time I was done, I was tired and sore, and happy to be making my way back to the comfort of my room.

I changed and slid under the barbed wire, brushed off my shirt and turned.

There, with a very stern expression on his face, stood Samuel, a man who served as combination father, counselor, teacher and group supervisor, and he was very strict. There were many rules in the school, and the keeping of the Sabbath was the most important of them.

"Well, David," he said, "where have you been?"

I tried to answer, but guilt and embarrassment kept the words from coming. I liked and respected Samuel very much, and I had always felt this was reciprocated. I worked hard and was known for the extra effort I put into my studies.

"Samuel," I said, "I'm sorry, I…"

The expression on his face silenced me. This man was a very important part of my life and the lives of my classmates. I could find no words to help the situation, and I had a lump in my throat that seemed almost to cut off my breath. With no further discussion, Samuel turned, and I followed him. Nothing more was said that day and I went to bed, but I didn't say anything to my friends, and I didn't sleep.

In the morning I was summoned to the principal's office, and I went with a heavy heart. The principal was a well-respected man among the students. He was also very strict, and I knew I had broken the most sacred of the rules. After all I had gone through, I felt as though I had thrown my new life away for a few dollars, and I wished very much that I had not gone that day to work in the fields.

To make things worse, when I entered the principal's office, I saw his wife seated at his side. I had written a poem about my mother that was published in the school newspaper. The principal's wife had read the poem and it impressed her, so much that she offered me her support. I was flattered by the attention, and the two of us had come to be close friends. To most of the students, she appeared cold and distant, but I had seen a different side of her. Having her there in the principal's office made my shame and embarrassment much worse. I wished, in that moment, that the earth would open and swallow me whole.

"David," the principal began, "of all the boys in my charge, you are the last I would have expected to find here under these circumstances. You've set an example through your diligence, applied yourself to your studies. Other students look up to you, and you have shown great promise.

"But this—this I would never have anticipated. You have gone outside the boundaries of the school, boundaries clearly outlined to you from the first day you set foot here. On top of that, you broke the sanctity of the Sabbath. You not only left the grounds, but you worked on the day of rest. I just cannot imagine why you would do it."

I stood, fighting back tears of shame. I wished I were dead. The principal said more, but at some point his words began washing over me without really registering. Nothing could have taken away the demoralizing guilt I felt.

Finally, apparently seeing the misery I felt, the principal drew to a close.

"In life, David, there are many things that are important. Your character and your honesty are sacred. The most important treasure you will ever possess is a good reputation. I have been thinking since last night about what an appropriate punishment for this offense would be. Many things occurred to me, but I believe I have hit upon the perfect thing. I have decided that, considering the way it has affected you to be caught, and the damage to your reputation both with the faculty and your fellow students, the best punishment is not to punish you at all. I will do nothing, but I feel very certain that you will not forget what you have done. I do not believe this offense will be repeated."

"No, sir," I said very quietly. I wished I could have been punished in some other fashion—a beating or a fast, anything. Something harder to bear would have given me the chance to endure and to work through the pain. This was much worse.

I saw then that if you make just one stupid mistake, it can ruin your life. It made a big impression on me that the principal figured out on his own that this would be the lesson I took. I wasn't a great student, but I was singing in the choir and taking part in activities, and I was a kind of semi-celebrity. Other students looked up to me. With that little thing of sneaking away to earn money, I had ruined my name and reputation. It was a tremendous lesson that stayed with me throughout my life. Even today I remember it. I return every phone call, pay every bill I owe, never lie. I treasure my good reputation.

After that, there was no more sneaking out to work. I buckled down and did my work, and I made the most of my studies. Every two months we rotated from one agricultural branch to another, and my turn soon came for plowing the fields.

The dirt was very hard, and the plow was drawn across the field by mules. They were stubborn, and the work was almost impossible, but this rotation was still the most anticipated in the school. When the work was done, those who did the plowing were allowed to ride the mules bareback from the fields to the school. This was a twenty-five-minute ride and, for the most part, an easy meander across the fields.

In addition to this agricultural training, we learned self-defense. We took lessons from a thin, young member of the Haganah, who taught us to fight. He took us out at night on patrols, sneaking quietly through the orchards and keeping watch on the village of Kalkiliah—the nearest Arab encampment to the school. We weren't just training.

We fired on Arab infiltrators who tried to sabotage the Jewish settlements. More than once I heard the whine of bullets. Snipers from Kalkiliah sometimes fired on the school. The patrol kept watch for strangers, and it gave us a taste of the real danger and combat we would face during the war that was coming. After several months of training we were deemed worthy of induction into the Haganah, provided we passed a vigorous combat test.

The talented, young man who made fighters out of us ended

up having a very interesting career. He was nominated to be the leader of the first and most elite commando unit in the Israeli army. He fought in all the wars and became the most decorated and most famous general in the army, eventually becoming prime minister of Israel. His name was Ariel Sharon. His wife, Margalit, was a fellow student at my orphanage.

One night, as I was sitting and reading in my room, I heard a knock on the door. I stood and opened it. Soldiers were outside in the darkness, and they told me to go with them. I did as I was told, stepping into the shadows.

"Where are we going?" I asked.

"Remain silent. Turn when we tell you. You will know all that you need to know soon enough."

They led me out of the gates of the school and into the orchards beyond. It was very dark, and after a few turns I had no idea where I was. I walked until one of the men told me to turn, and I turned. There I saw others—I wasn't the only one being led out—but there was no way to ask questions or to figure out who else was there. After walking for quite a while, we came to a clearing where a small hut had been erected.

I stepped up to the door of the hut, and someone appeared from the shadows to open it. I went inside.

The interior was lit only by candles, and the flickering light was dim. There was a low-slung table, and on the far side of the table sat three men, one of them Ariel Sharon. On the table I saw several small Bibles and handguns.

"David Karmi?" one of the men asked.

"Yes, sir," I answered.

"State your full name and your training."

I did as I was told. I briefly recounted the training in the groves, the patrols and the self-defense. I talked of my training in the school, the language and history lessons. When I was finished I stood quietly.

"This is an important night for you," one of the men said. "Are you ready to become one of the Haganah? Are you ready to stand and fight for your country and your people—to die, if it becomes necessary, in their service?"

I placed one hand on a Bible and the other on one of the handguns.

"I am ready," I said.

At that moment, my military career began. I was led back through the orchards and returned to the school, and shortly afterwards my life changed yet again.

Chapter Twenty-Four

As the end of the British rule over Palestine approached, it was obvious to the entire world that war was inevitable. From where my fellow students and I lived at the school, we could often hear bursts of gunfire from the direction of the nearby Arab village. It was the same all over Palestine—tempers were high, and the air was thick with tension.

At that point, all Jewish military or defense organizations were illegal. This did nothing to stop them from organizing, but it forced all of their operations underground. This prevented solid organization and made it difficult for the Jewish forces to be controlled by one command. To complicate things and tip the odds toward their Arab allies, the British took actions in their final days. They left all the police and fortressed locations under Arab control. They also left weapons for the Arabs to use as defense. At the same time, they aggressively confiscated any weapons or equipment found in the possession of the Jewish population.

The future looked bleak. It was widely believed that 600,000 Jews had no chance of standing against five Arab states and millions of trained, armed soldiers. But for me, and for all of those who had survived the Holocaust and made their way to Palestine, what was at stake was the most important thing in the world. We were fighting for a country that we could live in and call our own—a country where no one could expel us or lock us away. It would be a country we could be proud to be a part of, as our ancestors had been nearly 5,000 years before.

One day, a group of buses arrived at the school, and it was time for the oldest of the students to leave and begin their service. My friends and I had nothing material to give them, but we wrote poems and told them our hearts were with them and hugged them good-bye. Those moments were filled with fear and expectation; it was the beginning of something big, something world-changing, however it worked out. Not long after that, the buses returned again and the younger boys, including me, were taken away to serve. In the end, even the girls were taken away to serve, and only women and children were left in the school.

As I sat near the back of my bus and watched the road curve away behind me, I saw the school growing smaller and smaller, the orange orchards dropping away into the distance, and I committed their images to my memory. I had so many fond memories of that school, and I didn't want to lose them.

When the bus rolled to a stop, we had arrived at an army camp near Hadera, about an hour north of Tel Aviv. The camp was mostly made up of tents, smaller ones for sleeping quarters and larger ones for command and the gathering of groups. The new men, including me, were issued our khakis and then lectured on the daily routine of the camp. We had that one day to settle in; the next day we began our basic training. I worked my way through this quickly. I was determined to succeed, and the moment I finished basic I began my corporal's course. Upon completion of this, I received my first important assignment. I was put in charge of the supply tent, where uniforms and other stores were kept, issued and maintained for the entire camp.

Not long after assuming control of the supplies, I got a visit from the camp commander.

"Corporal," the man said, "we have a very important visitor

coming to camp. The prime minister, Mr. Ben-Gurion himself, is coming and we must be ready. I want every corner of this supply tent cleaned and inventoried. Our records must be spotless, as well as our tents and our equipment."

"Yes, sir."

"That's not all," the commander said. "I need one more thing from you, and it is very important. When the prime minister comes to this tent to see how you are maintaining it, I want you to tell him the things that we are short on, and the things that we need most desperately. Others could tell him, but it's better coming from the man who runs supply."

"Yes, sir," I said.

I took the task very seriously. I worked long hours sorting, stacking and straightening my inventory. I cleaned every inch of the supply tent and then did it again, and all the time I kept going over in my mind the words that I would say. I practiced my speech, and I worked carefully on my Hebrew, making sure that I would make no mistakes. I didn't want to embarrass myself. At last, when the expectation was almost too great to bear, the moment arrived.

Ben-Gurion toured the entire camp. He checked out our tents, our mess hall and every other aspect of the camp. When he finally made his way to the supply tent, I stood waiting. I popped to attention and offered a smart salute.

The prime minister was surprisingly short. His hair was bushy, and it waved about in the breeze. He walked through the tent, inspecting everything.

"What's your name, soldier?" he asked. "Tell me where you come from, where you've been. Have you been in charge of the supplies for very long?"

I replied carefully and when I was done, I launched into the speech I had prepared. As the commander had instructed, I began to list the supplies and equipment we were most short on.

"Young man," Ben-Gurion interrupted, "stop right there. When I was in the Turkish army, things were hard in every one of our camps—very hard. If we couldn't get something, we stole it. We are not provisioned to supply all of the things an army needs. If you don't have something, you try to get it. If you can't get it by normal means, you steal it. I'm afraid that's about as much help as I can be."

Later, when the camp had gathered to hear him speak, the prime minister expounded on this subject. He said that he'd heard the same complaints of lacks of supplies, armament, manpower and other things everywhere he had traveled. He wished that he could promise that he would buy all that we needed and have it delivered to us, but that was not possible. For the time being, he said, whatever we had was what we would have to make do with. If we needed more, we would have to find ways to get it.

The message was the same to everyone all over the Haganah. It was not going to be an easy fight—and it was not going to be a pleasant one. The thing that drove us on was that it would be an important fight, a life-changing fight, and we felt we were up to the task.

Shortly after Ben-Gurion's visit, I began my sergeant major's course. I went through basic training all over again but had to be much better than the average soldier. Everything was harder—the training, the obstacles that I had to jump over and go through, the walking. I had to learn how to take apart machine guns and weapons, and I also had to know how to teach my soldiers how to do this. I had to prove that I was capable of commanding forty soldiers and of leading them in war. Eventually the time came for the final test—the last one before graduation.

My assignment was very straightforward. I had to deliver a lesson to a group of students. The subject was how to assemble, disassemble and fire a machine gun. There was a strict sequence of tasks to be adhered to, and I studied hard, committing the lesson to memory to be certain I didn't slip up. When I gave the lesson, I was to be observed, and when the day came for me to teach the lesson my observer was none other than the base commander. I was nervous but confident. I knew the material, and I knew I was ready.

When we started, I stood in front of twenty students. The commander sat off to one side to watch and listen. Once the lesson was underway, I started to feel better. I followed the procedure exactly and made a very thorough presentation. When it was finally over, I glanced over at the commander, who was still seated along the side.

I felt the satisfaction that comes from a job well done, and I was actually looking forward to hearing what my observer would have to say. I dismissed the class, and after they had gone, I walked over to the commander.

The man sat there, shaking his head sadly, though he was smiling.

"David Karmi," he said. "You talk too much. I think you'd better become a lawyer."

Chapter Twenty-Five

After receiving my sergeant major's stripes, I received a new assignment. It became my job to train young men between the ages of seventeen and twenty, and some younger because they had lied about their ages in order to become a part of the Haganah. These men and boys came from a variety of backgrounds. Some came from Europe, others from various Arab nations such as Algeria and Egypt. They were nearly all poorly educated. Almost none spoke Hebrew, and they had little discipline. The lack of communication made training difficult, and I had little time with each group before it was shipped out and the next group was shipped in.

It would have been bad enough if it had been simple training, but they were being sent to war. Their lives would be at risk from the moment they left my charge, and I took the work very seriously. It was a very demanding post. The training was too short, very intense, and there were no breaks between groups. We struggled constantly against poor communication, and this exacerbated the discipline problems. It was frustrating for trainers and trainees alike.

The training squads were made up of about forty recruits each. Every new group was a veritable melting pot, with different backgrounds, different levels of education and ability, different languages. Part of the training they received was in Hebrew, enough to get them by and to make it possible for them to work together and fight together. The impossibility of making soldiers out of the recruits in a matter of weeks instead of months weighed heavily on our shoulders. The young men we trained were going to face off against trained Arab soldiers with superior equipment, training and supplies in a ferocious war.

My superiors were fully aware that we were turning our young men out too soon with too little, but it was 1947 and the Arab countries that bordered Israel—Egypt, Syria and Jordan—had declared war. Iraq, Algeria, Morocco and Saudi Arabia had sent volunteers, irregulars who fought with the Arab armies. There was no time to sit back and properly conduct training. We knew we were sending our soldiers into hell, but it was a price we felt we had to pay. Israel came first.

So I trained the recruits as hard and as fast as I could. We woke in the morning and started with long runs. We shot weapons and ran obstacle courses again and again. We learned to cross rivers and then ran again. We went out on night patrols, got little sleep, and got up to do it all over again.

Despite the seriousness of the work and the incredible strain of leading—and participating in—all the activities with the recruits, there were occasionally entertaining moments.

I entered the tents of my squad at 6:00 a.m. and rousted the recruits. I rushed them all out to the road and we started our day with a run. The standard run was between twenty and twenty-five minutes out and then the same back again. I ran ahead of the group. Since we went straight from our tents to the run, it was common for the men to have to relieve themselves before the run was complete.

At first, one man might step out of line, relieve himself by the road and then try to catch up to the others. Slowly, though, I noticed that more than usual of my men were stopping alongside the road. Many of them were not returning to the run, even when the group passed again on the way back to camp; they were sneaking off back to camp and avoiding the exercise altogether. Eventually, almost half the troop was dropping out, and I knew something had to be done.

One morning I lined them up on the road, but before they could take off, I addressed the group.

"This morning," I said, "we are going to do things a little bit differently. It seems that a number of you have found that you cannot run the full course without stepping to the side of the road to take a leak. That's fine. I don't want you to be uncomfortable. As a courtesy to those who need to stop, the rest of the squad will now run in place and we will wait for each man who feels the urge to stop."

This announcement was followed by silence. Some of them, I knew, barely understood me. Others would not believe that I would carry through with this new rule. We started out, and sure enough, after about half a mile, one man broke ranks and dropped off beside the road. I immediately stopped. I turned and ran in place, facing my men. I stayed that way until the man beside the road finished and, embarrassed, ran back into the group. Then we took off again.

This happened several times during the run, and by the time it ended, over an hour after we had set out, all of my men were exhausted. I was also very tired but I didn't allow it to show in my expression or demeanor.

The next morning we started out on our run, and I kept a close eye on the men. I dropped back and ran beside them, watching carefully, but not a single man dropped formation to go to the side of the road. We finished our run in the normal time, and from that point on there was no longer a problem with dropouts.

The training culminated in a six-day hike in full combat gear. The entire group, all the recruits graduating at once, numbered about 200. There were boys and girls on the maneuver, marching together. We started out in the morning and we marched steadily. We were fed from a truck that met us along the way, and then we continued the march. When it started to get dark, we slept for short periods in the open field. We would sleep and then wake and continue on for fifty minutes at a time, rest ten minutes and move on again.

The march led us across fields and through orchards; we avoided roads. It was very difficult and, over time many of the recruits grew too tired to carry their gear. Whenever the first of them was unable to continue, boy or girl, my fellow sergeant majors and I carried the recruit's equipment until he or she was rested enough to carry it. We did this to help, but there was also a desire to show how strong we were—that we were like supermen. It was an example that we set for the recruits. Even when the group rested for their ten minutes each hour, I remained standing. It wasn't easy—I was often exhausted—but I managed not to show it, though at times I couldn't help leaning on a tree when no one was looking.

And each time I returned from a long march, there was a new group of recruits waiting for me. It was grueling work, but we were driven by necessity; if we could not provide complete training, we had to do the best that we could. I continued the training until it almost became a blur. Then, one day, without warning, I was summoned to see the officer in charge.

I had no idea why I had been called in. I knocked and was told to enter. There was a chair across the desk from the commander. The man told me to take it, and once I was seated I felt a little better. If I had been in trouble, I would have been left standing. When we were both seated, my superior got right to the point.

"I've been watching you since you were assigned to train recruits, David. You've done a remarkable job. You've put in good service, and I'd like to reward that. I'd like to see you move up and become an officer. It's time you were promoted."

I was surprised and pleased. "Thank you, sir."

"There is one thing," the commander said. "Before such a promotion can be official, you'll have to go through officers' training school."

I sat back, a little stunned. What my superior was offering me was a career. I knew that if I went to that training and accepted that commission, I would be committing myself to the life of a military man. It was too important a decision to be made on the spur of the moment.

"Can I have some time to think about it, sir?" I asked. "I'm very honored, but this is a surprise. It's a serious decision."

"It is, and I understand," the commander said. "Why don't you go back to your recruits, give it some thought? Come see me next week and tell me what you've decided."

I nodded. "Thank you, sir."

I left the office and returned to my quarters, lost in thought. The offer had taken me by surprise, and I knew it wasn't going to be an easy decision either way I went.

Over the next week, I gave the matter serious thought. I asked myself, if I survived the war, where did I see myself in the future? Where did I want my life to go? I wanted to make the choice that best fit my character and, as I saw it, I had three possible choices.

The first was to return to the school at the orphanage. I had been offered a teaching position there, and I knew that I could do the work well. Still, it was a very sedate life without much change in its future. Then there was the choice of a military career. It would keep me involved in the affairs of the new nation, and in its battles, for most of my adult life. The last choice was to go to Tel Aviv and go into business with my brother, who was an architect and a designer.

A week later, I returned to the commander's office.

"I have been thinking about your offer," I said. "I am flattered that you see potential in me as an officer. I remember when I first made sergeant major—you told me that I should be a lawyer. I have decided, though, to be neither an officer nor a lawyer. For now, I will continue with my assignment. When the war is over, I have family and work waiting for me in Tel Aviv."

"I'm sorry to hear that," the commander replied. "Still, I wish you well. You have worked hard, and I'm certain that whatever you decide, you will do well."

The two of us shook hands, and I left the office. I didn't feel regret but instead a kind of relief and hope for the future. As it turned out, only a few weeks later headquarters decided the next portion of my fate for me. They created a new unit named Nachal. The name meant "young pioneer fighter," and the men and women assigned to this unit were charged with protecting the many kibbutzim that were located on the borders between Israeli and Arab lands.

At the same time, Nachal would help out with the agricultural work, a plan intended to groom those involved to remain on the kibbutz when the war had ended, supplementing the work forces. Since the students from the orphanage where I had studied were well versed in agriculture, it was decided that we would gather the first unit from our number.

Jacob, one of my roommates from the orphanage, and I were sent to a kibbutz on the Syrian border. Having someone familiar with whom to share our fears and new experiences made it easier for both of us.

The name of the kibbutz was Masada. In the beginning

of the war, the members of this kibbutz were evacuated. The kibbutz itself was overrun by Arab irregulars who stole what they could and set most of the buildings on fire. By the time we arrived, the kibbutz members had returned and were repairing the burned-out buildings. They had started to work in the fields with bulletproof tractors and were trying to get back to a normal life, which was far from easy. There were daily shootings by snipers and cannon fire as the Syrians tried to prevent the kibbutz members from working in the fields.

When Jacob and I arrived, we were placed in the trenches surrounding the perimeter. The trenches were manned day and night. Every time we were fired upon, we returned fire. There were occasional casualties. And there was always the danger that the Syrians would try to overrun the kibbutz and destroy it for good.

The Syrian border was a dangerous and volatile area. The kibbutz could have been overrun at any moment. In fact, had the Syrians known just how weak and poorly defended we were, it would certainly have happened. We worked and lived with the constant knowledge of that danger.

The kibbutz was on the eastern side of the Sea of Galilee, a couple of hundred feet below sea level. There were Syrian forts built into the surrounding mountains. With the kibbutz and the cities in the valley below and the Syrians on the high ground with snipers, even returning fire was almost impossible. Later, those forts were overtaken and manned by Israelis, but when I first went to the valley they were a serious and continuous threat.

I settled in quickly. Life in the kibbutz was interesting. A typical day began for all members at around 6:00 a.m. We would have breakfast and then we would receive our assignments in the fields or orchards or tending to the gardening or the livestock. We worked steadily through the day until about

2:00 p.m., when we would return home. Each member of the kibbutz was assigned a single room. If a member was married, he or she would be assigned two rooms.

All of our meals were taken together. We ate in a communal dining room. Our clothing was supplied by the kibbutz and all laundry was washed by those assigned to that work. There was no need for money. If we went to the city, we were allowed some pocket money, but other than that everything was shared.

The children of the kibbutz were cared for as a group. They were educated as if they were a single, large family. Some of the children even slept separately from their parents. The relationships between all members of the kibbutz were close and caring.

There was a library with plenty of reading material. There was also a recreation room. The space was occasionally used for lectures or presentations, and there were also concerts from time to time. It was a rich life.

The kibbutz was managed by committee. All major decisions were voted on by the members of the kibbutz. It was a very cultural, intellectual life with a great amount of time spent reading, discussing and attending lectures and concerts. There was no reason to have or covet money—you could live and work there from the cradle to the grave. It was a wonderful life for what it was, and the proof of its effectiveness could be seen in men like David Ben-Gurion, a kibbutz member who became prime minister of Israel, and in nearly all the great generals of the Haganah who had been raised on kibbutzim.

I enjoyed my time on the kibbutz. I could see that it was a rich and satisfying lifestyle without worry—or would have been if the Syrians had not been perched on the border. Still, such a life, while perfect for some, was not good for others, and I knew I was among them. When my family had been expelled from Poland and we had been deported to the camps, my freedom to make my own decisions and my ability to do what I wanted with my life had been removed. I could not see limiting myself again by choosing to live in the one small community on the kibbutz. I needed to find my way and my place in the world.

Chapter Twenty-Six

As often as possible, I took my furloughs in Tel Aviv so that I could spend time with my brother, Mendu. I would hitch a ride into the city and sleep on the ride to Bat Yam, the suburb of Tel Aviv where he lived. I spent my Shabbat there. As pleasant as the time was in the kibbutz, I still liked to get out, see more of the world and work on renewing the family connections so long denied me. As it turned out, my brother was not the only one in Tel Aviv with whom I would reconnect.

One day, while walking down a city street, I ran into another student from the orphanage. Of all the people to meet, of all those I had thought about and wondered about since leaving the school, I met the girl I had cared so much for, the one who had been the girlfriend of another and so off limits.

I saw her and my mind whirled back. I remembered the times when we had danced together, how we had sat so that we could touch and stolen moments to be alone—but never dated. I had ached to tell her my true feelings and to do more than hold her hand in secret. I had left her with a poem to remember me by. And now there we were, face to face on a public street, far from the school and anyone who might have been watching, or who might have cared.

"So," I asked, "what have you been doing?"

"I'm a nurse in the army," she said. "I'm here on furlough."

I told her about what I had been doing in the army. "I spent some time training recruits, and now Jacob and I—you remember Jacob?—are stationed at Masad, a kibbutz on the Syrian border. We spend our days just like in school—taking care of fields, tending livestock and, when we have to, shooting back at Syrians on the mountain."

We walked and we talked. Each of us knew what had happened to some of our classmates. We talked about who was where, who had done what with whom, who had died. The entire time we talked, I couldn't take my eyes off of her. After the long walk, during which all I could think of were the long days and weeks I had dreamed of being alone with her, we stopped and sat down on a secluded bench in a park.

"Do you remember when we said goodbye at school?" I asked.

"Of course I remember."

"I wrote to you several times," I said, "but I never got an answer. I thought about you all the time. Even though we were together at the school, it was an awful time. Every time I saw you I had to look into your beautiful eyes, see your hair falling down over your shoulders, and hold the ache inside. I wanted to hold you and to kiss you, but it was impossible. You never answered my letters, and I didn't know why... On the Syrian border, when we're out on night patrol, sometimes I think about you. I remember your face, and your laugh, and..."

I would have gone on talking maybe all night, but she didn't let me. She leaned in close, put her arms around me and kissed me deeply, cutting off my words and my breath. We sat there on the bench for a long time, hugging and kissing and making up for the time we had lost. All the while, I couldn't help thinking how strange it was—of all the times I had dreamed of a moment just like this, for it to all happen so suddenly and out of the blue was like a dream or a little slice of heaven.

By the time we stopped kissing and took stock of our situation, it was almost two o'clock in the morning.

"I didn't know it was so late," I said. "I'm staying with my brother, but I can't wake him now. I'm not sure what to do. I don't have much money, and there's no way to get a ride back to the base now."

"Let's walk, and we'll think about it," she said.

We started back into town.

"What about a hotel?" she asked.

I shook my head. "I don't have enough money for even a single room, let alone two." We stopped and pulled out what cash we were carrying to see what we had. We were standing beneath a streetlight. It was obvious that if we had enough money for a room, it was only going to be one. She stared into my face, studying me, and then she spoke.

"We will try to get the one room. We'll take that room, and we will have a wonderful time—a memorable night. But first I must ask you to make me a promise. And I know you. I know that of all the men I have met in my life, you will keep that promise."

"Anything," I said. "Just ask."

She continued. "I will walk into that room a virgin, and it is important to me that when I come out tomorrow, I must be the same."

She never dropped her gaze, and I met it steadily. My heart pounded in my chest, and at first it was a little hard to breathe.

"Of course," I said. "I promise."

She smiled. "If you are the one," she said, "the one I will marry, then tonight we will have a time you will not easily forget. It will be wonderful."

I understood her request. In our society, girls were expected to remain chaste until marriage. Most Jewish men would expect it, and it could cause problems for a girl who failed to retain her purity.

In the end, when we entered the hotel and brought out our money, we were still slightly short the price of a room. We searched our pockets again, checking for anything we might have missed, but there was nothing. Disappointed, we turned to leave.

"Wait," the clerk said.

We turned back.

"The two of you defend this country," he said. "While I'm here, handing out room keys, you are risking your lives to make sure I'm safe." He reached into his own pocket and pulled out the difference in the room price. "It's the least I can do for you."

I took the key, sort of in a daze, and we went to our room. I had no idea what to expect. I unlocked the door and we went inside. I turned then and stood thinking, trying to figure out what I should take off first, what would be appropriate. I felt a sudden rush of passion mixed with a strange awkwardness that made it hard to think straight. I turned back to find her standing before me, naked and beautiful. She looked like a Greek goddess, carved in smooth stone, with her long hair dangling over her shoulders.

I felt the blood pulsing slowly through my body. Everything was changed, as if I stood in a completely different world. I nearly forgot to breathe. In moments we were in each other's arms. I reached for the lights, but she stopped me. She told me she wanted to be able to see me, and she removed my clothing slowly.

We lay together on the bed and explored each other's bodies for hours. She told me that she had cherished the poem I had written for her. She remembered how we had danced together at the school, and she told me she had always made sure that she danced as near to me as possible.

The morning came too soon, and before we parted we exchanged addresses. We wanted to arrange to take our future furloughs together, but we knew it would be very difficult. Our commands were different, and time off had to be scheduled ahead of time. We kissed goodbye and returned to our separate bases.

Eventually she was transferred north, to an area near Galilee. We did meet a few more times. She finished her service before mine was complete. The next time we met, she mentioned marriage but I was still in the army, with no home and no so solid means of support. I told her that I had to establish myself. Later, when I was out of the army, I went in search of her only to find that she was already married.

For the time being, I returned to my duties guarding and working the fields of the kibbutz. Jacob and I often talked about the future, about transfers of duty and careers after the army. Eventually, my time in the kibbutz came to an end and I was transferred to a regular army unit.

By the time I returned to Tel Aviv, I knew I had to make some serious decisions about my future and my career. Though my friend Jacob was stationed in another unit, we were still in touch, and we talked often about what we would do next.

"They wanted to send me to officer's school," I said one day. "I knew that if I made that commitment, it would be more than just the school. It would mean a military career."

"You should be a teacher," Jacob said. "I've said that many times. You should go back to the orphanage. They would love to have you there as a teacher, and they would be lucky to have you."

I knew that I could have a career as a teacher. There had been times when I had thought about it, but somehow settling down so soon into such a job was not very appealing. There was limited potential for advancement at the school. I could teach for a while and then, if I did well, I might one day aspire to become the principal—and that was the end of that road. I had bigger ideas for my life.

"I think you should at least try it," Jacob said.

I told him that my brother had his own business in Tel Aviv. "He's asked me to come and work with him," I said. "I'm thinking that is what I'll do. There's no dead end in such a career. The only thing that forces you to stop succeeding or to settle down is your own decision to do so. My brother does interior design, but the fields of carpentry and construction are wide open. There are a lot of choices, and even if I start out in one field, I could change to another.

"What's important to me," I added, "is that I set my own limits. What I do, and how well I do it, is dependent on my own hard work, drive and capabilities. No one tells me what I can do, or, if they do, I show them that they are wrong!"

Jacob didn't seem convinced, but he dropped it.

I had only about $200 saved up from the times I had sneaked out of the school to work in the orchards. I took the money to my brother's house for him to hold for me. When I returned to Tel Aviv after being discharged from the army, that money and my clothing were all that I owned. I didn't even have a place to sleep.

In Tel Aviv after the war, it was almost impossible to rent an apartment. You could buy a place to live, but you had to have a lot of money to do it. There just wasn't anything available. My brother rented a very small apartment, and there was no room for another bed.

The shop where I went to work was in Yafo, which was very near Tel Aviv, though in modern times Yafo and Tel Aviv are one city. I made an agreement with my brother that worked out at first. By day I worked in the shop and then, at night, when everyone had gone home, I laid out my bedding on one of the benches and slept there. I had to make sure that I woke very early every morning and got my things put away so that the other workers wouldn't know that the owner's brother had to sleep in the shop.

After a while of this, I purchased a bike. At the time, owning a bike was like owning a car. I took off through Yafo in search of a better answer to my sleeping arrangements, and I found it when I ran into another old schoolmate. Jacob Amsterdam had been discharged sooner, and he'd managed to find a one-room, backyard apartment. It was a very small place, just the one room and a small terrace. There was no kitchen—but there was a sink on the terrace.

Jacob agreed that we should be roommates, but there was still a problem. The interior of the small apartment had Jacob's bed, a table and some chairs. There was no way to get another bed into it and still have the table and chairs. I studied the problem for a bit.

"I have the answer," I announced, "and I will show you soon."

What I did was to design and build a trundle bed on wheels. We were able to slide it under Jacob's bed during the day, which gave us plenty of room for the table and chairs and to move around. At night we rolled the bed out so we could both sleep.

Neither of us made a great deal of money, so we ate at home for economic reasons. We did our cooking over a kerosene lamp and shared our small accommodations by day. I quickly got used to this new arrangement, pulling out the bed at night, sliding it away by day—it was a huge improvement over sleeping in the shop, and I felt as if I had begun to build the foundation of my life.

The two of us got along very well. We started going out together and made a lot of friends. Jacob was an inspector in a winery, and he knew some people; I knew others. Between the two of us, despite our meager existence, we had some very good times.

On weekends in particular, we enjoyed life. We would find dates, get on our bikes and ride to the seashore. There were many outdoor cafes there, and they played music late into the night. There was dancing, and even if Jacob and I had no dates when we left home, there were more women than men in Tel Aviv in those days. There was always something to do—and someone to do it with.

We didn't always go out together. Sometimes we went on separate dates. I could always tell when he came home whether or not Jacob had scored because if he had, his pants would be inside out on the terrace. They were good times, and both of us lived life to the hilt. After the years of oppression and war, it was amazing just to be free to live.

Jacob was a tall man, dark and good-looking. He was good-natured and was well-liked at his job, and by the girls. One night he made a weekend date but forgot that he already had one. He talked me into filling in. Jacob kept his date with a girl named Hannah, and my date was Gladys, a girl from Brooklyn.

That was when the pattern of dating different girls every weekend changed. Both of us had a great time on that first date, and both of us continued dating the same girls. I saw Gladys every weekend and sometimes during the week. We would take long walks and stay up into the small hours of the morning talking. I often went to work on little or no sleep, but I got by. When you are young and having a good time, it seems as if you never get too tired to get through the next day and do it again.

There were only two months left before Gladys had to return to America. We spent as much of that time together as possible. When it was time for her to go, we kissed and we exchanged addresses, but in my heart, I knew that would be the end. Still, just in case, I gave her my brother William's address in Brooklyn. I didn't believe I would ever see her again.

I was surprised when, only a few weeks later, I received a letter from my brother. Gladys had come to see him and introduced herself. She had shared stories of Tel Aviv. I was happy to hear it. I wrote to my brother that he should make friends with her. I still didn't believe I would ever see her again, and I hoped she would like William.

The two did become friends. They dated for a while, but it never got serious. Meanwhile, I received letters from Gladys. They kept coming for about a year. She told me about America, about Brooklyn and about her work. She was a legal stenographer in Manhattan. Her mother's family had a house in Brooklyn. I read the letters and sometimes reread them. They reminded me of the time we had spent together, walking in Old Yafo. I thought, despite the continued communication, that we were just friends.

Then, about a year after we had parted, I got another letter. She was coming back to Israel for another visit. It was a shock—a complete surprise.

As I waited for the day Gladys would return, I thought about my family—those who remained and those I had lost. My sister Ilana had survived the war while living in Bucharest. She had married, and with her husband, Abraham Fuchs, had relocated to Belgium. Abraham was a renowned cantor at the temple in Antwerp, Belgium. Eventually the two moved to Israel, and Abraham became cantor at the Allenby Street Temple in Tel Aviv.

My mother and father had died in the camps. My brother Moses had been taken into slave labor by the army in Hungary and had died there. My sister Rachel and her husband had been in Budapest during the war. They were shot and thrown into the Danube by Hungarian Nazis only one week before the war ended.

My oldest brother, Armin, survived in Bucharest with Ilana. He married and moved to Santiago, Chile. He had a son, Marcel, and two daughters, Pepi and Alisa. Armin taught Hebrew, and his wife, Pookey, sold dry goods. It was a hard life. They made little money. Eventually they joined the family members who had moved to America.

William, the artist, moved to Italy after the war. He stayed there for a while and then immigrated to America. He became a portrait artist and eventually owned a sign shop in Brooklyn. Irene married Joseph Weiss in Kluj. Joseph had been working for Mendu, and my brother introduced Joseph to my sister. Joseph made his living building baby carriages. He and Irene had two children, Andrew and Lea. They had to wait fifteen years to get their exit visas, but they eventually made their way to the US. By that time, Mendu was married to Judit and had two sons, Gabriel and Amiram, as well as a daughter, Ronit. They lived in Bat Yam.

Ilana, her husband and her daughter Mariana lived in Petach Tikva, just north of Tel Aviv. Out of the huge family, only six remained. Three lived in Israel and three had spread out to various corners of the world. It was hard to imagine that, in the short years since I had first been taken to Poland, my entire world had shifted and changed.

Every Shabbat, I visited either my sister Ilana and her husband Abraham or my brother Mendu. I alternated weeks, enjoying my time with both siblings. I continued to live in the small apartment with Jacob. It was still impossible to find a place in or near Tel Aviv to rent.

I received a final letter from Gladys. It gave her date of arrival, and when that day arrived I met her at the airport. It was a wonderful reunion. I felt as if we had never been apart. I got a taxi and we rode to Gladys' cousin's home in Yafo.

The two of us started up immediately where we had left off, seeing one another as often as possible. We got along as well as before or better, and things grew serious very quickly. One evening, Gladys brought up the subject of marriage. It caught me by surprise. I still had very little to call my own and had honestly not even considered marriage. We talked about it at my sister Ilana's house, and my sister overheard.

"If you love her, David," Ilana advised me, "then marry her. What are you waiting for?"

Six months later, a package arrived from Gladys' sister in America. It contained her wedding dress. I managed to borrow a gray suit, a hat and a tie from a friend of my sister's. Gladys' mother sent over kosher salami; Ilana provided preserves, cookies and cake. The entertainment was provided by some musician friends. The cantor was my brother-in-law Abraham, and a friend who was a rabbi said the blessings.

We stood beneath a canopy, Gladys in her beautiful dress and me in my oversized gray suit and hat. We exchanged our vows and then she circled me seven times. At the end, I stomped on a wineglass wrapped inside a napkin, and everyone cried, "Mazel tov!" for good luck.

The guests were seated around long tables near the front of the canopy. There was a small plate in front for hors d'oeuvres and a larger platter in back for the salami and potato salad. There was cake and coffee, wine, and singing and dancing.

The guests included people from many walks of life, including Joseph Shprinzak, speaker of the house of the Israeli Parliament. He was a distant relative of my wife's. My brother Mendu and his wife were there, as well as people who I had worked with and those who Gladys knew. Some were important people, and others would become important people later in their lives.

It was late in the night when we finally said our goodbyes. A friend had a taxi, and he grabbed what was left of the wedding cake and put it in the car. We got in and pulled away, and I wondered if it was the first wedding ever where everyone—the rabbi, the cantor, the musicians—had performed their services without being paid. I felt very happy and very fortunate. We had good friends and good family.

Gladys had found a job as a legal stenographer and an English translator at the Israeli parliament. Despite the difficulty in finding housing in Tel Aviv, with the help of Joseph Shprinzak we were able to rent a one-bedroom apartment on Jerusalem Boulevard in Yafo. We arrived at the apartment a little after midnight. My friend gave us the wedding cake and said good night.

We walked to the door and I opened it, holding the door for Gladys. As we entered, I could tell she caught the scent of something sweet in the air. When I turned on the lights, she exclaimed at the sight of rose petals carpeting the floor. Gladys had stayed with her cousin the week before the wedding and during that time, I had prepared this special surprise and another for her.

Now I placed the cake on a table and closed the door. The rose petals trailed down the hallway and into the bedroom. They even covered the bed. Then came the other surprise. I had connected the record player to the bedroom door so that when I opened it, the record player started playing "How Deep Is the Ocean, How High Is the Sky." That was Gladys' favorite song.

Our honeymoon plans were to stay at Tiberius by the Sea of Galilee for a week, but Gladys and I ended up staying there for only four days. We spent the first three in the apartment, eating nothing but wedding cake. It was a wonderful beginning.

Chapter Twenty-Seven

After the wedding, Gladys continued her work as a stenographer. I moved from my brother's small shop to a much larger business that created interior furnishings for offices and businesses. I was always very conscientious in my work. I never felt as if I was doing enough or being productive enough. I worked long hours, and eventually my supervisors noticed. After only a few months I was promoted to foreman. Between the two of us, Gladys and I made a decent living and managed to have a lot of fun.

It took a while, but eventually Gladys got used to life in Israel. It was different from New York and not an easy transition, but we were very happy for the first couple of years. In time she grew homesick and began to miss her mother, so she started planning a visit to the United States. Soon after that, she began to talk now and then about the possibility of relocating. I did nothing to encourage this, but once she had the idea in her mind it stuck. She eventually made the trip, and when she returned she suggested again that we relocate. She said we should give it a try, and if we weren't happy we could always return to Israel.

I had mixed feelings, but I wanted her to be happy. We discussed it for about a year, and then Gladys left for the United States. After a short while, I joined her. Her mother owned a four-family home on East Ninety-Fourth Street in Brooklyn.

All of the rooms were rented, so at first we had to move in with her mother. It took more than a year to get the tenants out of one unit so that we could rent our own apartment.

I went to night school to learn English, and I studied hard. Eventually I could read the *New York Post,* though I could not quite get *The New York Times.* I took my union card to the Brooklyn Carpenter's Union and presented myself for work. I expected to get work immediately, but I met with disappointment. I was told that there were no jobs. The union had nothing to offer.

I said I was willing to do any job, and the man gave me the address of a private employment agency. He explained that they might have work, but if they did they would expect a week's salary in payment for the placement. I just wanted to get a foot in the door somewhere, so I went to the agency. I told the man there that I would take any work he had available and that I would gladly pay the fee.

The agency had only one position. It was a job in a small, non-union shop where the workers assembled and shipped staircases. I took the address, and the next day I presented myself to the shop owner, ready to work. The man was in his sixties, and he spoke with a heavy Eastern European Jewish accent. He asked a few questions and sized me up. I answered to the best of my ability and stood waiting for his decision.

"David," he said, "you cannot start working here today, I am sorry to say."

I was discouraged and confused. The man was still smiling.

"What's wrong?" I asked. "I will work very hard…"

"I am sure that you will," the man said. "What I mean to say is that you cannot start working here today because first I want you to go back to that agency. You will tell them that you didn't get the job. Come back here again tomorrow after you've done that. If you work hard, you will have a steady job."

"Can you tell me what my wages will be?" I asked.

"Work for me one week," the man said. "After we see how you do, then we will decide what to pay you."

I did as I had been asked. I returned the next day and worked hard through the week. When Friday rolled around, my new employer informed me that I would be making $2.50 an hour. This was the best news I had heard since coming to America. In Israel I had been making sixty cents an hour.

Besides me, there were ten middle-aged workers in the shop. I was the youngest. The work we did was much simpler than what I had done in Israel. In Tel Aviv I had made furniture and done precise specialty work. In this shop the work was lathing risers and cutting steps to size. Then we created grooves and stringers for each step riser. The stairs were assembled by hammering a wedge with glue in on either side, forced between the stringer and the step. Then they were nailed.

Each set of stairs was manufactured for a specific house. The lengths and widths varied. Sometimes we had to make open or circular stairs. This required more skill, and I wasn't allowed to work on those at first. After a couple of months, my boss came to me.

"David, we're going to have to lay you off. Your work is just too slow." I left the office discouraged. Then, before I reached the outer door of the shop, I turned and went back to the office.

"If my work is too slow for two dollars and fifty cents an hour," I said, "what would you pay me?"

The man thought for a moment. "I can keep you on at two dollars," he said. "That's all I can do."

"I'll take it, but I want you to make me a deal. When I am able to work the open stairs and the round stairs, I want the fifty cents an hour back."

The man agreed, and I left the office more determined than ever to do well at the job. I started thinking about what had been happening in the shop and realized that there was a good reason why my work had been slow. Some of the older workers had been giving me advice, and as it turned out, the advice was bad. They were afraid of losing their own jobs if I was too productive, so they told me things that made my work take longer.

Things went on this way for a while, and then one day the boss in charge of the more sophisticated stairs didn't show up for work. I took a chance and stepped in. I completed the work. The boss saw this, but he said nothing. That Friday, I went to him and asked for the fifty cents back. After some bickering, I got twenty-five cents. I accepted this, but it bothered me. It stung my ego that I had lived up to my side of the deal and the man I worked for had not. A couple of months later, I asked again and was refused. At that point, I decided it was time to move on.

I found another staircase shop and asked about work. They told me that yes, they needed workers. I asked what the salary would be and they told me, much like my boss at the first shop, to work for three days and they would see. I agreed, but because I didn't want to burn my bridges if it didn't work out, I played sick for three days at my other job while I worked at the new staircase shop. When the time was up, I was told they would start me at $3.50 an hour. I left my old job officially and moved to the smaller shop. There were only four or five men working there. I worked in that shop for about a year, but when the wintertime rolled back around, I was laid off for a couple of months. I didn't want to sit around and wait, so I began looking again.

I found a private employment agency that was looking for a foreman to work in another staircase shop. I took the job, and I liked it. After the winter I got a seventy-cent-per-hour raise, and I stayed on as foreman. We supplied stairs to new construction projects. I asked to be allowed to go along on the installs, and reluctantly my supervisors agreed.

This was an important turning point in my career. I was

able to see the method by which homes were built, and it didn't take me long to decide that this was what I wanted to do with my life—to build. I thought about it all the time. I didn't have enough money, and I knew that the only way it could happen was if I just took a chance and went for it. I even prayed occasionally to be fired, because if I was out of work I would have no other choice but to try.

I spoke about my plans with some of my coworkers, and one of them introduced me to a carpenter named Aaron.

The two of us planned for a while, and eventually we determined that one of us would give up his job. We would split the salary of the man still working and begin looking for some land on which to build. I had three or four thousand dollars saved. I did extra jobs whenever possible, and we finally found a block of land in Brooklyn large enough for four houses. We got a loan and set to work. We built two-family homes that were actually illegal because they were three-family apartments with extra apartments on the lower floors.

We couldn't move on and buy land for the next block of houses until we had sold the four, but after about a year we sold all four houses.

Once we did, we took our profits and bought eleven home parcels at two locations in the Flatbush area of Brooklyn. We realized that we had made a mistake on the first job: we had done all the work ourselves, and it had taken too long. This time we hired general contractors, and the work went much more smoothly.

We built the two groups of homes simultaneously. Aaron and I made great partners. We were both hard workers who attended to business ten to twelve hours a day, seven days a week. Both of us worked very hard to make sure our business was a success. Now and then we disagreed, but most of our disagreements were of a personal nature and not about business. Aaron was good at supervising construction and dealt well with general contractors. I was good at design and very good at dealing with customers.

With all of my money wrapped up in the eleven houses, I tried to figure out how to gather funding for another project. I thought about asking my mother-in-law, but I believed the chances of her agreeing were no better than fifty-fifty, and in the end I decided not to ask. It might have caused family problems, and they would not be worth it.

This only left me with my brother William to approach. I had no idea if William had money or if he would loan it, assuming he did. The two of us had not really seen each other since I was ten. He didn't know me as an adult. He knew I was his brother, but was I decent? Was I honest? Would I walk away and not give back the money? To give all his savings—and in those days it was a lot of money—how many would do that? I had mixed feelings about approaching William for money. It felt awkward, but I gathered my courage and moved forward.

When I asked him for a loan, there was a moment of silence. He walked to a closet, and when he came back he was holding a bank book.

"This is all that I have," he said. "But you are welcome to it."

The account held $4,800. I had a hard time controlling my emotions at that moment. I had been afraid to ask, and now I was overwhelmed by the immediate and positive response.

"I won't be able to pay you back for a year or two," I said. "I'll give you a promissory note, and I'll pay interest."

William smiled then. "There's no need for that," he said. "You're my brother."

With the additional money I got, I bought land for fifteen more houses. We were building in two locations simultaneously. After both jobs were completed and sold, I paid back the loan from William. Since he did not want to be paid interest on the $4800, I gave him double his money back. "You did me a great favor," I told him. "You're entitled."

Aaron and I looked ahead. We had accumulated profits from our early efforts and gained quite a bit of experience. This gave us the courage we needed to tackle larger projects.

We found a full city block—enough space for forty two-family homes—in the Canarsie section of Brooklyn. It was a big risk, and it took a lot of guts to commit to. If anything went wrong, we could have lost all our profits from our earlier ventures or more. But we were young, and we took the chance. We finished all forty homes and sold them in only eighteen months. The project was a great success, and we made a very good profit. Before we were even done with the project we bought sixty more lots so we would be ready to start immediately.

We kept on buying and building, and in the end we built on five city blocks in the Paerdegat section of Brooklyn—Fourth, Fifth, Sixty, Seventh and Eighth Streets—with 250 dwelling units completed and sold. After that, we built 140 units in the Brooklyn Seaview section off the Belt Parkway and Rockaway Parkway.

We went on to build 200 units in the Georgetown section of Brooklyn. Once these were completed we relocated to Staten Island and built 200 homes there. Before completing our last project of over a hundred homes, interest rates shot up and all home sales came to a halt.

I decided to try something different. I found a local Ford dealer on Highland Boulevard on Staten Island and struck a deal. I offered a free, stripped down Ford—no radio, no air conditioner, no automatic shift, just four wheels and the body—with each house purchased. The cars sold for about $5,000 apiece. I then advertised in the newspapers, and the response was good. We sold a few homes and cars—not as many as I had hoped, but a lot of people came out to see the crazy car giver and to look at the homes.

Eventually the gimmick helped to sell a number of homes, and other developers, seeing what was happening, grew jealous. One day I received a letter from the Better Business Bureau accusing me of false advertising. A representative of the BBB came to view one of the model homes. He asked the price, which was $35,000. Then he asked what the price would be if he didn't want the car, and he was told $31,000. It was illegal to advertise that the car was free if the price of it was being figured into the cost of the house.

There was no use arguing. I changed the advertisement, and the homes continued to sell slowly. It took about two years, but eventually we sold all the homes, making a little profit. That was our last venture into building on Staten Island. After that we built a couple of projects in Brooklyn. Then Aaron suffered a massive heart attack, which brought our fifteen-year partnership to an end. He passed away a couple of years later.

Chapter Twenty-Eight

When I'd arrived in the United States, Gladys was working as a legal stenographer. She held that job for about a year, and then our son Glenn was born. Eleven months later, Glenn was joined by a sister, Cora. After that, Gladys no longer worked. She stayed home and took good care of our children, our home and me.

Once I had started in business, I never looked back. I kept long hours and worked hard, usually from seven in the morning until nine at night. Some days were pleasant; others were hectic. Sometimes the construction and the business went like clockwork and other times there were problems, setbacks and challenges. We learned from our mistakes, fixed them if we could on the next project, and moved ahead.

After staying for many years in my mother-in-law's four-family house on East Ninety-Fourth Street, my family and I finally moved out on our own to a new house in Seaview. By that time Cora and Glenn were attending high school. Glenn also attended Hebrew school for a while. Cora proved to be the better student of the two. She was able to watch television and do her homework at the same time.

Eventually the two went off to college. Glenn went to Pace University to study marketing, and Cora was accepted to Boston University to study occupational therapy. During this period, the family was very close. We gathered for dinner every Friday at either my sister Ilana's house or at my sister Irene's.

Gladys and I became members of the Seaview Jewish Center. I was happy to oversee the construction of the shul's extension, and as its biggest contributor I was named the guest of honor at a fundraising dinner held at the Waldorf Astoria. I may not have been an observant Jew, but I believed in Jewish tradition and wanted our kids to grow up as Jews. We kept a kosher home and went to synagogue on holidays. I was, and always will be, a Zionist. I would have lived in Israel for the rest of my life if I hadn't met my wife.

On Saturday nights Gladys and I often went out for dinner or to a club, but for the most part I was busy. The family took no long vacations. We spent occasional weekends at a resort in the Catskills during the summer, and Glenn and Cora went to a sleepaway camp every summer. The one exception was the last summer before Glenn went off to college. That summer I sent him to a camp in Israel, where he met Mendu's children and toured the country.

It took my sister Irene fifteen years to obtain her exit visa from Romania, which became a communist country after the war. Eventually she managed it, and she and her husband Joseph immigrated to New York City with their children. I had built an apartment building in Brooklyn, and Irene and Joseph lived there rent-free. Eventually they bought one of the homes I built.

Irene's daughter Lea went to The Juilliard School to study the violin. She subsequently became a music teacher. Andy, Irene's son, went to Columbia Engineering School and became one of the top engineers in the Trump Organization. After twenty-five years, he remains with that company in a very high position.

At that point in time, with the exception of Mendu, who still lived in Israel, all of my surviving siblings had moved to New

York. William had come over from Italy; Ilana and her husband, Abraham, and daughter, Mariana, had come from Belgium; and Armin, with his wife, Pookey, and their children, Pepi, Alisa and Marcel, came from Santiago, Chile.

Throughout the trials and triumphs of our lives, we remained a very close-knit family. We helped one another out financially and otherwise. In retrospect, I am unable to think of a time when differences or jealousy drove us apart. From the time we had grown up together in Halmi, Romania, to the time we were all reunited in New York, rich or poor, successful or not, it had never made a difference. We were always there for one another.

By the time Glenn and Cora had gone off to college, Gladys and I found ourselves drifting apart. We had been married for twenty years, but those years had given each of us a different outlook on life. We had simply outgrown one another, and so we separated. There was no day in court. We met in a lawyer's office and signed some papers, and that was it. I believed we were both happy with the new arrangement. We settled our assets amicably. A year later, Gladys remarried and moved to Florida.

After this, Glenn and Cora moved in with me and shared one of my unsold houses. Cora studied hard, graduating summa cum laude and becoming an occupational therapist. Glenn, after graduating from Pace College, entered a career in retail.

A short time after my divorce, I started to date a lady who was also recently divorced. She was pretty and intelligent, with a well-rounded personality. We seemed to hit it off from the very start and shared many good times together. We danced, played tennis, skied and traveled on vacations together. We were both in love, both still young, and I was thinking about starting a new family.

She came from a very bad marriage. She wanted a house with a white-picket fence—something she'd never had. I was prepared to give that to her, but she wanted to marry right away. I wanted to wait some time. Eventually we parted, both in love and both with broken hearts.

As a rule, I try not to look back or to spend time regretting things I might have done in the past. Perhaps this case was an exception because throughout the following years, I only dated three ladies for extended periods of time. I kept thinking of the one who had wanted the house with a white-picket fence. But then I laid eyes on a lady while she was dancing. I liked the way she moved. She had excellent rhythm. She was very attractive, with a beautiful body and a warm personality to go with it.

We dated for a long time, dancing away the nights together. Eventually, the dancing turned to love. I taught her the sports with which I was involved. We traveled around the world. As time went by she got to know my family, my children and my grandchildren. She got along with all of them very well. All of this happened more than fifteen years ago. That lady is still at my side. Her name is Emily.

Chapter Twenty-Nine

I built the last group of two-family homes in the Paerdegat section of Brooklyn on my own. There was one block left. Without a partner, I had to handle all aspects of both the business and the construction. All the decisions were mine, and I had no one with whom to consult. The job was much harder alone.

Through all of this, I knew I was a very lucky man. No matter how hard I worked or how long the hours, I honestly enjoyed my work. I had taken raw land and in just a matter of a year or two provided paved roads, sidewalks and residences to couples and families who moved into their dream homes. Knowing that I had created something that people might enjoy for decades to come, and that I did it all by myself, gave me great personal satisfaction.

That was my last residential home project. My next project was in Manhattan. I purchased an industrial building on Broadway and Worth Street and converted it into an office condo. At that time it was one of the first office condos in Manhattan, with retail stores on the ground floor. After some difficulties obtaining various permits and difficulties with marketing, I got a break and a law firm bought the entire top floor, which had a beautiful panoramic view of Manhattan. They spent a few hundred thousand dollars to fix and furnish the interior.

After completion it served as the model, and soon after I sold all the units except for the ground floor, which still held the retail stores. The project was very profitable. Now, thirty years later, I still own the stores in partnership with the lady who invested with me, Doris Lener.

My next project in Manhattan was at 82 Beaver Street, off of Wall Street. It was an eighteen-story building, similar to the famous Flatiron Building. The idea was to convert it into an office condo, the same way I had done on Broadway. In order to purchase this building I needed a partner. Between the two of us, we would have enough resources to purchase and renovate the entire building.

The search for a partner took months. Finally, I was introduced to a Greek gentleman who lived in London. I spent the day showing him the completed projects. I took the man to the airport, and he told me that he would look through the papers I had given him and let me know in a couple of days whether he was interested. After saying goodbye, I felt as if I had just wasted another day.

This time I turned out to be wrong. The man sent a wire: "I am in. I am betting on the jockey, not on the horse." We purchased the building, and I worked on it for over a year. Before the renovation was completed, we got an offer from Barclays Bank, who needed that particular location. They bought it for double our investment. It was the most profitable project I had been involved with up to that time.

I kept building but no longer considered single-family homes because commercial property was more lucrative, and there was less stress involved. My next project was at 170 Seventh Avenue South, on the corner of Perry Street in the West Village. The property housed a very old gas station. There were old cars all over the place. Any building on that site had to be approved by the Landmark Commission. I submitted plans for a fourteen-story condo. The local board was against any building on that land. After months and months of negotiation, I got permission to build a seven-story condo. The community board was overruled.

I built the condos first class all the way. Each came with a marble bathroom and a fireplace. There was a sun deck on the roof and all the amenities I could pack in. My son Glenn, who owned a large retail store at the time, sold his business for a profit and got his feet wet by supervising the construction of the condos. He did a good job and, after this project, went on to build a four-floor condo unit in Brooklyn Heights, which sold for a good profit.

In the early 1990s, the commercial real estate market collapsed. During that time I didn't do much, but I kept my eyes open and was always looking for something—though I wasn't sure at the time what that something might be.

One day I was introduced to a lawyer by the name of Glen Schor. He was looking for investors to purchase office buildings that he would manage. After several meetings with him, I showed him some of the projects I had worked on and completed. After more talk, we came to an understanding. I would be an active partner, though the others would be silent. The name of the partnership was Treeline Company. We started out by purchasing small office buildings. A couple of years later we sold the smaller ones and began to buy much larger office buildings.

The idea was to buy a building, make improvements, raise the rent and eventually refinance it, and, if possible, take out all of our investment or more. In most buildings we did just that. At the present time we own a group of five office buildings in downtown Brooklyn, and another group of nine office buildings on Long Island. I have been partners with Glen Schor for about fifteen years.

Overall, it's been a good partnership. As in all partnerships, there are sometimes disagreements, but in the end we always work it out. Glen has a large ego and I have a smaller one, so things even out in the end. Glen runs a tight ship. His wife, Fran Schor, lends a helping hand. To give credit where it's due, when it comes to putting together a creative finance package for a real estate deal so that it becomes viable and profitable, Glen Schor is the man to do it. Not to shortchange myself, I was intelligent enough to pick a partner like Glen.

Chapter Thirty

My sister Irene, who is the closest to me of all my siblings, took care of me when I was a baby; she was my second mother. Irene and I were the only ones of all my siblings who were deported to Poland and afterward transported to Auschwitz, where my mother and father were murdered. After sixty years, Irene and I decided to revisit the death camp.

Irene and I, with Emily, arrived in Krakau, Poland. A tour bus took us to Auschwitz, the largest graveyard in the world though you won't find a single grave there, nor a tombstone. All you can see are mounds of ashes and bits and pieces of bone. That is what is left of all those people who were brought to Auschwitz in cattle cars day after day and year after year.

Our first stop was at the main entrance to the camp. On top of the gate, the words *arbeit macht frei* were still there, as they had been when I passed through the gates when I was just a boy, not knowing that thousands of people who entered the gate daily would never come out again.

I looked down. I was standing between a pair of railroad tracks. The long train of cattle cars that brought us to this place so long ago had traveled on these same tracks. We were standing in the same place where Dr. Mengele, the famous Nazi doctor, stood and chose who would go to the slave camps, and who to the gas chambers.

The gas chamber was where my mother and father went.

We were standing at the gate to hell.

Our guide was a nice Polish lady. She took us around the camp. The main crematorium and the gas chambers had all been blown up by the Nazis. They had tried to hide the atrocities as much as they could. In one location there were thousands of barracks made of wood that housed the prisoners. They were all in bad condition by the time of our visit.

We passed the section of Auschwitz called Birkenau, where Irene and I were prisoners. The electric fence that separated the men's camp from the women's camp was gone. That was where Irene had thrown over a wood chip with a message written in charcoal on one side—*Papa*—and on the other side *Irene*. When I had picked up that bit of wood, I knew that she was alive.

None of us knew until after the war ended who had survived from our family. As we continued with the tour I tried to remember where my barrack had stood. It was difficult. I looked for the group of boulders that had been in front, where the old German prisoner Hans had once been sitting. Hans, whose few words to me became a great part of the reason I'm still alive today. Hans, the one who had pointed to the chimneys and said, "They smoke twenty-four hours every day. The terrible odor that you smell, and the soot that sticks to your skin, is not from burning rubbish but from burning human beings. If you stay in this place, it is just a question of time. You will wind up as smoke from those chimneys. Because where you are now is hell. But if you get out on the other side of the fence, you will be in heaven."

As I stood there in Auschwitz, I remembered how, one morning, I had been placed in a separate barrack of forty youngsters. What Hans had said to me reinforced my instinct to sneak out of the barrack and rejoin the adults, with whom I'd been originally. None of the other youngsters had survived. All of them were taken to the gas chamber and killed.

Irene had been in Auschwitz much longer than I had. Every couple of weeks she saw the selection. This meant that an SS officer checked everybody in the roll call. Anybody who looked too skinny or sickly was immediately put on a truck, and with other sickly prisoners they were taken to the gas chambers and killed.

While we were walking between the barracks, Irene told us about her friend, who had a younger sister about thirteen years old. The younger sister was very sickly and skinny. At that time, in Irene's barrack, everybody knew that if you were selected out of the roll call, within an hour you would be dead. During one of the roll calls, the friend's younger sister was selected. She was clinging with both hands to her older sister and refused to go on the truck. Both girls were crying, and it broke the older sister's heart. She couldn't stand to see her younger sister crying, so she went with her sister and they died together.

We continued our tour. Emily was beside me, holding my hand. Irene was on my other side. We were all very emotional. Sometimes we cried, and Emily squeezed my hand to give me support. Irene's memories of the misery in the camps were sharper than mine and affected her more deeply.

In my case, I found myself remembering the turning points in my camp life, the events that made a difference. As always, I tended to forget or repress the everyday suffering as something I didn't want to remember. Instead, I remembered that I had tried not to give up hope even if it seemed hopeless. I had tried to believe that tomorrow would be a better day. What I did not forget was that while learning to survive, I was also learning to live.

Finally, the tour ended. We sat down in the bus, emotionally drained. As the bus left, I took one more look at the gates of Auschwitz, and I knew that I would never go there again. Other people visit that place every year. On Yom ha-Shoah, Holocaust Memorial Day in the Jewish calendar, high school students from Israel, the US and other countries go to Auschwitz to commemorate the Holocaust and to remind the world what happened there. This huge graveyard, surrounded by barbed-wire fence no longer electrified, is a witness to the atrocities of which mankind is capable.

On one Holocaust Memorial Day, the silence of Auschwitz was shattered by Israeli F-14 fighter jets. I saw pictures in the newspaper and on television; I saw the Star of David insignia on their wings as they zoomed over the death camp. When the fighter jets broke the sound barrier, it was as though they were saying, "For all of you who died in this place because of the one crime—that you were Jewish—we will make sure that what happened here will never happen to your offspring. Now we have Israel, the country of our forefathers, where every Jew is welcomed with open arms. And we, the Israeli armed forces, will defend our borders and protect and guard our safety for as long as it takes to achieve a lasting peace with our neighbors."

That is how I want to remember Auschwitz—with Israeli fighter jets zooming overhead, the Star of David insignia on their wings.

Afterword

I had no intention ever to write the story of my life, but my son Glenn made all the arrangements to publish this book as a birthday gift to me. I was reluctant to undertake this project, but after Glenn made the arrangements, he left me no choice.

It took me a long time to write my story and great effort to remember and sometimes relive the horrible things I went through. I had avoided thinking or talking about them to anybody, including my wife and my own children. Perhaps it was because the events were too painful, or maybe because of my nature—I always look forward to tomorrow and try to forget yesterday. Now, in hindsight, I know that this way of thinking helped me to endure and overcome the difficulties that came my way through the years.

Experience taught me to get on with my life quickly. I've also found that if I disagree with anybody or get angry, it might last an hour, a day or a couple of days, but never longer. I can honestly say that this part of my nature has never changed, even to this day.

I always looked at life as consisting of individual days, each with its own events. Once a day is over, the day is gone. If it is a bad day, I always hope that tomorrow will be a good day. Now, decades later, I see all those days and tomorrows, good or bad, adding up to my lifetime, and that it is up to me to make those days good ones.

While writing this book, I was forced to think back through all I have gone through in my life and to reflect. I see things now that I never thought about—events that had strong influences on my life. I see now, for example, that my mother and father had enough love in their hearts for all of their eight children, and that I got a bigger share than I deserved since I was the unplanned, unexpected child with the nickname "Leftover."

My siblings and I sometimes fought, but we always cared for one another. From the time we lived in the small town of Halmi in Romania to the time we all ended up living in New York, this remained true. A helping hand was always there for whoever needed it.

I can also see that I was destined to be in business. By the time I was five I sold candy to my friends in Hebrew school. At the age of eleven I was cleaning the barracks and shining shoes for the Hungarian soldiers stationed in Poland. When I was liberated in Germany I was selling American cigarettes. When I was living in Italy I sold American uniforms. When I lived in pre-state Israel I worked in orange orchards, sneaking out from school and earning money.

So, since the age of five there was never a time that I did not have some money. Even while I was in the concentration camps I possessed my mother's gold ring hidden in my belt, and despite the temptation to trade it for food or better treatment, I stubbornly held on to it until the day I was liberated. A couple of years after arriving in the US, I took a chance with a few thousand dollars I'd been able to save up and went into business on my own. About fifty years later, I'm still in business. In real estate, as in any other business, there are good and bad days. I can sincerely say that throughout all these years I have enjoyed every single day of it, and still do. To succeed in business, I've found, you must choose something that you like to do, no matter how hard it seems to get started. Don't be afraid; take a chance and give it all you've got. Be persistent and you will succeed.

I have been asked many times, "How did you survive those horrible times?" Decades later, I can only guess. Perhaps it was that I came from a loving family. My siblings and I lived a very secure life, and we always knew that the family would be there for us no matter what. I always felt that if I survived, some of my family would be out there waiting for me. The trick was to survive, and I did my best to do so.

I tried to live one day at a time and always hoped that perhaps the next day all of the pain and suffering would end. To think otherwise would have meant that the miserable life I was living would go on for years. I would have had nothing to look forward to or live for, and I couldn't have borne that. I saw that in the camp, practically everybody did the same work, got the same food and had the same clothing, but thousands perished while a few survived. The difference, as I saw it, was that the few had hope and willpower. If you lost hope, then you lost your life. The ones who believed that tomorrow was a day that might bring liberation and a reunion with loved ones had the best chances to survive. The ones who believed they would eventually die, if not from starvation then by just being killed, had less chances. If you let those thoughts of death seep into your mind, you were already dead, just waiting to be carried out and placed on a big pile of bodies in front of the barrack.

Some prisoners suffered for years, then eventually couldn't take the pain any longer and gave up hope that their suffering would ever end. They walked over to the fence and were shot. They died just days before the liberation.

When I was liberated from the concentration camp, I didn't feel like drinking, dancing or celebrating. Instead, I just felt lucky that I was among those who had survived. Even though

I was skin and bones and could hardly stand on my feet, I was alive.

Why didn't I celebrate? Perhaps, after all the years of suffering and hopelessness, I had been so dehumanized that I wasn't capable of celebrating. Perhaps it was because I found myself in a strange land, my parents, siblings and friends all gone, most likely dead, and I felt a little guilty for all of those who had not survived while I was alive. What was there to celebrate?

It took me a long time to comprehend emotionally that I was truly a free man. I could do whatever and go wherever I wanted. The most surprising feeling of all was the realization that as my suffering and starvation were gone, so were my hatred and anger. Days after my liberation I could have easily walked over to any German on the street, accosted him and said, "This is for killing my parents. This is for wiping out my family, and this is for the years you starved and tortured me." I could have killed the German and nobody would have stopped me or taken a second look. It never happened. The feeling of "an eye for an eye" just wasn't there.

I had no desire for revenge. I had no desire to get even. Instead I found that the experience had an opposite effect on me. It made me more sensitive to other people's pain and suffering. This feeling of just being content to be alive, without the need for revenge, was common among the survivors.

About four months later—it took me that long to get back to my hometown Satu Mare in what was then Romania again—I experienced the saddest day of my life. The thousands of Jewish families who had once lived in this city were all dead, including my parents, two of my siblings, all my relatives, my neighbors and my best friend Solomon. I wandered around in the street, passing all the familiar places—my home, my school, synagogues, my relatives' and friends' homes. The buildings seemed just as I remembered them, but the people were strangers, cold and hostile. I could not find a single familiar face.

When I'd been liberated, I had looked forward to this moment when I would be reunited with my family, relatives and friends. Now, there I was in the city where I had spent my childhood, and I had to face the unbearable truth: that what I had hoped to find there was just wishful thinking. The people that I had once known I would never see again. I decided to leave Satu Mare immediately. Within two days I found out where my surviving siblings were and I left my hometown in Romania, never to return.

When I met up with my sister Irene and my brother Mendu in Kluj, we had a very emotional reunion that was both happy and sad. They wanted me to stay with them longer, but I was in a hurry to leave Romania as soon as possible. I made up my mind that my next destination would be Palestine, the land of my forefathers. It was a country I would be able to call my own. That is the place where I wanted to settle down and live my life peacefully, without the fear that someday I might be kicked out.

It was a long journey to Palestine with many stopovers in Romania, Czechoslovakia, Austria, Greece and finally Italy, where I spent many months doing business, studying and finally embarking on a fishing boat with 700 other survivors. After thirty treacherous days we saw the shores of the Promised Land, our final destination. Thanks to the British, who refused to let us disembark, we were instead transferred to a prison camp on the island of Cyprus. After some months, I finally went to Palestine.

A year after my arrival, the War of Independence broke out in Israel. All of us from the orphanage where I lived participated in that war to defend our homeland. Some boys from my school were killed, others wounded, and the rest of us served in the Israeli army for three years.

Fifty years later I received an invitation from Israel that said: "You are hereby invited to a fifty-year reunion of all the students from Magdiel, to take place at that same location." Since I had left Israel, I had never visited the orphanage. I was very excited by the prospect of seeing that place again, my first home after the Holocaust. It was the place where I had said to myself, *These are the best times of my life.*

The thought of meeting all of my friends and fellow students after fifty years also excited me. I grabbed a plane with Emily, and ten hours later we were in Tel Aviv.

The next morning Emily and I drove forty-five minutes through most of Tel Aviv and to Magdiel. The two-lane highway from Tel Aviv had become an eight-lane highway. All the fields on both sides of the road were now built up with forty-story condos, office buildings and international companies like Intel, Motorola, Microsoft, Sony and others. The narrow, little country road that had led to Magdiel was gone. Now it was a wide, paved road. The beautiful orange orchards that had surrounded the school as far as the eye could see were gone. They had been replaced by housing, roads and subdivisions. Even the sign on the school had been changed.

The beautiful, scenic little village was now a large town. Once we passed the school gates, the first thing I saw was the only thing that had stayed the same: the memorial that had been erected to my fellow students who were killed in the War of Independence. I stood in silence in front of the memorial and read their names. When I closed my eyes, I could still see their faces, a group of teenagers who sacrificed their lives so that their fellow Jews could have a country of their own, and so that there would never again be a Holocaust.

Next we passed a large building that had been the girls'

dorm. It had once been filled with teenage girls wearing khaki shorts and white blouses. Some were brunette, some blondes, all with different hairstyles. They were all orphans. Despite the horrors they had lived through, they always made sure that they looked pretty and attractive. Just like the boys in the school, they tried to forget the past and look forward to a better future.

Next I came to the boys' dorm. It consisted of a group of smaller buildings. I passed the room that I had shared with Jacob and Kostik, two of my best friends. Jacob, who took his studies seriously, but who was always ready to have fun and was always happy. Kostik, the born artist who studied painting and sculpture, who was skinny and blonde with blue eyes, a real lady-killer. Studying and money were the last things on his mind. We were called the three musketeers. We dressed alike and always hung out together.

Next I came to the building that had been the dining room, where periodically I had to be a waiter for my fellow students. We moved through the dining room and on to the recreation room where there had been folk dancing until 10:30 every Friday night after dinner. Then, it was curfew.

I went inside the building. The recreation room was a classroom now. I closed my eyes and could still hear the music and see the girls and boys dressed in their freshly ironed Shabbat clothes. All of them in white shirts, they danced away the night, having a wonderful time. I tried to look a little harder and there she was, sitting on a bench next to the window, with her black hair dropping down past her shoulders and her beautiful blue eyes. I found myself staring at her, and she looked back at me. Without saying a word to one another, we both walked over and joined a group of dancers. Our hands touched, and I fell in love with her. From that night on we had a secret love affair no one was aware of. We had to wait a long time before we could spend a night together in a Tel Aviv hotel room, where between the two of us we didn't have enough money for the room until the hotel concierge chipped in.

Then I opened my eyes, and I was back on the school grounds. I was fifty years older. I continued walking, looking for the places where I used to work—the vegetable garden, the flower garden, the stable where we kept the mules that we used to hook to the plows, the barn where we milked the cows every morning, the coops where we fed chickens and collected eggs. I kept reminiscing for Emily about the wonderful times I had working in these places.

Working in the gardens, whether it was digging in the melon fields or the orange orchards or removing cow manure on a hot and sweaty summer day, was part of my training. I was always happy and content in this place.

But all of the places were gone. The orphanage had become an ordinary high school. For the couple of hundred of us who came to the reunion after fifty years, hoping to take one last look at the place that had been our home after surviving the Holocaust, the place where we had enjoyed our teenage years, Magdiel the agricultural school the way we'd known it was no longer there. The place was just a local high school now. All there was to find were memories, but they were wonderful memories and they will last me a lifetime.

The reunion took place in a large conference room. There were welcoming speeches from past students of Magdiel. Some had become officers, pilots, lawyers and businessmen, and one had become a judge. After the official reception we were invited to the dining room, where everybody mingled and looked for old friends. I met my best friend whom I hadn't seen for fifty years—Kostik, who was no longer blonde or skinny but whose eyes were still blue. His outlook on life was still the same: have a good time and laugh. Money still didn't matter to him. He had become a well-known sculptor in Israel.

I also met Jacob, my other roommate. He had become a communications officer in a very high position in the police department. I had been in touch with him, and he had been to my house in New York to stay a couple of times. I had also visited his home.

Next I met Jacob Amsterdam, who had shared his one-room apartment with me after my service in the army. Though his room had been so small that when my bed was pulled out from beneath his, the only room left was for a small table, I was forever grateful to Jacob for letting me share that tiny room. Jacob had become a customs officer in Israel. I had been in touch with him also, and he had visited me in New York a couple of times.

After meeting my friends and exchanging addresses, it was time to sit down and eat. Emily and I were sitting at a table, and I heard a lady's voice in the distance asking someone, "Where is David Karmi?" The voice was familiar. I looked up to see who she was and saw a man pointing to my table. A lady with dark hair stood at his side, and despite her age she was still attractive.

It was the girl I'd fallen in love with fifty years earlier at the Friday night dance. She didn't realize that I had heard her asking about me. When the man pointed toward my table, she looked at me, then slowly turned and walked away. She did not look back. I was about to run after her, but something held me back. I realized that she must have had a good reason for wanting to walk away. Did it upset her that I was with Emily? *Leave her alone,* I said to myself, and out of respect for her feelings, I did. That was the last time that I saw her.

After dinner we all chatted, promised to visit each other, and swapped phone numbers. When the reunion finally came to an end, I suddenly felt a deep sadness in my heart. I realized that this reunion, the last and only one except for more private reunions with a couple of friends, was the last time I would see most of these people. Slowly, the room emptied. As I walked out with a heavy heart, I was glad that Emily was walking beside me. It made me feel that I was not alone.

For me, this reunion had caused a deep, empty feeling to reemerge, a feeling of guilt I'd carried within me since the day I had left Israel. This small country, consisting of only 600,000 Jews at the time, had accepted me after the Holocaust with open arms, given me a home and an education, taken care of all of my needs and provided some of the best years of my life. I fought in its War for Independence, and I had sworn on the Bible that I was ready to give my life if necessary to defend it.

After all of that, how could I have left? Of those in my class at Magdiel, I was the only one who had left Israel; all of my friends and fellow students had stayed, married, had children and grandchildren, and still lived in Israel. In the Hebrew language, a person who immigrates to Israel is called an *aliya*, which means "ascending." A person who leaves Israel is called a *yored*, which means "descending." The word *yored* carries a stigma with it. It is something that I was never proud of being. None of my friends could believe that David Karmi would ever do a thing like that. Although my close friends never confronted me about it, I always knew how they really felt about my leaving the country. From the day I left until today, after all the decades, my heart is still there, where I spent my formative years. I arrived from a burning hell and got a second chance at life. For that I will be forever grateful.

One night after the reunion, I invited about fifteen fellow students and their spouses to have dinner with me in my hotel. It gave us time to reminisce intimately about old times at Magdiel. During that dinner, Emily got the chance to meet my closest friends and their wives: Jacob, my roommate, Jacob Amsterdam and his wife Hannah, and Kostik the artist, who was the only one who came without his wife. He told Emily that he was single. Later, when we visited him in an expensive neighborhood in a one-family house, we knocked on the door and a blonde lady let us in. We didn't know who she was, and she didn't know who we were. After a cup of coffee, we found out that she was a retired colonel in the Israeli army and was Kostik's wife, Ilana. They also had a daughter, Karen. Why had Kostik told us he was single? Maybe he was joking. He was always a Bohemian. From that time on, Ilana and Emily became very good friends. Kostik and Ilana stayed with us for a week in New York, and when Emily and I have the chance, we visit with them.

After the dinner I also visited Mendu and his family—his daughter Ronit is a teacher, his son Gabi is in electronics and his son Amiram is a well-known rabbi. Mendu has a total of nineteen grandchildren and a couple of great grandchildren.

After saying goodbye to all my friends and relatives, Emily and I were soon on our way back to New York. I've since gone back to my daily routine of going in to the office. On Friday nights, Emily and I go to my sister Irene's home for Shabbat dinner. She always was, and still is, my second mother and my best friend. On Sundays we usually meet my daughter Cora, who is an occupational therapist, her husband Mike, and her youngest daughter, Kimberly. Her older daughters, Lauren and Jessica, are in college. I try to follow in my parents' footsteps and be very close to my family, to love them and to be there for them with a helping hand, whether it is with my time or with resources.

My son Glen, who is in the retail and real estate businesses, has two apartments, two cars and two businesses, but no wife. There are girlfriends galore, but of all the girls he's dated, none seems to have the qualities he expects in a wife. My sister Ilana, my brother William and my brother Armin have passed away. Of all my siblings, only three of us remain, but we have a total of forty-four children and grandchildren.

Being an optimist helped me to endure and overcome the

unbearable suffering of the Holocaust. I was left with the feeling that even if you find yourself in the most hopeless situation, some decent human being might be there with a helping hand. So, as I end this book, I would like to mention some of the people to whom I will be always grateful—those who touched my life, each in a different and significant way. Without the help of some of these people, I would not have survived the camps.

I'm grateful to Hans, the old German man in Auschwitz who showed me where hell and heaven are and gave me the right advice. I'm grateful to the camp commander in Landsberg, who I approached and asked for a job as a camp runner. He could have beaten me or worse, but instead he gave me the job.

I'm grateful to Lieutenant Werner, for whom I served as an orderly, who took me with him when he visited his family in the town of Landsberg. I dined with them as if I were a member of their family. For that short time, they made me feel like a human being. To this day I do not know of any prisoner who was ever permitted to leave the concentration camp and dine with a German officer and his family.

I am grateful to the German officer whose motorcycle headlight fell on me while I was attempting to escape from a death march at night. He came after me with his gun pointed at my head. I was sure that I was going to die. Instead, he ordered me back to the march.

I am also grateful to the German family who invited me to their home after the liberation to live with them. They made me feel like part of their family. They shared with me whatever they had. These were Germans who treated others and me with compassion.

I would love to see these people again, walk over and shake their hands and say, "Thank you for helping me stay alive through those torturous, hopeless times."

But of all the people and places I am grateful to, I am most grateful to the country of Israel. My only crime for being in a concentration camp was my religion. Six million Jews from all over Europe were exterminated because of their religion, some by shooting, some by gas chambers. For the last 2,000 years the Jewish people were blamed for being Christ killers, for using Christian children's blood to make matzot for Passover, for causing the Black Death plague in the Middle Ages, for starting all the wars in the world, for wanting to rule the world, for controlling the banks of the world, for being anarchists, communists, capitalists. The list of misdeeds goes on and on.

There was a time when the Jewish people were an independent nation with their own government and homeland and army. That all changed when the Romans conquered the country, enslaved the population and brought most of the Jews in chains to Rome. Others were dispersed to the four corners of the world. They were driven from country to country. They lived through the pogroms in Russia, the ghettos in Italy, the Inquisition in Spain. Then, 2,000 years later, in 1948, the Jewish state was reborn. The homeless Jew finally had a homeland of his own called Israel.

This tiny country has achieved tremendous progress since its founding. It has world-class universities, Nobel laureates, high-tech industries and world-famous armament and pharmaceutical industries. It is one of only five countries in the world that has launched satellites into outer space. Hebrew, the language of the Bible, was not spoken for centuries and is now spoken by over seven million people who live in Israel. Despite all the suffering I lived through because of my religion, I feel great satisfaction about being Jewish and proud of the outstanding, disproportionate success Jews have achieved in science, medicine and art.

I'm particularly proud of what Israel did: it gathered the Jews from the Diaspora, from the concentration camps all over

Europe and from the Arab countries and created a vibrant, modern democracy, the only one in the Middle East. It achieved all that in less than fifty years. The 600,000 Jews who lived there before Israel was declared independent are now over seven million. I feel privileged to have been able to participate in its War of Independence and to have lived through the historic time when this old-new country was reborn. Every Jew, wherever he lives, should get real satisfaction from the existence of Israel and support it. Should Jews be mistreated anywhere in the world, all they would need are plane tickets, and the minute they land in Israel, they are citizens.

I believe that a strong Israel, economically and militarily, should be in everybody's interest, Jews and non-Jews alike. Israel is the insurance policy for all the world that a Holocaust will never happen again. I further believe that Israel will be a role model for other countries in how to turn land that was desert and sand into a modern, vibrant, high-tech industrial country. Someday, when peace comes to the Middle East, I am sure that Israel will be the one to help out its Arab neighbors and guide them to become modern industrial countries. In that process, Israel might become one day the Switzerland of the Middle East.

I will be forever grateful to Israel, the country that adopted me as a Holocaust orphan and gave me a home, an education and self-confidence and reinforced my belief in decency and humanity. I always contribute generously to different causes and projects in Israel, and every couple of years I visit there, but every time I say goodbye to my family and friends and step on the plane, I realize that I left something behind. Part of me will always be in Israel.

I cannot complete my life's story without mentioning my gratitude to another country: America. It is known all over the world as the country with unlimited opportunities, a country where you can arrive with empty pockets and, with ambition, perseverance and a willingness to work hard, achieve success. The measure of your success is only limited by your will.

I am a living witness to the above. I left for America in my early twenties on a thirty-day journey on a cargo ship with exactly ten dollars in my pocket. I spent three dollars on the way here. I left the ship with seven dollars in my wallet. I had not much to speak of in resources or in education. What I did have was plenty of ambition and perseverance, and the will to succeed in my life. Toward that end, I was prepared to do anything, to do any kind of work, no matter how hard or how long it took to achieve my goals.

It wasn't easy. There were times when I worked seven days a week on two jobs. I always said to myself, *If you want to be in business and to be successful, this is the only way you will get there.*

After one year of being in America, I was drafted into the armed forces. I got an A-1 certification, and I chose the Navy. I was supposed to present myself in six months, but by that time my second child had just been born, and I was told I had to wait. That was the only reason I ended up not serving in the US armed forces. I wanted to serve, just as I had served in Israel. I was grateful to this gracious and generous country for having given me a chance to become a citizen and the opportunity to prove myself.

When I started in business I did not expect the amount of success I ultimately achieved. I would like to believe that I have shown my appreciation to America by building neighborhoods where hundreds of families will be living for decades to come.

I feel today as I felt when I was liberated. I still have no animosity toward anyone. When you are in a situation where you face death every day, you stop hating. It's a waste of energy. All you want to do is stay alive. When you are finally a free man, you realize that hating is just another way of hurting yourself for what someone else may have done to you. Despite the hard times I went through, or perhaps because of them, I find myself more tolerant and understanding of other people and their feelings.

Many times I tell my children, grandchildren and friends: when you are angry at somebody, you are the one who gets hurt, not the one you hate. Even if somebody did something to offend you, don't dwell on it. You be the smart one and don't hold it against them. Just forget it and go on with your life. You'll be a much happier person for it, and so will your friends.

I strongly believe in this philosophy. I have tried to live by it all my life. Perhaps that is why I can say with all sincerity that I carry no grudges toward anyone. I lived through the greatest genocide in human history—a time when people were starved, tortured, beaten, burned and shot to death. Every morning, as I left to go to work in the camps, I would see a large pile of dead bodies in front of my barrack. Those were the prisoners who died overnight. As I passed by, questions always popped into my mind: Is that where I'm going to wind up? And why? Because I do not have the right religion?

I forced myself to ignore those thoughts. With whatever strength I had left in me, I refused to believe that I would die. All through my suffering, I tried hard to believe that with perseverance, strong will and hope, I had a good chance of seeing my family again. I believed that this insane world would come to its senses and that the nightmare I found myself in would end.

More than anything else, the constant refusal to give in helped me to survive the tremendous suffering and pain.

I hope that the world has since learned a lesson: that ethnic cleansing may start with a dictator against a particular minority, but eventually the ethnic cleansing engulfs everybody, not just the minority. It leads to a Holocaust.

Despite all that I lived through, I want to believe that there will never be another Holocaust. I hope that schools everywhere will continue to teach future generations about the Holocaust so that they will understand what hatred and discrimination can lead to. And, most importantly, I hope that our children and their children will live in a better world, a world where hatred—whether religious, racial or any other kind—will disappear.

David Karmi
New York, 2010

About the Author

After being liberated from a Nazi concentration camp by the Allies in WWII, David Karmi made his way to Palestine, fought in the war of independence and became part of the army that created the Nation of Israel.

After moving to the US, he pursued a thriving career in construction, building numerous residential developments and condos in New York City. David is still involved in the ownership and management of commercial buildings in New York City and Long Island.